# The Simplicity Reader

## ELAINE ST. JAMES

SMITHMARK

**First published in the U.S. by Hyperion.**

This edition published in 1999 by SMITHMARK Publishers,
a division of U.S. Media Holdings, Inc.,
115 West 18th Street, New York, NY 10011.

SMITHMARK books are available for bulk purchase for sales
promotion and premium use. For details write or call the manager
of special sales, SMITHMARK Publishers, 115 West 18th Street,
New York, NY 10011.

ISBN: 0-7651-1676-6

Printed in the United States of America

10 9 8 7 6 5 4 3 2 1

Library of Congress Catalog Card Number: 99-71083

# Simplify Your Life

∽

## 100 Ways to Slow Down and Enjoy the Things That Really Matter

### Elaine St. James

SMITHMARK

To Wolcott Gibbs, Jr.

And to Michelle and Bill, Jessie and Megan,
and Lisa and Eric

# Acknowledgments

I'd like to thank Marcia Burtt, Dave Sowle, Marisa Kennedy Miller, Jackie Powers, Judy Babcock, Phil Babcock, Jim Cummings, Meg Torbert, Linda Miller, Albert Chiang, and Ira Weinstein for their support and encouragement in the writing of this book. I'd like to thank Felix Fusco, Sue Pettengill, Cyndy Van der Poel, Hope Kores, Kathy McDonough, Beverly Brennan, my mother, Dorothy Kennedy, and my favorite aunt, Kathleen Schiffler, for always being there. I'd like to thank Sam Vaughan for his advice and inspiration, and for connecting me with my wonderful agent, Jane Dystel. And most of all, I'd like to thank my husband, Wolcott Gibbs, Jr., for everything.

# Contents

∽

Introduction /3

## One: Your Household

## Two: Your Life-Style

# Three: Your Finances

# Four: Your Job

# Five: Your Health

# Six: Your Personal Life

# Seven: Special Issues for Women

# Eight: Hard-Core Simplicity

# Simplify Your Life

# Introduction

*ᴄ⃘*

Let your boat of life be light, packed with only what you
need—a homely home and simple pleasures, one or two
friends worth the name, someone to love and someone to
love you, a cat, a dog, and a pipe or two, enough to eat and
enough to wear, and a little more than enough to drink, for
thirst is a dangerous thing.

—Jerome Klapka Jerome

Several years ago I was sitting at my desk, idly glancing at my
daily schedule, which was laid out in a time-management
system roughly the size of Nebraska. This binder was burst-
ing with "to-do" lists, phone logs, time-organizers, meeting-
maximizers, goal-stabilizers, high-tech efficiency charts, and
five- and ten-year life planners. Suddenly, I realized I no
longer wanted my life to be that complicated.

I immediately picked up the phone and scheduled a long

weekend retreat. I left my time-management system at home, but I took a notebook. I had a lot of thinking to do.

Like many others of our generation, my husband, Gibbs, and I had bought into the Bigger is Better and the More is Better Yet philosophies of the 1980s. We had the big house, the big car, most of the conveniences, and many of the toys of the typical yuppie life-style. Then we gradually began to realize that, rather than contributing to our lives, many of these things complicated them far more than we had been willing to admit. We had always known the Joneses weren't worth keeping up with, but we finally had to face the fact that the only thing we'd ever gotten from a power lunch was indigestion. The time had come for us to get off the fast track.

Over the next few days I sat alone in the peaceful silence of that retreat house, and came up with a list of things we could do to improve the quality of our lives while decreasing the complexity. When I got home, I sat down with Gibbs and went over the list. Fortunately, he agreed with all of the major and most of the minor changes I proposed.

The first thing we did was get rid of all the stuff we didn't use anymore (#1). We took a giant step and moved across country, so we could work where we wanted to live (#51), and do what we really wanted to do (#52). In the process we moved to a smaller house (#19). Over the next few years we

simplified our eating habits (#57), consolidated our investments (#46), sold the damn boat (#21), rethought our
buying habits (#40), and drastically reduced our needs for
goods and services (#42). Step by step, we gradually imple-
mented most of the ideas outlined in this book.

When we launched our simplicity program, we had three
specific goals in mind. First, we wanted the things in our
lives—our home, our cars, our clothes, our diets, our finances—to be small enough and few enough and simple
enough that we could easily take care of them *ourselves*.

Second, we wanted to free ourselves from the commitments, the people, and the obligations that kept us from
having time to do the things we really want to do. We made
the decision early on to stop doing the things that we'd always
done because we felt we *should* do them. Not only has this
increased the time we have for ourselves, but it has greatly
reduced the stress that comes from doing things we don't
want to do.

Third, we wanted our lives to be consistent with our desire
to live in harmony with the environment.

For us, simplifying was not the "going back to the land"
movement of the 1960s—though we did want to include
more nature in our lives, and we have. Nor was it about living
cheaply, though close to half of the suggestions in this book

will reduce your expenditures. For us, living simply meant reducing the scale, maintaining the comfort, eliminating the complexity, and minimizing the time demands of life as we had known it in the 1980s.

When we first started to simplify, I longed for guidance from others who had been there before us. I combed libraries and bookstores in search of help. While a fair amount has been written about the *philosophy* of the simple life, I was unable to find anything of a *practical* nature that outlined specific things we could do to simplify. So we plodded along on our own.

Each time we completed a major step in our simplification process, we discovered some other minor things we could do to simplify, and we added them to our list. I decided that if the two of us—for the most part rational and reasonable people—had gotten so caught up in the frenetically paced lifestyle and rampant consumerism of the eighties, there must be other reasonable people out there who had done the same thing, and who were now looking for practical things they could do to simplify their lives. And so I decided to write this book, which is a compilation of those steps we've taken to simplify, and the things we've learned from other like-minded people along the way.

It's possible your life is complicated enough—as ours was—to warrant implementing many or all of these suggestions. Or, it might be that taking just one or two of these steps—like cleaning up your relationships (#72), or changing your expectations (#88)—will provide the level of simplicity you need to more fully enjoy the other areas of your life. Whatever the case, keep in mind that one person's simplicity is another's complexity. Bowing out of the holidays (#33) was tremendously liberating for us, but it might complicate your life beyond words. You get to decide.

Wise men and women in every major culture throughout history have found that the secret to happiness is not in getting more but in wanting less. The nineties appear to be presenting one of those golden moments of change, the opportunity to freely give up the things that don't make us happy and to incorporate the lessons of the eighties into a simple but elegant life-style for the nineties—and into the next century. So, to paraphrase Henry David Thoreau, take advantage of the movement of the times and simplify, simplify. And enjoy.

*One*

# Your Household

# 1. Reduce the Clutter
# in Your Life

A giant step on the road to simplicity is to eliminate the odds and ends that clutter up your home, your car, your office, and your life. If you're moving to a smaller home (#19), paring down will no doubt be a necessity. As you start your program to reduce the clutter, the guideline is easy: *If you haven't used it in a year or more, get rid of it.*

Getting rid of it can mean any number of things: give it to a friend, give it to Goodwill, take it to a consignment shop, sell it at a garage sale, or put it in the Dumpster.

Start with your clothes closets and branch out from there. Clean out every closet, every drawer, every shelf, in every room of your house, including the kitchen. Do you really need a full-sized Cuisinart *and* a mini-Cuisinart *and* a hand-held chopper *and* a mixer? (See #35 for some ideas on how to get rid of these things.) Don't forget the front hall closet, the linen closet, tool chests, and the medicine cabinets. (See #66; it will save you a lot of time trying to decide what to keep.) Remember the laundry room, the garage, the attic, the basement, your office, your car, and any storage space you may be renting or borrowing.

When Gibbs and I started to simplify, we went through this exercise and were amazed at the amount of "stuff" we had accumulated that we simply didn't use anymore. Getting rid of it all was a tremendously liberating experience.

Soon after that, we came to the realization that we really had far more living space than we actually needed or even wanted, so we moved from our house to a small condominium. In the process of moving, we went through a second uncluttering exercise, and managed to free ourselves from another load of things we would no longer have room for.

We've found, as we've refined our simplification program over the past couple of years, that we're getting better and better at letting go of the things we know we'll never use again. You may not be ready to get rid of everything in your closets on the first uncluttering round or two, but I promise that once you begin to experience the exhilaration and the sense of freedom such an exercise generates, uncluttering will become easier and easier.

You can complete the initial stage of an unclutter program in a couple of Saturday afternoons. Be sure to have your children go through this exercise with you. It's a great way for them to learn at an early age how to keep their lives uncluttered. Just schedule the time and get started.

Remember, the idea is not to deny yourself the things you want, but to free yourself from the things you don't want.

# 2. Use Dave's Uncluttering System

⌒

Our friend Dave swears by this method for getting rid of things he no longer needs, but can't bear to throw out: Put them in a box with a label indicating a date two or three years from now—but don't list the contents on the label. Store the box in the attic or the basement, or wherever is convenient. Once a year, examine the labels. When you come across a box whose date has passed, throw it out without opening it. Since you don't know what's inside, you'll never miss it.

Of course, it's much easier to keep your life free of clutter if you make it a habit not to hoard in the first place. You can stop things from accumulating by getting in the habit of throwing them out now, rather than later. Every time you start to store something in the back of your closet or in a dark attic, ask yourself, "Do I *really* want to save this, or will it end up adding to the clutter?" Then discipline yourself to throw it out now.

# 3. Use "Speed Cleaning" to Clean Your House

$\backsim$

If you've reduced your needs for goods and services (#42), you may already have let the cleaning lady go. But, whether you clean your house yourself or hire someone to do it for you, you should read *Speed Cleaning,* by Jeff Campbell and the Clean Team (available from Dell Publishing). You can read it in less than thirty minutes and it will cut your housecleaning time and expense by more than half.

I consider myself fairly efficient, but I'd never even thought of some of the simple time-saving techniques described in this book. For example, easy-to-follow, step-by-step diagrams show you exactly how to set up the cleaning process for your home, room by room, so you can move from top to bottom and from left to right, all the way around a room and the entire house *without backtracking.* This tip alone will reduce your cleaning time drastically.

It's actually possible for one person using the Speed Cleaning system to thoroughly clean a 1,200-square-foot house in little more than an hour. Once you have set up your home for speed cleaning, you don't *have* to do the cleaning every week:

these methods are so thorough that cleaning every other week or even once a month—depending on your circumstances—will suffice.

The book shows you how to save time, energy, water, cleaning supplies, and, best of all, your Saturdays. It discusses environmentally safe products and the latest tools and cleaning techniques. It even shows you how to get the best from your cleaning service.

It might seem that letting the cleaning lady go would complicate rather than simplify your life, and, if you've got a five-bedroom house, it probably would. But if you're moving toward a human-scale, low-maintenance life-style, you can easily take care of the routine cleaning without outside help, especially if you include all the family members in the process. Teaching your children efficient cleaning and household maintenance techniques will not only make your life easier, but will give them skills for keeping their own lives simple.

# 4. Cut Your Grocery Shopping Time in Half

∽

Most people I know find themselves running to the supermarket at least two or three times a week, and many shop more often than that.

One extreme case is a friend of mine who shops for food every day of the week. She is a married career woman with no children who spends close to a thousand dollars a month on food for herself and her husband. Though she claims to detest shopping, she has never got herself organized enough to plan ahead for meals and for grocery buying. (Her excuse is that she wants to be sure her produce is fresh every day. As I see it, that's what refrigerators are for.) Consequently, she spends far more time, money, and energy on shopping than necessary, and she ends up throwing out an unbelievable amount of food because she buys on impulse things she doesn't really want or need.

When we started our simplification program, one of the first things I looked at was how I could simplify our grocery shopping chore, since dawdling in a food store is one of my least favorite ways to spend time. I made it a goal to cut by at least half the two or three hours I spent shopping each week.

So I sat down at the computer and typed up a list of all the food items I might possibly buy. Then I arranged them in the order they appear in the aisles of my favorite grocery store. I ran off a couple dozen copies of the list, which I keep in one of the kitchen cabinets so a fresh one is there when I need it. It can easily be updated as our eating patterns change.

Now, before I go shopping, I sit down at the kitchen table and draw up a quick meal plan for the week. Then I go through my computer list and check off the items I'll need. Since I'm right there in the kitchen, I can quickly see what we're out of, and note those items on the list.

The entire process, from making the list to doing the shopping to putting the groceries away, takes a little less than an hour, and I almost never have to run back to the store during the week for items I've forgotten. Of course, we've also simplified our eating habits (#57), but, just by keeping a list, we've substantially cut our monthly food expenditure, and created more free time for ourselves.

Another advantage of using a computerized list is that if you're the primary shopper and have to be away on shopping day, it's very easy for your mate or one of your kids to check off the list and take care of the shopping in your absence.

# 5. Buy in Bulk

$\wp$

Another way to simplify your grocery shopping is to buy in bulk. For years I resisted this idea. We never seemed to have the storage space, and I just never took the time to sit down and figure out what we could buy in large quantities. Then, when we started making our own oat bran muffins (#61), we went through so much oat bran it became much easier to buy it in bulk.

When I saw what buying oat bran this way saved in time and energy and packaging—not to mention money—I began to think about other things I could buy in quantity. I was surprised at how extensive the list was. Now, I have a separate list for our bulk purchases: paper towels, Kleenex, detergents, cleansers, pet foods, toothpaste, shampoos, shaving creams, rice, grains, legumes, nuts, and baking supplies.

Once or twice a year I make a trip to our local wholesale house to stock up on these items. Since we've eliminated so much of the clutter in our closets and cabinets (#1), we have plenty of room to keep these supplies on hand, and we never run out of things we need.

When buying in bulk keep in mind that not *everything* offered at a wholesale market is necessarily less expensive, so you should have a good idea of regular prices on the items you wish to purchase. Otherwise, you could end up paying too much. While cost savings is only one of the advantages of buying in bulk, why pay more than you have to? Secondly, you'll find it much easier to shop for bulk items with a detailed list; otherwise there's an overwhelming temptation to buy things you don't really need but that you can't pass up because the price is so good.

In addition to the time and money we've saved, one of the most rewarding benefits of buying in bulk is the reduction in packaging materials to be recycled. In fact, many wholesale houses, especially cooperatives, encourage customers to bring their own shopping bags and containers, which reduces packaging materials even more.

# 6.  Plant a Garden

～

We have friends who have simplified their grocery shopping by planting a garden. Their entire yearly crop is raised in planters on their front deck. They have fresh tomatoes, peppers, green beans, artichokes, cucumbers, and several types of squash, as well as an extensive herb garden. They've set up a drip irrigation system on an automatic timer. They never have to till the soil; when a crop is finished, they pull out the old plant, add some fresh mulch, and put in a new one. The planters are on wheels so they can be rotated easily to get the maximum sun through the season. They seldom have to spray for bugs, but when they do they use an organic mixture of one part detergent to ten parts water.

They're professionals who both work long hours. They decided some years ago they'd rather spend time on their deck tending their plants than running to the market every time they need a tomato. They get a tremendous amount of satisfaction from being the source of much of the produce that goes on their table, not the least of which comes from the fact that it is organically grown. What little work they do to tend this simple garden gives them a lot of enjoyment, and they love the feeling of being in touch with nature. Also, they've made a point of involving their teenage son in their gardening routine. Not only has he been a big help to them, but he has developed an appreciation for plants and nature he might not otherwise have had. And they've come to treasure the opportunity to work together as a family at an activity they all enjoy.

If you have the space for a deck or patio garden, planting one might not only simplify your grocery shopping, but add a great deal of satisfaction to your life as well.

# 7. Run All Your Errands in One Place

Ɔ

I used to spend an inordinate amount of time doing my routine errands. Each week, without giving it a second thought, I drove all over town to my favorite little shops, which I patronized more out of habit than convenience. I would drive seven miles to one side of town for groceries, five miles back into town to the bank, two blocks away to the post office, another six miles to the opposite side of town for the dry cleaners, and then to a shopping center several miles beyond that, where I took care of almost everything else: video rental, hardware store, bookstore, and pet supplies. And, of course, don't forget another short drive to stop at the fish market, the bakery, and the flower stall.

Now, fortunately, we live within one block of a shopping area where we can take care of everything in one stop, and also have the vet and the pet groomer, a photo lab, a pharmacy, and even a half dozen good restaurants we can walk to. It has cut at least an hour and a half off the time it takes to do our weekly errands.

If you don't live in close proximity to a shopping center

where you can take care of all your weekly shopping needs, find the one closest to you and drive there, even if it's halfway across town, for the simplicity of one-stop shopping.

The automobile, like the washer and dryer (#8), is another convenience we tend to misuse. Because it's so easy to hop in and drive away, we don't think about all the extra time we spend doing things we wouldn't do, and maybe don't really *need* to do, if we didn't have the car that makes it so "easy."

# 8. Cut Your Laundering
# Chore in Half

In his excellent book *Timelock,* Ralph Keyes points out that there are many supposedly time-saving devices that, because of the way we use them, don't save us as much time as we think they do. The automatic washer and dryer are perfect examples.

Studies have been conducted over the past fifty years comparing the time our grandmothers and mothers spent on certain chores with the time we spend on them today. It's interesting to see that even though our washers and dryers greatly reduce the amount of time it takes to clean and dry a load of clothes, we're spending just as much time on the clothes washing chore as our grandmothers did, and in some cases more. Why? Because we're doing more loads.

In the old days, for example, Grandpa would put on a clean shirt on Monday and, after wearing it carefully through the end of the week, it would go into the clothes hamper for Grandma to take care of on wash day. Now we think nothing of wearing two or three shirts a day, one for exercise, one for work, one for casual wear, and throwing them into the laundry basket the minute we take them off.

The same is true of towels and linens. Today, without batting an eye, we use a towel or maybe two or three per person per day. After all, it's so easy: just run another load through the machine, right?

It's one thing if you have household help to do the laundry, though there is still the water, the detergent, the gas, the electricity, and the expense to think about, not to mention having to supervise the help; but it's another matter entirely if you're the one doing the laundry, and you're spending far more time each week in the laundry room than you want or need to.

If that's the case, sit down and rethink your use of clothes and other launderable items. An easily attainable goal would be to cut back your laundry to the equivalent of one load per person per week. After you've done that for a while, it'll be easy to cut back again, to one load every two weeks, especially once you've simplified your wardrobe (#22), and have mostly dark colors that don't need to be laundered so often! Wear your clothes to the max and teach your kids to do the same. Assign one towel and one washcloth per person per week.

And who says we have to change the sheets *every* week? Our mothers did because it was the accepted way then. But, with so many mothers working outside the home, in addition to also working in the home, things are different now. I'm here to tell you it's possible to go for two weeks (or more) without changing the sheets on your bed and live to tell about it. Just don't tell my mother.

## 9. Stop Buying Clothes That Need to Be Dry-Cleaned

Obviously, there are a number of occupations with dress codes requiring clothes that must be regularly dry-cleaned. If you're an investment banker, you have to have your three-piece suits, which don't respond well to being run through the washer and dryer. Fortunately, most of us in the 1990s no longer need to be slaves to the Dress for Success code that ruled the 1980s. From now on, at least until the Revolution, the code should be Dress for Comfort and Convenience, which means, for the most part, wash-and-wear cottons and natural fabrics.

I have a friend who argues that taking a load of clothes to the cleaners is much simpler than having to run a comparable amount of clothes through the laundry, and for some that may be true. It comes down to a life-style choice, and how simple you want your life to be. For years we made weekly trips to the dry cleaners to pick up the shirts and to drop off the week's cleaning, and never gave it a second thought. Now that we've simplified our wardrobe, it's much easier to avoid the dry cleaners. I love being able to run a load of clothes through the washer/dryer, hang them up, and know they're ready to wear. And we take some satisfaction in knowing that we've reduced, even if only by a small fraction, the use of environmentally harmful dry-cleaning solvents.

## 10.  Leave Your Shoes at the Front Door

‿

Get in the habit of removing your shoes before you enter your house. This simple practice has some incredible benefits. By reducing the amount of outdoors that is brought indoors, you reduce the amount of dust and other unwelcome particles on the carpet and the floors. Your house will be visibly cleaner: dirt stains on the carpets and rugs are kept to a minimum, carpets are much easier to keep clean, and the overall dust quotient throughout the house is greatly reduced.

But perhaps the greatest benefit for the simplicity-oriented is that taking off your street shoes at the front door helps to create the sense of your home as a sanctuary. It's almost magical: when you leave your shoes at the door, you start to feel you can leave your troubles there, too.

A variation on this idea comes from an acquaintance who owns a computer software firm. Because of the importance of creating a dust-free environment in his workplace, he started many years ago requiring his employees to leave their shoes outside. He even went so far as to buy each employee shoes or slippers to be worn indoors and maintains a shoe budget for his staff. His employees and visitors are trained from day one to check their shoes at the door.

*Hint:* Build or create (or, as a last resort, purchase) a small box or rack where you can leave your shoes when you come into your home. Keep a supply of socks or your slippers there if you're the type who has to have something on your feet. Also, keep some extra socks or a supply of airline slipper-socks for guests, and encourage them to leave their shoes at the door, too.

# 11. Go for Patterned Carpets

When I think back to the time I decided to have light taupe carpet installed in our newly remodeled home, I wonder why I didn't have my head examined. It was the mid-eighties, and the taupe and gray and off-white carpets were a fashionable rebellion against the dark brown and orange shags of the seventies, and possibly even the sculpted greens of the sixties.

Yes, the light, low plush carpets are fashionable and, if well maintained, look beautiful, but simple they ain't. They show every spot, every fleck of dirt, every cat hair, every crumb of toast, and every slosh of coffee that ever passed over their supposedly stain-resistant fibers.

When we moved from our house into the condo, I replaced the light carpet that was there with a multicolored flecked carpet that looks like sand. It was the best decorating decision I ever made. There are many such patterned carpets available today, and if you find yourself changing carpets, I strongly urge you to consider one. Or, consider a multicolored Persian or Oriental rug that will achieve the same results. It's not that they stay so much cleaner, it's simply that they don't *show* the spots, the specks, the drips, the dust, and the smudges as easily as the plain light-colored ones, or even the solid-colored dark ones, for that matter. If you want your carpets to look good without having to spend a lot of time on them, a speckled or patterned or multicolored carpet will hide a multitude of sins and will make your life a whole lot easier.

# 12. Use Food Trays

∾

When I went on my private retreat at the beginning of our simplification program, I spent a wonderfully quiet and refreshing weekend in a beautiful old stone house up in the hills. The house comfortably accommodates anywhere from eight to ten guests at a time and is usually booked months in advance. Guests can have their meals in the communal dining room, or can take meals to their rooms. Coffee, teas, fruit drinks, and all manner of non-dietetic, drippy, crumbly, gooey snacks are available all day long. Guests laden with these spillable foodstuffs make regular treks across carpeted hallways, up and down polished stone stairways, through rooms covered with gorgeous Persian and Oriental carpets, and over beautifully maintained hardwood floors. Yet the floors and carpets and rugs are spotless.

Why? There is only one rule in the house: Any food or drink leaving the kitchen has to be on a tray. When I think of all the time I used to spend blotting up spills from the light taupe carpet and brushing crumbs off the hardwood floors, I wonder why I never thought of this myself. We now have one rule in our house regarding food: Any food or drink leaving the kitchen has to be on a tray. It is such a simple, and elegant, solution.

## 13. Keep Your Plants Outdoors

～

Have you ever lifted one of your houseplants to move it to a sunnier spot, and found a ten-inch-diameter water stain on your newly refinished hardwood floor?

Is your coffee table spotted with water marks that were made when you failed to notice the base of the planter holding your favorite orchid had overflowed?

Do you find yourself looking at the philodendron hanging over the kitchen sink and wondering when you'll ever have the time to take it down and dust the leaves?

Are you tired of brushing against the ficus next to the couch and dislodging another layer of dead leaves to litter the carpet?

How often do you come home to find your cat has thrown up on your sofa again because she's been eating the schefflera?

Interior decorators and serious plant lovers won't like this idea, but the rest of you know what I mean: houseplants are a pain in the neck. It's time we realized that the photographs in the home-and-garden magazines don't necessarily reflect reality. They make having indoor plants look so easy, when they're anything but. And I'm speaking from years of being a plant lover, surrounded by indoor plants that took up a lot of my time. It was the water ring on the cherrywood bookcase and the third infestation of aphids on my flowering hibiscus that made me think there might be a better way to get in touch with nature.

If you don't have a yard or a patio where you can enjoy natural greenery, consider a window box. If that's not possible, visit your local botanical garden or neighborhood park when you need a plant fix. At the very least, don't replace your Creeping Charlie next time it dies. You'll be amazed at how simple your life can become when you keep nature outdoors where God intended it to be.

# 14. Get Rid of Your Lawn

⌒

Unless you're one of those weekend wonders whose passion is huffing and puffing behind a push lawn mower, or worse yet, walking behind a noisy, smelly, environmentally damaging, pollutant-spewing power mower, why would you have grass in your yard? Neighborhood custom? Social expectations? Habit? Do you really *like* having a lawn? Is it worth having to keep it trimmed, clipped, mowed, fertilized, aerated, raked, and watered?

Even if you have someone else, such as a hired gardener, to take care of your lawn for you, you still have to expend the effort to get it done; at the very least you have to write the check for the work. Wouldn't it be simpler to get rid of your lawn altogether?

You could save a great deal of time, money, effort, energy, water, and other natural resources (gas or electricity for the mower), as well as unnatural resources (chemical fertilizers and weed killers), by replacing your lawn with ground cover.

Many beautiful, drought-tolerant, fast-growing, low-maintenance ground covers—pachysandra, dichondra, ivy, and numerous low-growing evergreens, for example—are available as effective lawn replacements. Check with your nurseryman for the one best suited to your locale.

Imagine never again having to concern yourself with a lawn. Just get rid of it.

# 15. At the Very Least, Simplify Your Lawn Maintenance

⁀

If you feel you absolutely have to have a lawn, consider making some changes in the way you keep it:

1. Make it smaller—just enough space for the kids to wrestle with the dog.

2. Most people overwater their lawns by up to 40 percent. Remember to water slowly and deeply. This is more effective than shorter, frequent sprinklings. The best time to water is early morning.

3. Mow it less frequently. Not only does this save time and energy, but most types of grass develop healthier roots when allowed to grow up to two or three inches high. The longer the grass, the more shade for the ground around each plant. This helps the soil retain the moisture longer, which in turn means less watering.

4. Don't rake the grass clippings. Leaving them on the lawn not only saves you time and energy, it helps to retain the moisture and creates a natural fertilizer for the grass. Also,

recycling the mowed grass into your own lawn reduces the amount of clippings that are added to your local landfill.

5. If you must use pesticides, use organic rather than chemical ones.

# 16.  Pets Simplified

⁓

The second year into our simplicity program Gibbs brought home a little Shih Tzu puppy. Though we have two very low maintenance cats, neither of us had ever had a dog before. We didn't have a clue what we were in for.

One evening at the end of the first week, we sat and watched in amazement as Piper ran around chewing on everything in sight, messing up the carpet, terrorizing the cats, and generally creating havoc in our peaceful home. Gibbs looked at me and said, "Maybe we overdid the simplicity bit." Had our lives gotten so simple that we had to bring in this little ball of fur to stir things up?

Well, perhaps. But what it came down to is that we'd finally simplified our lives enough so we could enjoy the pleasures, and put up with the hassles, of owning a dog, something we'd never had time to do before.

Pets won't simplify your life, but there are things you can do to make pet ownership easier:

1. Unless you love pet grooming, stick with short-haired pets. Even with short-haired animals, take a few minutes each day to brush your cat or dog; this reduces the amount of hair that ends up in your carpet, or as fur balls on the hardwood floor.

2. If at all possible, keep your pets indoors. Obviously, this is easier with small dogs than with large ones. But indoor pets are much less likely to get into fights with other animals (requiring expensive and time-consuming trips to the vet), and the chance of them being hit by a car (which can be not only expensive but fatal), is greatly reduced. Also, indoor pets have fewer problems with fleas.

3. If your pets do have fleas, the best method for getting rid of them (both in the house and on your pets) is Flea Busters (1-800-767-FLEA). This is an environmentally safe, simple, nontoxic method guaranteed to rid your house and your pets of fleas for up to one year. Most pet stores offer a product similar to that used by Flea Busters that you can use yourself at considerable savings.

4. Take the time to train your dog. Whether you have a new puppy or an older dog, all dogs can be trained to obey basic commands such as COME, SIT, STAY, HEEL, QUIET, and STOP CHEWING ON THAT TABLE LEG! Contrary to what many veterinarians will tell you, puppies can start basic train-

ing at three months (and house training should start the minute you bring them home). Call your local Humane Society for information on training classes in your community.

A well-trained dog, while not simple, can be a true joy to have in your life. Because of Piper, we make absolutely certain that we take our brisk walk every day (#63). And, taking her out at first light in the morning and the last thing at night has brought us in closer touch with nature. We now regularly see many phases of the moon and stars that we hadn't seen before, and the quiet sights and sounds and smells of dawn and night are special gifts that we've come to enjoy every day of the year.

# 17. Moving Simplified

We've moved eight times in fifteen years. Here are some things we learned along the way:

1. Before you move, go through the uncluttering exercise outlined in #1.

2. Most people start packing long before they need to. As a result, the house looks like a disaster area for weeks before the actual move. The average household can be packed up in less than a week. If you hire movers to do the packing, it can usually be done in one day, but get an estimate from them as to how long they will take. Set aside one room in the house in which packed boxes can be kept out of the way while you are packing up.

3. When packing, start with treasures such as vases and art objects (of course, these are now going into the mathom box, #35); then do books, linens, clothes, and personal items. Pack the kitchen last, preferably on the morning of the move while the movers are loading everything else into the van.

4. Make sure the place you are moving to is cleaned and ready to live in.

5. Set up a system of colored labels for the movers to use. All boxes with red labels go to the kitchen, all boxes with blue labels go to the living room, etc.

6. If you're moving across town, move the kitchen things you'll need for your next couple of meals—dinner tonight and breakfast in the morning—the clothes you'll need, and an overnight kit, in your own car. These will be the things you'll unpack first.

7. Use the large wardrobe boxes for your clothes, and load them directly from the closet in the old place into the closets in the new place. If you've simplified your wardrobe (#22), you'll have little to pack.

8. When packing books, start with the top shelf of a bookcase, and move from left to right all the way down to the bottom shelf. Take a stack from the shelf and put them right into the box in the same order. Label the boxes by bookcase and by number. Don't worry about filling every square inch of space in the box. You may use a few more boxes this way, but it is so much simpler.

Instruct the movers to set up the bookcases in the new house, and to stack the book boxes next to them in numerical order. Start with box number one, and stack the books on the shelves exactly as you packed them, in the same order.

9. Whenever possible, use a mover who'll sell you boxes and then will take them back at half price. Many moving companies also sell used boxes at considerable savings.

10. Board pets and young children for the day. Older kids can help with the unpacking of their personal things.

11. Draw up a rough schematic showing the rooms in the new house and where you'd like the furniture to be placed. Run off enough copies so you can post one copy on the door of each room. This will save you from having to be on the spot each time the movers bring in a piece of furniture or a stack of boxes. That means you can be in the kitchen unpacking and organizing for dinner that evening, or at least for breakfast in the morning.

# 18. Recycling Simplified

One of the wonderful side benefits of simplifying your life is how easy the process of recycling becomes. By simplifying your eating habits (#57), you'll greatly reduce the packaging that automatically comes with processed foods. By making water your drink of choice (#60), you'll greatly reduce the number of cans, bottles, and plastic containers you have to dispose of. By eliminating the daily newspaper (#28), cutting back on your magazine subscriptions (#27), and stopping your junk mail (#26), you'll greatly reduce the amount of paper you have to recycle.

You'll also cut back on bottles and packaging by throwing out everything but the aspirin, and by reducing your use of prescription and over the counter remedies that don't work (#66). Rethinking your buying habits (#40) and your need for goods and services (#42), and bowing out of the holidays (#33) will reduce not only the packaging, but also the number of items that clutter up your life. And of course, uncluttering (#1), staying uncluttered (#89), and gift-giving simplified (#35) are automatic recycling processes in themselves.

Experts agree that for all its promises, recycling is only a part of the world's waste disposal problem. Reducing waste in the first place, which simplifying will do, will be a major part of the solution.

*Two*

# Your Life-Style

# 19. Move to a Smaller House

 ∽

How has it happened that the size of the average American home has gone from the roughly 900-square-foot, two-bedroom, one-bath home of the 1950s to a roughly 2,000-square-foot home with three bedrooms, three and a half baths, an eat-in kitchen, a dining room, a library, an exercise room, a "great" room, a TV room, at least a two- but often a three-car garage, and an entry hall that rivals the size of the Sistine Chapel? It certainly did not happen because of the need to house larger families; the average family size has gone from 4 in the 1950s to 2.5 in the 1990s.

The monthly financial burden of maintaining these behemoths has more than doubled, and in many cases tripled, from the 1950s. Today, many homeowners are spending more than half their monthly income on housing. In order to have larger houses, we've had to move farther and farther away from our jobs and community services. This in turn means we have to spend more time commuting and more money on gas and cars.

Many people are beginning to realize that what they've had

to give up in terms of time, energy, and money to own a large house is just not worth it.

When Gibbs and I moved from the smog and the congestion and the four-hour commutes of the big city and suburbs to a more rural environment where we could live where we worked (#51), our first move was into a 3,000-square-foot house. We'd unwittingly bought into the eighties mentality that bigger is better. Besides, we needed that space to house all our stuff.

Once we had got rid of the stuff (#1), we realized we no longer needed all that space. When we moved to our small condominium, our goal was to scale down to easily manageable size in our accommodations, without loss of comfort or conveniences. It's been a tremendous emotional and psychological relief not to have to worry about that big house, the big yard, and the ever increasing complexities of owning an oversized home that no longer fits our life-style.

# 20.  Drive a Simple Car

⏤

When it comes to simplicity in the car department, Gibbs and I are partway there.

A few years back, in typically upwardly mobile fashion, I bought one of those high-powered foreign sedans. While it has for the most part been a reliable car and, for me, a real joy to drive, it would be a stretch to call it simple. It's a fair amount of trouble and expense to maintain, I have to be careful where I park it, and the gas consumption—26 miles to the gallon in town—is difficult to justify in this day of 50-mpg cars.

Gibbs, on the other hand, has a ten-year-old Plymouth. He grew up in New York City on subways and buses and never even owned a car until he moved to the suburbs. Then he bought an old station car that barely made it back and forth to the train. Unlike me, he has absolutely no ego tied up in the car he drives. For him, a car is a sometimes convenient means for getting from one place to another.

The insurance and taxes and registration fees on his car are half of what they are on mine. He can take his car anywhere and not have to worry about it being broken into or stolen. (As he is the first to admit, no one would want it.)

My car is in the shop nearly twice as often as his. Even the smallest part costs three times what it would for his car, and often takes twice as long to get.

Recently, after experimenting with our local bus service, Gibbs found it quite adequate for his needs, and, like our friends in San Francisco (#96), he is seriously considering getting rid of his car altogether. In addition to reducing his transportation expenses by two-thirds, it would relieve him of the task of driving, which he's not fond of to begin with.

No doubt the simple thing would be to replace my car with his. Though I hate to admit it, I'm not quite ready to do that. But I do plan to replace my car as soon as technology is advanced enough to produce electric cars that are reliable for reasonable distances.

# 21. Sell the Damn Boat

This suggestion is addressed to men. Women, for the most part, don't have these toys.

Fifteen million Americans own boats. Anyone who's ever been to a boating community on any weekend knows that only a very small percentage of these boats actually get used. Many are running up expenses in slips or storage lots around the country. The rest are taking up space in driveways or garages or the owner's backyard.

The same thing is true for many of the other sporting and recreational gadgets we Americans collectively have spent billions of dollars acquiring: downhill and cross-country skis, scuba gear, backpacks, fishing tackle, golf clubs, camping equipment, you name it.

If you've reached the point where you're beginning to doubt the bumper sticker that said "He who dies with the most toys, wins," maybe it's time to think about unloading some of them.

## 22. Build a Simple Wardrobe

This suggestion is, for the most part, addressed to women. Men already have simple wardrobes.

After years of trying to come to grips with the elusive concept of "fashion," I've come to one overwhelming conclusion:

When a man and a woman are together and comparably dressed in any style, from dressy to casual to unbelievably casual, almost without exception the man looks better than the woman. There are two reasons for this:

One: When it comes to fashion, men have it easy, and because of this they almost always get it right, and,

Two: Women have it difficult, and they almost always get it wrong. And some get it more wrong than others.

Let's face it, men have basically only four options: suit (with shirt and tie); slacks (with shirt and, sometimes, a jacket); casual pants, jeans (with polo shirt), or sweats; formal wear.

Women have unlimited options:

Suits, the jackets of which can be short, medium, long, or

very long; fitted, loose, boxy, or peplum; broad-shouldered, narrow-shouldered, drop-shouldered, or puff-shouldered; single-breasted, double-breasted, belted, or open, with collars, of every variety, or without collars; they can be round-necked, square-necked, scoop-necked, or V-necked; and are available in any fabric or combination of fabrics, and in any color or combination of colors imaginable.

Likewise, the options for the women's equivalent of the other categories—slacks and casual wear and formal wear—are also available in an infinite variety of styles, fabrics, and colors. This is the reason women have three times the amount of clothes in their closets as men do. They've got a dozen different fashion statements, and few, if any, of them work together.

My suggestion for creating a simple wardrobe is to take a lesson from the way men dress:

First, pick a simple, classic style that looks good on you, and then stick with it. Forever.

Second, build combinations of outfits that work as a *uniform:* Two or three jackets of the same or similar style but in different, muted shades, with two or three sets of the same or similarly styled skirts and/or slacks in different muted shades, and a couple of coordinating shirts/blouses/tops. *Each item should go with every other item.*

Third, remember that men, for the most part, don't wear jewelry (see #94), don't carry purses (see #93), and wear only one heel height (see #91).

This is not to say women should dress like men. But it's certainly possible to create a simple, functional, feminine wardrobe by following the same *principles* men follow when it comes to fashion.

## 23. Reduce Your
## Go-Go Entertainment

If you began your simplification program out of the need or the desire to cut back on your spending, your entertainment expenses were probably among the first to be reduced. If you're seeking simplicity as part of getting off the fast track, then reducing your need for outside entertainment will no doubt be high on your list. In either case, cutting back on your nightlife, and looking within yourself and to your family for entertainment, is a positive step toward simplification.

The financial rewards of avoiding such activities as movies, plays, theater, opera, concerts, cabaret, and nightclubs are obvious. The personal rewards may not be so apparent at first. After all, we've been compelled in recent years to go, to do, to be on the move, to experience all that money can buy. Oftentimes, in the process, the things we really *like* to do have been overlooked.

I was recently in a meeting with a dozen high-powered professional people. We started talking about our goals for our leisure time, and how seldom we allow ourselves to truly enjoy our own quiet moments. We each decided to make a list of the things we really liked to do.

The lists included things like:

Watching a sunset. Watching a sunrise. Taking a walk on the beach or through a park or along a mountain trail. Having a chat with a friend. Browsing in a bookstore. Reading a good book. Puttering in the garden. Taking a nap. Spending quiet time with our spouse. Spending quiet time with our children. Listening to a favorite piece of music. Watching a favorite movie. Spending time with our pets. Sitting quietly in a favorite chair and doing *nothing*.

We were surprised and delighted to see most of the things we listed required little or no money, no expensive equipment, and were available for anyone who wants to take advantage of them. For the most part, our favorite pleasures were the simple pleasures.

I don't pretend that this small group represents a major sampling. But as I travel around the country talking to people about simplifying their lives, I hear the same stories over and over again. People are tired of being driven by entertainment market forces. They're coming to realize the best things in life *are* free, and that doing less can mean having more—more serenity, more happiness, more peace of mind.

I urge you to make your own list of the things you and your family really love to do. And then arrange your life so that each day you have time to do as many of the things you like to do as possible.

## 24. Rethink Your Meals
## with Friends

$\infty$

One of the things Gibbs and I had to take a hard look at when we started to simplify was having people over for dinner. We enjoy spending an evening with special friends, but since meal preparation is not a high priority for either of us, we found the time and energy required to have even a casual dinner at home were more than we were willing to expend. Fortunately, after suffering through our home cooking, most of our friends agreed.

Now, we regularly meet friends at a local restaurant for a dutch-treat evening out. We avoid the shopping, preparation, cooking, and cleanup, and our time and energy have been freed so we can enjoy each others' company. It doesn't have to be expensive, and if you split an entree (#58), it doesn't have to be fattening. It doesn't even have to be an evening; Saturday and Sunday mornings are a great time to have a relaxing meal out with friends.

On the other hand, we know several people who've recently sworn off restaurant meals completely. They're tired of the expense, the noise, the secondhand smoke, and the lack of privacy at most restaurants. Like us, they're not all that fond of cooking, so, when they get together with friends, they've gone back to the potluck dinner where everyone can pitch in. They've instituted some new rules for that time-tested social gathering, however: people can bring whatever they like, as long as it's low in calories, moderate in quantity, and lacking in the competitive spirit.

## 25.  Turn Off the TV

Studies have shown that in the typical American household the TV is on approximately seven hours per day. If you've been on the fast track these past years, the chances are good you haven't had a lot of time to spend in front of a TV. But you may be spending more time watching television than you realize. You may not have stopped to consider how your television viewing may be affecting you and your family, and how it's dictating your purchasing and life-style choices. I urge you to give some thought to it.

Think about whether the lives portrayed on your favorite sitcom contribute anything positive to your life, or whether repeated exposure to crime and violence contributes to your peace of mind. Think about whether the "thirty-second sound bite" format of most television news gives you any real information. Think about whether the addictive habit of watching television contributes to your aliveness, spontaneity, and sense of freedom.

And, if you've made the decision to reduce your need for

goods and services (#42), think about the overpowering effects of television advertising:

By far the largest percentage of the over $125 *billion* spent last year by advertisers was spent on television commercials. Christopher Lasch, in his best-selling book, *The Culture of Narcissism,* points out that modern advertising creates a consumer who is "perpetually unsatisfied, restless, anxious, and bored." Judging simply by the percentage of advertising dollars spent, it's reasonable to assume that television has done more to foster the consumer spending of the eighties, and what Lasch refers to as "the new forms of discontent peculiar to the modern age," than any other medium.

If you suspect the habit of watching television might be playing a significant role in the complexity of your life, I suggest you read *Unplugging the Plug-in Drug,* by Marie Winn. This book explains TV addiction, and offers an easy, step-by-step program both you and your children can use to reduce or eliminate the use of television.

Come up with a personalized list of things you can do, either by yourself or with your family, to take the place of watching TV, such as reading the classics again, or reading out loud from your favorite plays. Set up some board games or other types of games you can play with the family, such as charades, Twenty Questions, Monopoly, or Trivial Pursuit. Or, find a hobby that will consume you.

If you're addicted to television, kicking the habit will certainly simplify your life. People who've done it say it's one of the best things they've ever done.

# 26. Stop the Junk Mail

Americans receive close to two million tons of junk mail every year, half of which is never opened or read. For the half that is read, we spend an average of three or four days a year just *opening* it. One can only guess at the amount of time we spend each year reading unsolicited catalogs full of items we have no use for. What a waste. And what an annoyance. Especially if you are anything like a good friend of mine who feels guilty every time she receives a charitable fund-raising solicitation she doesn't respond to.

In addition to the personal nuisance junk mail creates, it also makes tremendous demands on our environment. If we stopped the unwanted junk mail we receive, we could save close to one hundred million trees every year.

Fortunately, there is something we can do to reduce the amount of junk mail that litters our mailbox each day.

First, write to Stop The Mail, P.O. Box 9008, Farmingdale, NY, 11735-9008. Request that your name and all variations of your name not be sold to mailing list companies. This will reduce your junk mail by up to 75 percent.

Second, whenever you request a catalog, ask that your name not be added to the mailing list. Or, if you want to receive that company's catalog but no others, request they not sell your name. Most legitimate companies will honor such a request.

Third, until you get your name removed from the mailing lists you don't want to be on, at the very least you can sort your mail over a waste basket or a recycling bin. Learn to be ruthless here. Rather than having to throw it out later, when the clutter has gotten out of hand, avoid the clutter process in the first place, and throw it out now.

If you could cut by even 50 percent the amount of mail you have to handle each day, wouldn't that simplify your life?

# 27. Cancel Your Magazine Subscriptions

I have a friend who reads dozens of consumer magazines each month. She has an exciting and satisfying career, lives in a beautiful home, has two lovely and talented daughters, and they're all healthy. She has all these and many other reasons to be ecstatic. Yet she recently went through an extended period when she was consumed with the idea that she wasn't happy, and that her life just wasn't what it should be.

One day I happened to be looking through the stack of magazines on her desk. All of a sudden it hit me: One of the reasons she thought she was so unhappy was she was gauging her life by the unrealistic life-styles portrayed in these magazines.

Most consumer magazines are little more than vehicles for Madison Avenue. One of their primary purposes is to get us to buy the products they advertise. Month after month, year after year, they create expectations about our lives we're often not even aware of.

Indeed, with the possible exception of television, there are few places where the idea of unbridled consumption is more subliminal and more seductive than the advertising found in these magazines. Advertisers are now spending *billions* of dollars each year in print advertising. It's not surprising that, through the lure of page after page of enticing four-color ads, advertisers set our fashion and cooking and eating trends, and regulate and promote our social lives. They encourage us to smoke, drink and drive fast cars, and to buy expensive clothes, jewelry, furniture, and hundreds of other products that, for the most part, we don't really want, often can't afford, and which seldom live up to their advertising claims. Is there even a remote possibility, for example, that drinking Johnnie Walker Red will make a woman more appealing to a man?

You might want to consider how the magazines you read are affecting the way you spend your time and your money. If you can trace many of your buying patterns to your magazines, perhaps it's time to cancel your subscriptions. This is one of the easiest ways to reduce the number of "Buy! Buy! Buy!" messages you are exposed to every day and to free yourself from consumer addictions.

If you're a magazine addict, go cold turkey on this one. Find a new interest or hobby or reading program to fill in the time you used to spend poring over magazines. You might be amazed to see how much time you'll have to do the things you'd really like to do.

## 28.  Stop the Newspaper Delivery

We have good friends who have never been in the habit of reading the daily newspaper. He is a physicist; she is an artist. Until they recently purchased a VCR to watch their favorite movies, they never owned a TV. They've never watched the news on television. While most other people are reading the morning news, this couple is reading their favorite novels.

They keep up to date in their professions and with what is happening around the globe by reading professional journals. They feel they are each making a contribution to the world through their work, and do not feel obliged to meet other people's expectations with regard to being up on current events.

They are well educated, literate, interesting, vital people who long ago came to the conclusion that reading the daily newspaper did not contribute to their mental or emotional well-being, and they arranged their lives accordingly.

If you're tired of bad news, but can't face the thought of giving up your daily newspaper completely, you might consider giving it up for even a month or two. Having done it, I can tell you that taking a break from the news from time to time makes it easier to discriminate between the news I want or feel I need to know and the negative information that complicates my life without enhancing it.

Over and over again, when I first suggest to soon-to-be-former fast-trackers that they try eliminating the daily newspapers from their schedule, they are shocked by the very idea. But as they begin to experiment, especially if they've set up a satisfying replacement activity, they find breaking the newspaper habit is not as difficult as they first imagined. Cutting back on the negative input you're subjected to every day is a positive step toward simplifying your life.

If you're trying to reduce your need for goods and services, keep in mind that advertisers spend over $8 billion a year on newspaper advertising alone. Cutting back on your daily exposure to that level of consumer programming may be sufficient reason to stop the delivery of the daily newspaper.

## 29. Drop Call Waiting

ᴄᴏ

I know not everyone will agree with me on this issue, but I can think of few "conveniences" of the modern phone age that are more irritating than the contrivance "call waiting." Not only is this system a rude form of interruption, but people who have it have to *pay for it.* And of course, if you have call waiting, the telephone company wants you to believe you also have to have—for a couple dollars more per month—the service known as "cancel call waiting"; and if you have that, you also have to have—for another couple dollars more per month—"priority call waiting."

Have we so lost touch with the art of communication that we can't just come directly out and say, "Excuse me, can I call you later? I'm expecting an important call now"? Or, perhaps more accurately, "Sorry, but there is someone else I'd rather be talking to." Are the phone calls we're receiving today so vital that we can't be satisfied with having just one call in progress, but we have to have two? Have our schedules gotten so out of control that we have to pay the phone company to keep us in line?

For small businesses that want to avoid the added expense of multiple phone lines, call waiting can perhaps be justified. But I can't believe that juggling two phone calls on the same line at the same time has ever made anyone's personal life simpler. If you agree, you can cancel this "service" and save approximately five dollars per month on your phone bill.

# 30. Don't Answer the Phone Just Because It's Ringing

∽

I know there are people out there who are constitutionally incapable of letting a ringing telephone go unanswered. I am married to one of them. And I admit it took many years of almost constant telephone use to reach a point where I could harden my heart to a ringing phone. But now that I'm there, there's no going back.

It's a minor point in a simplification program, but just because it's convenient for someone to call you at this particular time does not necessarily mean it's convenient for you to answer. Just think of all the times a ringing phone has interrupted a sound sleep, a good soak in the tub, a hot meal, an interesting conversation, some important work, mad passionate sex, or simply a quiet evening of welcome solitude.

All I can say is thank goodness for the answering machine. Now it's at least possible to monitor your phone calls so that you can talk only to those you wish to talk to, when you wish to talk to them. If you don't have an answering machine, you can turn your phone off so you don't have to hear it ring when you don't want to be disturbed.

There's no question that the telephone is one of the greatest conveniences of the modern world. But it can be one of the greatest nuisances unless we learn to use it for our *own* convenience rather than someone else's.

## 31. Don't Answer the Doorbell, Either

There's something so importunate about a ringing doorbell. It's different from a ringing phone: whoever it is is *right there* on the other side of the door. I can't tell you how many times I've had a perfectly good meal ruined by a knock on the door. We've all been trained to be polite to guests, even uninvited ones. Often we think nothing of inconveniencing ourselves and other family members, letting our dinner get cold, for example, by answering a ringing doorbell to speak to someone we may not even want to see.

I've come to regard a ringing doorbell in the same way I do a ringing phone. Unless I have an appointment or am expecting a friend or a delivery, I simply don't answer the door if it's inconvenient. My friends know not to drop by without calling first.

"But what if it's the postman delivering a certified letter?" a friend asked me. Have you ever had *good* news by certified mail? As far as I'm concerned it can wait. "But it is so rude not to answer the door," she protested. Certainly we've been brought up to think that way. But I've come to feel that, in fact, it's rude for someone to show up at the door unannounced and expect me to drop whatever I'm doing and answer it just because it happens to be convenient for them.

I admit it does take some hardening of your social graces. But if you're regularly bothered by unannounced callers at your front door, learning to just let the doorbell ring can make your life a lot easier.

Or, consider installing a spyhole, so at the very least you know for whom you're opening your door and your time.

# 32. Get Rid of Your Car Phone

∽

You already know that I'm not fond of the sound of a ringing telephone, so please forgive me a certain level of prejudice on this issue.

I know many people who caved in when the price of car phones dropped below five hundred dollars. Some people, like the half-dozen real estate agents I know who have car phones and say they couldn't do business without them, presumably have a legitimate need to have constant access to a telephone. But most of the people I know, including even some of the real estate people, say car phones are another one of those "conveniences" that are more trouble than they're worth.

First, there's the safety factor, which has never been adequately addressed by the manufacturers, the regulatory agencies, or the media. More than one person I know has given up their car phone because of near-miss accidents that occurred when engaged in a heavy-duty conversation while barreling down the highway at sixty-five miles per hour. Worse yet are the clowns who are busy punching in a seven-digit phone number while maneuvering through rush-hour traffic with a five-speed stickshift car.

At the very least, use caution and common sense where you use a car phone. If you have to make a call en route, pull off to the side of the road to place your call. Or, if possible, have a fellow passenger make the call for you.

Second, there's the frustration of the as-yet-unperfected technology that causes conversations to fade in and out, or to be cut off altogether if you pass outside your calling area. This is convenience?

Third, safety aside, there is the sheer lunacy of committing ourselves to yet again doing at least two things at the same time. Have we really gotten *that* busy?

Fourth, there's the expense. If, as my father used to say, you've got more money than brains, there's probably no real harm done spending it frivolously on calls that could in most cases more easily and at far less expense be made from a stationary phone. But if you're working within a tight budget, you might want to seriously reconsider what having a car phone really saves you.

# 33. If You Don't Like
## the Holidays, Bow Out

~

Major holidays are among the most stressful, and therefore least simple, times of the year. Be honest. How often have you fervently and possibly not so secretly wished that you didn't have to go through with today's commercialized Christmas and all the shopping, presents, cooking, office parties, family dinners, overeating, overdrinking, and overspending that's a long way from simple and in fact complicates your life a good deal?

I know there are people out there who actually love celebrating Christmas and all the other holidays. If you're one of them, that's great—do so, and enjoy. But if you can't bear the thought of sitting through another Christmas dinner, you're not alone. Studies show that for many people Christmas is the most depressing time of the year. Now that we're in the enlightened nineties, we know we all come from dysfunctional families. It's no big deal to finally admit that the holidays are a pain in the neck and move on to other things we'd rather do.

Imagine how you'd like to spend the time you've previously spent on holidays—ensconsed on the sofa with a stack of good books, relaxing in front of the VCR with your favorite movies, hiking, skiing, or even using the time for private reflection with your family—then set it up exactly as you'd like it to be. We know a couple with three teenage children who have forsaken the holidays altogether and go camping instead. It's a chance for closeness with each other and with nature and an opportunity to escape the commercialism they no longer want to have in their lives. We know another couple who decided years ago that Christmas was for children. They buy or make special Christmas gifts for the kids in their life, and make a donation to their favorite charity each year for the grown-ups.

To make the transition as easy and as painless as possible, announce well ahead of time to all your family and friends that you no longer want to do Christmas (or Thanksgiving, or Easter, or birthdays, or any one or all of these), or that you want to do it differently from now on and explain why. Let them know you'll be making other arrangements for the holidays.

Realize that not everyone is going to understand your position, and some might even be hurt by it. If the guilt becomes too heavy, you may have to compromise: Do Thanksgiving but not Christmas. Or whatever.

Also realize that while some may pretend to be hurt, they might actually be delighted that they don't have to suffer through another Christmas, but they're too tradition-bound to admit it.

Just think. If you act now, you can free yourself from one of the most stressful events of the year. Don't waste another moment. This year do Christmas your way.

# 34. Stop Sending Christmas Cards

∽

"Stop sending Christmas cards? You've got to be kidding," moaned a friend of mine. "It's my favorite thing about Christmas."

If, like my friend, you love sending Christmas cards, by all means do it; this suggestion is not addressed to you. It is addressed to all those people who start grousing in mid-July that they haven't picked out their Christmas cards yet, and to all the ones who are still mumbling by the end of November that they haven't gotten around to addressing their cards yet, and to the ones who are still grumbling by the middle of December that they haven't had time to pick up the Christmas stamps from the post office yet, and they don't know how they'll possibly get them mailed in time for Christmas.

This is also addressed to those people who send printed-signature cards. Hand-picked or lovingly hand-produced Christmas cards are a joy to receive. What is surprising is that in these days of environmental awareness there are people and businesses that year in and year out are still sending the printed-signature, rubber-stamped, or signed-by-their-secretary Christmas cards. I've never been able to figure out what the message on these cards is, or why anyone would bother sending a card they didn't have the time to at least address, sign, and stamp themselves.

For many people, the printed-signature holiday card has become the symbol for what's wrong with Christmas. It's impersonal, it's commercial, it's expensive, the real message is not a positive one, it clutters up our lives, and it's an environmental waste.

If you're ready to stop sending Christmas cards, you can begin to let people know that this is your last year for doing cards. Or, cut your list by half or more and send cards only to those you truly want to keep in touch with. The chances are good the other people on your list will understand, and it may free them from feeling they have to send cards as well.

# 35.  Gift-Giving Simplified

~

I have a friend who has quite a large extended family and they all remember each other's birthdays and anniversaries, not to mention Christmas and other holidays, with gifts. Hardly a month goes by without my friend agonizing over what to give some member of her family whose birthday is approaching. Invariably, she ends up settling on something she is not happy with. Usually, neither is the recipient, though neither of them would ever admit it.

In trying to simplify the perennial problem of gift-giving, I've come to the conclusion that the Hobbits, in J.R.R. Tolkien's epic fantasy, were right: mathoms are the answer. A mathom was an object of any value for which a use could not be found, but which the owner was not prepared to discard completely. A Hobbit would never *buy* a gift; they gave mathoms instead.

When we started the uncluttering process of our simplification program (#1), I set up a section in our linen closet for items that would make good mathoms. It included things like vases, trays, decanters, little decorative bowls and boxes, toasters, a mini-Cuisinart, games we no longer used, and any extras I was getting rid of (#99) that might be appropriate.

I also announced to family and friends that from this day forward I'd be giving mathoms rather than buying presents. I figure if you're going to give someone you love something they probably have no use for, it should at least be blessed by having a history with you first.

Now, when special occasions arise at which a gift would be appropriate, I search in our closet for a suitable mathom. I've also let my friends know that they are free to pass on (or possibly fob off) these "treasures" to someone else whenever appropriate.

If you have the knack of gift-giving, please share it with those of us who don't. But if you find gift-buying an occasion for pulling out your hair, consider setting up a mathom box. Rather than spending untold hours shopping for and agonizing over gifts that are never quite right, you can go straight to your mathom box and find something that's absolutely not right.

And by the way, an excellent source for mathoms is all the gifts *you've* received over the years that have never been quite right either.

Don't forget to have your children set up a mathom box of their toys and games they no longer use. Have them get in the habit of thinking of other possibly younger children who would be delighted with a new-to-them toy. This creates a natural recycling process for your kids' toys, and is another lesson in uncluttering.

# 36.  Traveling Simplified

∽

Gibbs is, among other things, a travel writer. In the fifteen years we've been married we have traveled tens of thousands of miles all around the world. We've crossed huge oceans on tiny yachts; ridden trains across desolate continents; paddled up quiet waterways; rafted down whitewater rivers; hiked over scrub-covered mountains; and walked through many of the major capitals of the world.

If there is one thing we've learned in all these years, it's how to travel light, and still have everything we need. Well, almost everything.

The bind many travelers get into is, in addition to packing all the things they'll need for a two-week trip, they also pack all the things they *might* need for a two-week trip. Here are some ways to avoid that.

For most vacation travel, start by making a list of the different types of clothes you'd like to take, such as dressy, casual, sporty, and loungewear. Then cross off everything but the casual clothes. That's all you use for most trips.

Go to your closet and pull out all the appropriate casual clothes. (Now that you've simplified your wardrobe [#22], you won't have a lot of clothes to confuse you.) Fold them, and arrange them in piles on the bed, shirts in one stack, slacks in another, etc. Then put at least one half of the items from each stack back in your closet. Let's face it: if you get there and think you need something, in most cases you can get along without it. THIS IS THE SECRET TO TRAVELING LIGHT: THERE IS SO LITTLE WE REALLY NEED AND YOU CAN ALWAYS GET ALONG WITHOUT IT. (This is also the secret to simplifying your life.)

Wear and take only dark-colored clothes.

Make sure each piece of clothing you take can be worn with every other piece.

Always, even in hot climates, wear or take a blazer or jacket or vest with all the pockets you can get, and one that can go from casual to dressy, if need be.

Take only what will fit in one of the rollerboard-type cases with wheels. We recommend the TravelPro 727, available at most luggage stores. It's lighter in weight than the hard cases and holds more, though if an elephant sat on it, you'd have to get another one. Also, it has a plethora of outside pockets for conveniently stowing tickets, reading material, and other goodies, so you don't need any other bag. Best of all, it meets FAA regulations for carry-on luggage on all domestic flights and many, though not all, international flights.

Use a toilet kit or cosmetics bag that unfolds and can be hung on the back of a door or on a towel rack and that fits right into your TravelPro. (If you're a guy, you've probably already got a simple kit; if you're a woman, and have learned how to be drop-dead gorgeous in ten minutes [#90], you won't need a hair dryer, or any of that other stuff.)

Take only two pairs of shoes, both of the same height, preferably low-heeled, and both of them comfortable.

Imagine how simple it would be to take off for a month and go halfway around the world with only one small bag you can easily roll through busy traffic, up and down stairs, across railroad tracks, around grassy knolls, through cobbled streets, and over the Nullarbor Plain.

# 37.  Take a Vacation
## at Home

Some of the most fun and relaxing vacations Gibbs and I ever had we've taken at home. If you're just getting started on your simplification program, a vacation at home is a perfect way to begin.

You could start your vacation by getting rid of all the clutter in your life (#1). Making a family project out of this step is not only fun but a good way to set up a check system so that no one cheats.

Taking a vacation at home is also a good time to start a new hobby (#53), or to get your house in shape for speed cleaning (#3), or to plant a garden (#6), or to do any number of the things you've been wanting to do, but haven't had the time because you've been too busy and you're never home.

We spent one vacation getting to know our local community. We realized at one point that there were many visitors to our area who knew our town in some respects better than we did. So we took a day and went to all the art galleries and museums. We took another day and walked every street in the downtown area. We saw new stores and changes to old ones that we hadn't known about. We took another day and walked through several residential areas; we saw new houses and additions to old ones, and got a firsthand look at the local flora and fauna of our neighborhoods. We also had picnics on the beach and in a couple of our local parks. All of these things contributed to a new feeling of pride and familiarity with our town.

You could take a vacation at home to get caught up on your reading list. If you wanted to take a break from reading, you could watch new videos of favorite movies you've been wanting to see. A home vacation is an excellent time to organize a simple eating program (#57), to begin your daily exercise plan (#63), or set up the model ship building project you've been promising to do with the kids. Or, you could take a vacation at home and learn to do absolutely nothing (#82).

*Hint:* It's often easier if you tell your co-workers, friends, and especially your family that you'll be "away" on vacation. Otherwise, your vacation time may well be taken up by other people's crises.

*Three*

# Your Finances

# 38. Get Out of Debt

෮

There's a good chance that your parents, like mine, were survivors of the Great Depression. Throughout their lives my folks had one inviolate rule when it came to finances: If they didn't have the cash in hand, they didn't buy it. With the exception of the mortgage on their home, they never had a debt in their lives. They simply refused to take advantage of the post–World War II buy now–pay later mentality that has made us a nation of consumers and debtors. Whenever they needed a new piece of furniture or a major appliance, they took money from their "contingency" fund, or, if the fund was depleted, they *waited* until they had set the money aside by saving a little each month.

Many people from our parents' and our parents' parents' generation lived that way. Considering the fact that debt is one of the leading causes of emotional and psychological stress in our lives, many of us would do well to live that way today.

If you're one of the more than fifty million Americans for

whom credit card or installment debt has become a problem, there are a couple of things you can do:

1. *You can take steps to get out of debt on your own.*
This means sitting down and figuring out exactly how much you owe, then setting up a plan so that you can pay it off as quickly and as methodically as possible, even though it may take several years to do it. It also means making a promise to yourself to stay out of debt in the future. This solution is doable, but it requires discipline, determination, and a total commitment to getting out from under the stress caused by debt.

2. *If you suspect you're in over your head and you're beginning to think you'll never get out on your own, you can get help.*
Jerold Mundis, in his excellent book, *How to Get out of Debt, Stay out of Debt & Live Prosperously* (Bantam Books, available in paperback), offers a time-tested system for getting out of debt. Based on the principles used in Debtors Anonymous, the program he outlines has been used successfully for years to free thousands of people from a life of debt.

This solution also requires discipline, determination, and

commitment, but the book provides a proven, step-by-step program to help you along the way.

I can't promise you that getting out of debt will be easy, but it will certainly simplify your life.

## 39. Live on Half of What You Earn, and Save the Other Half

෴

It's estimated that less than 10 percent of Americans are in the enviable position of having all their present and future financial needs taken care of. A large percentage of the people who will be retiring over the next twenty-five years will have little more than their Social Security payments to sustain them. And there aren't many people who are betting money that Social Security will be an adequate or even a viable source of retirement income in years to come.

We've become a nation of spenders rather than savers. While it's true that many people have been forced to live beyond their means because of the increase in the cost of living and the decline in the value of the dollar, it's also true that we spend far more than we need to on stuff we don't really require.

If you're feeling so out of control in terms of your spending that you think you couldn't possibly save a significant portion of your income, take a close look at *how* you spend your money. If you feel you can't make major cuts in your spending, start by cutting back by only 10 or 15 percent over the next year. Then cut back another 10 or 15 percent beyond that the following year, gradually building up to 50 percent.

Close to half of the items in this book will help you reduce your spending. Living simply is not a matter of living cheaply or of feeling deprived. On the contrary, it's an opportunity to get in touch with what is really important in your life, and to reach a level of moderation that will create not only a feeling of contentment and security, but also a sense of being in control.

If you've been living on the edge, getting to the point where you can stash away a good portion of your income each month to take care of your future needs will put you back in the driver's seat, and go a long way toward simplifying your life.

# 40. Rethink Your Buying Habits

~

Several years ago, Gibbs and I decided we needed to get a set of hand-held weights to use on our daily walks. So we rushed right down to the sporting goods store and spent fifty dollars on a set of Heavy Hands.

Over the next two weeks we used the set half a dozen times and then put them aside and never touched them again.

Six months later I gave the Heavy Hands to a friend who mentioned she was going to rush down to the sporting goods store to buy some hand-held weights. She has used them once and, if my guess is right, she'll never pick them up again, except possibly to pass them on to the next person she hears about who is going to rush down to the sporting goods store to buy a set of Heavy Hands.

This is just one example of the dozens of things we've bought over the years that we really didn't need and, after we'd used them for a short time, didn't even want. You no doubt have your own list of similar purchases, some more expensive than others, but all bought with the same compulsive "I've got to have this *now*" syndrome. For the average

American, our lives—and our homes, our cars, and our work spaces—are filled with the flotsam of our buying habits.

Once Gibbs and I could face the fact that we had yet again bought one more thing we didn't need, we decided we should rethink our buying habits. So we sat down and drew up a list of ways we could do things differently:

*1.* We designated one day a week for shopping; this includes groceries and anything else we think we might need.

2. Now, before we buy something, we think it through. Many of the things we buy are simply momentary gratifications. We've gotten into the habit of asking ourselves, "Do we *really* need this whatever-it-is?" "How *long* will we need it or want it?" "Will this be just one more thing to end up in the back of a closet?"

3. We delay all major purchases—and many of the minor ones—for at least two weeks, or even a month. We've found that by the time the end of the month rolls around we've figured out that we didn't really need the item, whatever it was, in the first place.

4. Or, alternatively, we see how long we can live without whatever it is we currently think we can't live without. Making a game out of this gives an extra boost to our determination *not* to acquire more clutter.

5. We try to come up with a creative solution rather than a buying solution to a perceived need. For example, there were many ordinary household items—books, or a pair of socks filled with sand—we could have used instead of running out to *buy* a set of Heavy Hands.

# 41. Change the Way You Shop

If you have trouble controlling the urge to buy, make it hard on yourself: go shopping if you must, but leave your cash, checkbook, and credit cards at home.

For many people, buying is nothing more than a habit. The way to break any habit is to replace the offending activity with another activity. Draw up a list of things you can do instead of shopping so that next time you get the urge to spend money on things you don't need, you'll have something else to do instead.

For example, take a walk, get together with a friend, go to the library, or take a cold shower—anything to avoid spending time shopping. Though initially you may feel deprived by the absence of shopping in your life, there is ultimately an exhilarating freedom in getting to a point where you don't *have* to buy.

Use the Buddy System. If there is something you've decided you absolutely must have, take a friend who is familiar with your buying habits and who is sympathetic to your desire to change them. Have your friend police your purchases so you buy only the item you set out to acquire. Make sure you pick the right buddy, though. I used to go shopping with a friend, and we'd spend time encouraging each other to buy things neither of us needed as a means to justify our own spending habits.

Pay for everything you buy by check. This makes it slightly more difficult than if you pay by cash or credit card, and also makes it easier to keep track of what you buy, and how you spend your money.

Practice looking at advertising with a jaundiced eye. It's the "thrill" of buying that is addictive. Once the thrill has worn off, you've got to do it again. That's what advertisers count on. Once you become aware of the control advertisers have over your money it's much easier to hold on to it.

## 42. Reduce Your Needs for Goods and Services

One of the myths of the eighties was that the more goods we had and the more help we hired, the simpler our lives would become. In the process of simplifying I have found just the opposite is true.

Rethinking your buying habits (#40) and changing the way you shop (#41) will reduce the "goods" that clutter up your life. Many of the other steps outlined in this book will reduce your need for "services."

For example, once you start simplifying, your house will be so easy to take care of you won't need the cleaning lady; your meals will be so basic you won't need the cook; your errands will be so organized you won't need the chauffeur; your wardrobe will be so minimal you won't need a fashion consultant; your investments will be consolidated so you won't need a bookkeeper; your purchases will be limited so you won't need a shopping service; your entertainment will be reduced so you won't need a babysitter; your phone system so direct you won't need an answering service; your lawn will be eliminated so you won't need the gardener; your home will be uncluttered so you won't need a professional organizer; your relationships will be cleaned up so you won't need a psychotherapist; and your health and fitness program will be so easy you won't need a personal trainer.

Just the scheduling (not to mention the rescheduling), arranging for transportation, getting people to do things right, arranging to pay them, and finding someone to take their place when they quit (which they don't do until just about the time you've gotten them trained) is complicated enough to make me want to avoid most of these "services" like the plague.

Again, we're talking about personal choice here. We each have to decide for ourselves the point at which the goods and services we have in our lives cease to make our lives easier, and begin to become a burden. Our own goal was to arrange our lives so that we could easily take care of most of our personal needs and possessions on our own. We've created a whole new sense of freedom for ourselves by eliminating most of the goods and services we once thought we couldn't live without.

## 43. Get Rid of All But One or Two of Your Credit Cards

*∽*

$B$y the time we decided to simplify our lives, Gibbs and I between us had nine credit cards. We didn't *need* nine credit cards. We didn't *use* nine credit cards. We didn't even *want* nine credit cards. We had them because, like Everest to the climber, they were there. We could have had many more. They arrived, unbidden and with increasing frequency, in the mailbox. It was so easy to just add one more card to our system on the theory that you never know when you might need an extra one.

In fact, the only time we've ever used credit cards is for dining out and for traveling—and we always paid the bill in full each month. Not only were all these cards a nuisance to keep track of, but we had to pay anywhere from $25 to $100 a year for the "privilege" of carrying them.

It wasn't until I started reducing our junk mail (#26) that I began to realize that getting rid of all but one of our credit cards would be another step in simplifying our lives. Not only would it eliminate at least a dozen or more pieces of mail each month (in addition to regular statements, there are routine promotional pieces as well), but it would save us several hundred dollars a year in annual fees, as well as the hassle of carrying and rotating the cards.

After doing some research, we canceled all of our cards, and got one Visa card. We used one of the many banks that offer a choice of a $25 annual fee and an interest rate of 9 percent above prime on the unpaid balance, or no annual fee and a slightly higher interest rate. Since we pay off the balance each month, we chose the no annual fee. We now have a card that costs nothing and is very easy to keep track of.

It took us a while, but we finally figured out that having one or two credit cards is a convenience. Any more than that is more trouble than it's worth.

# 44. Consolidate Your
# Checking Accounts

*ᴄᴏ*

Early in our simplification program, I realized that my banking system had gotten out of hand. I had four or five separate bank accounts, which I had gradually been acquiring over the years: one for household expenses, one for business, one for contingencies, one for investments, one for savings. A banker friend told me that it's not at all uncommon for people to have multiple bank accounts these days; some at the same bank, some spread around banks all over town. Like many multiple account holders, I had deluded myself into thinking multiple accounts were a convenience.

In terms of the excess mail that multiple accounts generate, not only are there the regular monthly statements for each account, but there are all the additional monthly promotional pieces, credit card offerings, and other inducements that have to be sorted through with the real mail.

In terms of the banking, not only did each of those monthly statements have to be reconciled, but I had to keep track of four or five separate checkbooks in addition to having to keep track of which account was to be used for which expenditures.

More than once I had created major hassles for myself by writing checks on the wrong account.

Then, of course, there was the complication of making sure there were sufficient funds in each account to cover the checks.

If you find you are burdened by multiple checking accounts, getting rid of all but one of them will greatly simplify your banking chores. If you like the idea of keeping your savings fund and your contingency fund separate from your household funds—or whatever different accounts you have—you might want to consider adopting my simplified check register system outlined in #45.

# 45. Use This Simple Check Register System

୶

When I got rid of all but one of my checking accounts I still found it convenient to have separate categories for my expenditures, so I set up those categories in one account and used check registers to keep those categories separate.

For example, now I maintain three categories in my checking account: Household, Savings, and Investment. I use two standard wallet-sized check registers, fitted together on one side of my checkbook; on the other side I keep the checks.

Since I write more checks from the Household category, I label the first check register "Household." Then I divide the second check register into two categories, "Savings" and "Investments."

For ease in reconciling bank statements, I enter all my deposits in the "Household" section, and then "transfer" funds to the other sections, as needed. To do this, I simply make an entry in the "Household" section that reads "Transfer to Savings" and then list the amount, one thousand or whatever, in the debit column, and *deduct* that from the Household balance. Then I immediately turn to the "Savings" section, and make the appropriate entry, "From Household," and indicate the amount in the deposit column, which is then *added* to the balance in that section. If we decide to make a purchase with the money we have set aside in Savings, I simply record the check in the Savings section of the check register, and then deduct the amount from the total shown there.

It's the same with money shown in the Investment section. When we have built a sufficient investment balance, I write a check, say for a mutual fund purchase, and record the check in the Investment section of the check register, and deduct it accordingly.

When it comes time to reconcile a bank statement, I first sort the checks by category (Household, Savings, Investment), then go through each section of the check register and cross off the checks accordingly. Since all the bank deposits are shown in the Household section of the register, it's easy to confirm that each deposit is shown on the statement.

By maintaining these divisions internally in one account, I've eliminated all the other bank accounts, the other checkbooks, the other bank statements, and the need to reconcile them all. Obviously, you can set up any other categories that suit your personal needs. Just don't get carried away. Remember, the objective is to keep it simple.

## 46. Consolidate Your Investments

～

Over the past fifteen years or so, mutual funds have become the investment haven for small investors. I have a friend who woke up one day and realized she had funds in more than a dozen different mutual fund accounts. Actually, of course, she'd known all along that she had a number of different accounts, she just hadn't realized how much such diversity in her investments complicated her life. Dealing with the account statements and regular promotional mailings from each of the funds was a major headache, and tracking each of the accounts had finally become overwhelming. But it was the amount of time her accountant had to spend each year calculating the dividends and capital gains on all these accounts that was the nightmare.

Things had started out simply enough. When she started investing, she did some research, came up with a couple of funds she thought were good, and set up accounts in them. As time went on, she discovered other funds that sounded good, so she gradually started spreading out, both with her IRA funds and with her regular investments. Each time she heard of another stellar performance in a fund, she'd open another account.

Most investment advisers agree that as long as you pick a reputable family of funds, it almost doesn't matter which one you invest in over the long haul. The important thing is to set aside funds and invest consistently, year in and year out. If you want to diversify, say among income funds, growth funds, and tax-free funds, do so within the family of the fund you choose.

My friend has started gradually to consolidate her investment funds. Her accountant has thanked her. Her mailman has thanked her. Even her trashman has noticed the lighter load.

## 47.   Pay Off Your Mortgage

If you're living in the house of your dreams, you plan to stay there, and your mortgage payments are within your means, you might want to think about taking steps to pay down your mortgage early. Or pay it off entirely.

For years we've had it drummed into us that the tax savings of home ownership make carrying a mortgage worthwhile. You'll need to look at your own situation, and perhaps run it by your accountant, but when you do the numbers, the savings are actually not that significant. Besides, many people are beginning to realize that the freedom of owning their home outright far outweighs whatever tax savings there might be.

There are several ways you can approach mortgage paydowns:

1. Lump sum payments. If, in addition to your regular salary, you receive sizable cash infusions from time to time, consider using them to pay down your mortgage. Before you make a large payment, however, make sure your lender will

re-amortize your loan so that your monthly payments will be reduced.

2. Extra principal payments. You can significantly reduce the term of your mortgage and save many thousands of dollars over the life of your loan by making the next month's principal payment each time you make your regular monthly payment. You will need to get a copy of the amortization schedule from your lender. Or, if you have a variable rate loan, ask your lender for the calculation they use to figure the next month's principal payment.

3. Since the amount of the payment that is applied to principal increases with each payment, there may come a time down the road when the increased principal payment becomes more than you can handle. If that happens, you can simply pay whatever amount is comfortable for you toward the principal each month. You'll still save a substantial amount in interest payments, and be able to pay off your mortgage sooner than you would have otherwise.

4. Sell your home and move to a smaller, less expensive home. Depending on the equity you have in your home, and on real estate values in the area where you now live and in the area you would be moving to, it is possible you could use the proceeds from the sale of your current home to pay for your

new home in full, or at least significantly lower the amount of the new mortgage. Again, you'll want to check with your accountant. If you're approaching age fifty-five, keep in mind your $125,000 tax exclusion.

Any of these mortgage paydown plans assume that you have paid off all other outstanding debts, such as credit cards or installment loans, and that you have sufficient funds set aside for emergencies and investments. Paying your mortgage early will not necessarily *immediately* simplify your life; but it will get you out from under the eternal psychological pressure of monthly mortgage payments.

## 48.  Next Time You Buy a Car, Get It Secondhand

∾

When you consider that a new car loses 30 percent or more of its value the moment you drive it off the sales lot, you have to wonder why anyone would ever purchase a brand-new car.

A high percentage of new-car buyers trade in their cars every two to three years. These trade-ins are an excellent source of used cars. Often, they've been carefully driven and diligently maintained, so it's relatively easy to pay a mechanic to determine if there are any major defects. Generally speaking, if a car is going to develop problems, it'll happen in the first ten to fifteen thousand miles.

Also, keep in mind that after two years, a car has dropped another 30 percent from its original value. So, if you buy directly from the owner—never from a used car dealer— you can save 60 percent off the original sticker price of the car.

Not only will buying a secondhand car save you money and, one hopes, the hassle of financing and monthly payments, but, if you buy carefully, you'll have a car that has already had the bugs worked out of it, and that you can probably count on for many thousands of miles of trouble-free driving.

# 49. Teach Your Kids Fiscal Responsibility

*ᵕᵕ*

I have a friend who recently found herself in reduced circumstances because of a divorce. As part of the divorce settlement she agreed to give up her high-powered foreign car, and to buy a somewhat more modest set of wheels. She took her ten-year-old son with her to pick out the new car and ended up, at her son's importunate urging, buying the most expensive model with leather seats, pinstriping, and, for an additional fifteen hundred dollars, gold trim. She was lamenting that she had spent all this extra money because she hadn't been able to tell her son that she couldn't afford it.

We all want the best for our children, and certainly there are times when it's hard to say no. But I can't help but wonder what kind of lessons we are teaching our kids by spending money on glitz and glitter "image builders," especially when we can't afford them.

As we are forging new spending habits for ourselves, either by desire or necessity or both, we should also be building sensible buying habits for our kids. Children are adaptable, and can learn to adjust quite well to a reasonable set of limits.

We just have to make sure they know what the limits are.

Teach your kids to save half of what they earn from their allowance or parttime jobs. Kids can learn, just as we are learning, that we don't have to have everything we see or everything the Joneses have. Kids can learn, just as we are learning, that there are options: if they get the gold trim on the car they can't have the new dirt bike. Kids can learn how to budget so their expenses don't exceed their income. Kids can learn, as we are learning, how advertisers appeal to our emotions rather than our needs. Kids can learn that if they don't have the money, they can't afford it, and that buying on credit can often lead to serious financial difficulties.

Teaching our kids how to handle their money is one of the most powerful gifts we can give them. And not only will it ultimately simplify their lives, but it'll simplify our lives, too.

*Four*

# Your Job

## 50. Stop Being a Slave to Your Day Runner

*ᴄ⁓*

I first started making "to-do" lists when I was in the third grade. Over the years, I graduated from simple 3″ × 5″ spiral notebooks to an 11″ × 16″ black leather briefcase-type three-ring-binder time-management system with a two-page spread for my daily schedule and up to a dozen tabulated sections for goals, priorities, strategies, decisions, communications, addresses and phone numbers, forward planners, backward planners, mind maps, expense summaries, personal information, daily (and monthly and weekly and yearly) calendars, and a priority management overflow chart (whatever that was). Any yuppie worth his salt is familiar with this or a similar system for personal organization.

I actually spent a day and a half and more dollars than I'm comfortable admitting learning how to use this organizer. It required a commitment of at least thirty minutes each day to evaluate progress, check off completed items, and transfer unfinished business to the next day's two-page spread. Fully loaded, the binder weighs over five pounds, occupies 4.2 square feet of desk space, and I couldn't go around the block without having to lug it with me in case I was overcome with a brilliant idea, or remembered something I had to add to my Communication Planner Sheet.

For some people, these organizers probably serve a useful function (in addition to making money for their franchisers). I made zillions of phone calls each day, scheduled appointments around the clock, had a handful of projects going at any one time, and definitely needed a way to keep track of it all. It was just that, like many other yuppie Type A personalities, I'd overdone it.

Fortunately, I looked at my planner one day and realized I didn't want my life to be that complicated. This was the beginning of my simplification program.

Gradually, over time, I simplified not only my home and personal and business life, but my planning system as well. I went from that gargantuan book to a 3″ × 5″ appointment calendar, which can fit into a small pocket, but stays on a tiny corner of my desk most of the time. There were several stops in between, but I finally reached a size and a system that was compatible with my simple life.

If you're controlled by your time-management system, maybe it's time to look at how you can change it so that you control it instead.

## 51. Work Where You Live or Live Where You Work

$\infty$

A few years ago Gibbs worked in a major metropolitan area and we lived in the suburbs, nearly two hours away by commuter train. This meant that he, like millions of other commuters, often spent more than four hours each day just getting to and from his office. Usually, he'd leave the house at 6:30 in the morning and return home around 7:00 in the evening. Is this madness? Yes. Why do we do this to ourselves? For many people it comes under the category of "getting ahead." We finally faced the fact that we were trading our present for a questionable future. So we made some major changes in our lives.

We moved to a part of the country where we could live in the same town where we worked. What a difference. Now we can linger over breakfast in the morning after we've taken our brisk three-mile walk along the beach. Gibbs leaves the house around 8:15 and arrives at his office before 8:30. At least once a week he takes off early on a Wednesday afternoon and spends several hours climbing to the top of our local mountain peak to clear his head. He's always home by 5:30 in the evening, and when the days are long we frequently go for a paddle, or perhaps take another walk before dinner. Maybe we'll spend some quiet time together reading, or watching a beautiful sunset; things that are important to us, and which we could never do when he was trapped on a steamy, smelly, overcrowded, frequently late, and always uncomfortable commuter train. These things are also hard to do when one is stranded in commuter traffic on the freeway.

Yes, we no doubt gave up some career "advancement" by moving away from the hub, but the vast improvement in the quality of our lives more than makes up for it. The only thing we wonder is why we didn't make the move sooner.

## 52. Do What You Really Want to Do

*~*

$F$ew things complicate your life more than spending eight to ten hours a day, five to six days a week at a job you don't like, doing something you don't want to do.

Unfortunately, the *process* of figuring out what you want to do and then doing it isn't necessarily simple. Unlike canceling your newspaper subscription (#28), which can be completed with a phone call, setting up your life so that you're doing what you really want to do can take months.

Your task will be easier if you know what you want to do. Simply make up your mind to make the switch, and then do it. The process will no doubt include research, making new contacts, updating your résumé, possibly going back to school, maybe making a move across town or across country, and in some cases starting all over again.

If you don't know what you want to do, you have the added burden of figuring it out, which could mean research, testing, counseling, experimentation, and then, as above, figuring out *how* to do it, including most likely starting all over again. But having just spent two years figuring out what it is I want to do, and then arranging my life so I can do it, I can promise you it will be worth whatever complications you have to go through to get there, and it will definitely simplify your life in the long run.

# 53.  Turn Your Hobby
## Into Your Job
*⁓*

One of the wonderful benefits of simplifying my life is that
I have created more time to devote to my hobby, reading. But
it can work the other way, too—making time for your favorite
pastime can simplify your life.

A few years ago my friend Sandra, an attorney, took a leave
of absence for the entire summer to visit her sister, who lives
in Italy. They were in a small village in the mountains with not
a whole lot going on. Her sister suggested they visit a neighbor's sculpting studio. Sandra knew nothing at all about
sculpture and wasn't really interested, but because there was
nothing else to do, she agreed to go along. She didn't know
it then, but she'd found a hobby that would eventually change
her life.

She spent every day for the rest of her vacation in that
studio, learning everything she could about sculpting. When
she returned home, she enrolled in a sculpture class. She
resumed her legal practice during her workday, but her evenings and weekends were now devoted to her stone. Gradually, she began to acquire the various tools she needed, and,

eventually, she set up a studio in her home. Before long she was selling her work at local art shows. Recently, she resigned from her law practice and is now a full-time sculptor. She exhibits her work regularly at galleries around the country. Sandra says her life has never been better—or simpler. Before sculpting, her life was filled with phone calls, appointments, depositions, briefs, court appearances, and the endless number of other things required by the legal profession. Now, her life consists of getting up in the morning, pulling on her jeans, and going to her studio to sculpt. Her gallery manager handles all the mundane details of her business. Of course, the fact that she is doing something she truly loves also contributes to the simplicity in her life.

I have another friend who combined his hobby, helicopter flying, with his profession, physical therapy. He set up his new business in a remote resort area where there is a lot of hiking and other physical activities and, consequently, vacationers with physical injuries who need to be flown out to medical facilities. He simplified his life so he could do what he wanted to do, and his life has never been busier or more complicated. But it's a complication he loves, and that makes all the difference in the world.

In any case, if you're not already doing what you love, starting with a hobby is one way to get there.

# 54.  Work Less and
## Enjoy It More

Once I decided to simplify my life, one of the first things I did in terms of my business life was to cut back on my workday by 10 percent. I simply scheduled my day to end an hour earlier. I was surprised at how easy it was, and how little difference one hour less made in terms of my productivity. In fact, if anything, my productivity increased. Gradually, I cut back another hour or so, with little loss in production and a great increase in satisfaction. As I began to look at why this was so, I found that I had fallen into the trap of believing that I had to do everything today, or at the very latest, by tomorrow, so I was constantly working under unnecessary pressure, which is no fun.

Bit by bit, I learned to prioritize phone calls. Not *every* call had to be returned immediately. Some could wait a day or two; some could wait a week even. I found, to my delight, some never had to be returned at all.

In terms of projects, I learned to set up more realistic time-frames in which they could be completed, and began to realize, as with the phone calls, not everything had to be done today. I started doubling the time I estimated a particular project would take for completion. Not only was it easier to finish things on time, but there was less stress involved because I wasn't struggling to meet an impossible deadline.

I decided to build time into my schedule—at least an hour each day—for interruptions such as phone calls, unplanned meetings, searching for misplaced papers, and other time-robbers that are unavoidable in today's business world, but that we seldom account for. This meant even another hour of "unproductive" time, but these interruptions had always been there. Scheduling them simply forced me to admit they existed, and reduced the consequent anxiety about them.

Admittedly, because I was working for myself, I didn't have a boss breathing down my neck. But at the same time, anyone who has done it knows that we often create much more unrealistic schedules for ourselves than any boss ever would.

Whether you've been working ten- and twelve-hour days for yourself or for someone else, working less—even if you start by cutting back an hour or two only one or two days a week—is a realistic and effective way to get more out of your workday.

## 55.  Stop the Busy Work

Busy work is the nonproductive time we spend sharpening pencils, cleaning out our desks, making unnecessary phone calls, getting another cup of coffee, organizing our schedule, drawing up reports, doing research, making more unnecessary phone calls—things we convince ourselves have to be done before we can get down to our real work. Some busy work is unavoidable and necessary. What I'm talking about here is the avoidable kind.

There are two reasons for busy work. One, we don't want to do what we're really supposed to be doing. Two, we don't have anything that has to be done, but we want to look busy. In this age of workaholism, busy work has been elevated to an art form. It is the phenomenon that in many cases makes it seem imperative that we spend ten to twelve hours a day in the office.

One of the first things I gave up when I started working less but enjoying it more (#54) was busy work. It's difficult to define exactly what that would be for you, since the actual activities vary from person to person, and from job to job. But at some level you know if you're doing it, even though you probably wouldn't want to have to admit it publicly. I can only tell you that when you stop the busy work it'll simplify your life, not because you'll be doing less, but because a greater percentage of your work time will, I hope, be spent doing work that is much more satisfying. If you prioritize before you start work, and then don't do *anything* unless it's on your list, a lot of busy work will just evaporate.

## 56.  Include Your Family in Your Work Life

⌒

I have a friend who is a successful television producer. She works long hours in her office and on the set and is very good at what she does. She is married to a freelance artist who works at home and is Mr. Mom to their two young children.

One of the things Catherine and Jack decided to do to simplify their family life was to involve their children in their work life. The children are familiar with their father's work, since they're free to come and go in his art studio at home, and they've been to the galleries where his work is sold. At least two afternoons a week Jack takes the children to Catherine's office for lunch, and then to spend an hour or so on the set, watching their mother at work. They've met all of Catherine's co-workers, and most of their families, since Catherine encourages her staff to bring their children into the studio as well.

While having two young children in her office during her workday has been time-consuming for both parents, Jack and Catherine feel it's well worth the effort. The children have a good understanding of what their parents do when they are away from them, and they feel connected with work-related conversations between the parents. Before Catherine started involving the children in her work, they cried furiously when she left for the office and hated her leaving. Now that they know where their mother is going, the people she will be spending her time with, and approximately what she will be doing, they're much more amenable to her daily departure for the office.

An added and, at least to Catherine, unexpected benefit of having young children in the workplace on a regular basis has been that it helps to relieve the stress of a hectic and demanding job environment. Many of her harried executives have found it's a special treat to be able to walk into the office and spend even a few moments holding a laughing, bouncy baby, or to take the time to explain a procedure to a wide-eyed curious child. Having the children around has brought the staff closer together, too, since they have had an opportunity to get to know the special talents and needs of the other family members.

Obviously, not every workplace is set up for visiting children. But it might be worthwhile to think about ways you could involve your children in your work life. Perhaps you can take them to the office on the weekend, when things are less hectic. Have them meet your co-workers and, if possible, their children. Explain to them what it is you do, and show them samples of your work, or the results of your work. Keeping families together is certainly one way to relieve the complexity of today's world. Involving your children in your work life is a good way to start.

*Five*

## Your Health

## 57. Simplify Your Eating Habits

It's only fair to confess that my idea of gourmet cooking is slicing a peanut butter and jelly sandwich on the diagonal. I realize my opinions about simple eating habits may not appeal to the gourmets out there—but once we started to simplify, I decided to cut, by at least half, the time I spent in the kitchen cooking. Now, it's ten minutes, max, from fridge to table. (I mean, why should I spend a lot of time cooking when our favorite meal in all the world is a bag of blue corn tortilla chips with fresh guacamole?)

In addition to cutting our meal preparation time in half, I had two other objectives when it came to simplifying our eating habits:

One, even though at heart I really am a junk-food junkie, I wanted our diet to be healthy and nutritious. To us that meant primarily fresh fruits and vegetables and grains.

Two, I wanted it to be low in calories, fat, and cholesterol. Again, that meant fresh fruits and vegetables, in as close to their natural state as possible—no whipped, frothy, sugary concoctions for the fruit, and no cheese sauces or gravies for the veggies. It also meant cutting back on meats, especially red meats.

Also, I wanted to eliminate processed foods from our diet entirely.

Now, our meals look something like this:

Breakfast: fresh squeezed orange juice or fruit in season, and homemade granolas, or fresh homemade oat bran muffins. (For a simple recipe for delicious fresh fruit muffins see #61.)

Lunch: Fresh fruit and/or vegetable crudités, with whole-grain bread sandwiches, such as sliced roasted turkey or avocado, tomato, and sprouts.

Dinner: Huge fresh salad or cold soup, such as gazpacho in summer; or hearty veggie soup and salad in winter; or steamed veggies with rice dishes.

There are no surprises here. This is basically the diet food and health specialists have been recommending for years. The real surprise to us was that in simplifying our diet in this way, not only did we cut our meal preparation time in half, we also cut our monthly food bill by more than half. I'm constantly amazed, as I go through the grocery store with our computerized shopping list (#4), at all the things we *don't* buy. And now that we've come close to eliminating packaged foods from our diet, we have greatly reduced the amount of trash we have to dispose of each week.

# 58. Always Split a
# Restaurant Meal

When Gibbs and I were first married, we thought nothing of going out for a restaurant meal once or twice a week. We'd each order an appetizer with our before-dinner drink, then we'd scarf down the fresh baked bread (slathered with butter, of course) while waiting for our salads and the first bottle of wine. We'd each order an entrée, such as steak, veggies, and baked potato (with butter *and* sour cream). Then we'd finish off the dinner with a 1,000-calorie dessert and an after-dinner liqueur. Boy, are those days gone forever.

Gradually, the numbers on the scales began to get higher and higher, and we realized we'd have to make some changes. It took some experimentation, but we've finally over the years developed a system that works for us:

Both of us have stopped drinking alcohol; we got tired of the fuzzy head the morning after, and we'd rather save the calories for dessert. We've learned (reluctantly) to ask the waiter to remove the basket of fresh baked bread and the butter. Now, we split the entrée or, if we can't both agree on the same one, we each order an hors d'oeuvre. This, with a salad, is usually more than enough for one person, especially when we have a dessert—split, of course.

It is the rare restaurant that has learned how to serve reasonably sized portions for people who are concerned about their health and weight. Even rarer is the restaurant that takes into account the fact that, generally speaking, women need smaller portions than men. I know few clean-plate clubbers who, when faced with a heaping plate of what might be their favorite dish, can resist eating every single bite. And besides, there are all those starving children in China.

These days, most restaurants will allow you to split an entrée. Even if they charge a "split fee," it's well worth paying when you consider that if you order a whole entrée, and eat only half of it, the other half goes to waste; if you eat the whole entrée, it goes to your waist. If you find yourself in a restaurant that either doesn't serve human-sized portions or that won't split, don't patronize it and let the management know why.

We love eating out from time to time. Splitting a meal makes it possible for us to do so without the guilt and the distress of overeating.

# 59. Have a Fruit or Juice Fast One Day a Week

#### ✍

Another way to simplify your eating habits is to have only fresh fruit or fresh fruit juices one day a week.

I did this for years when I was single. I picked Saturdays because that was then the least demanding day of my week. I was usually at home, where I had easy access to the blender, and I could create the feeling of a "spa" weekend by relaxing and taking it easy.

After I got married, I switched my fruit day to Monday. Not only had the nature of my weekend changed, with a husband and an instant family, but eating only fruit on Monday seemed like a proper balance to the excesses of what was developing into our weekend pattern. Having nothing but fresh fruit one day a week certainly was a help in maintaining our weight.

Now that we've simplified our eating habits, we still have all-fruit days on a regular basis. One of our favorite treats is a drink made from an apple, a banana, a couple of oranges, and a handful of fresh strawberries or blueberries, or maybe a fresh peach. Obviously, any fresh fruit of your choice would work. We toss everything into the blender and press the button. It makes a fresh frappé that is a filling meal by itself. It's so good it almost feels sinful, and it couldn't be simpler.

# 60.   Make Water Your
# Drink of Choice

The most widely consumed liquids, in the order of preference, are coffee, sodas, diet sodas, milk, alcoholic beverages,
carbonated fruit drinks, and teas.

There are many reasons to make water your drink of
choice, but perhaps the best reason is that very few of the
alternative liquids are good for you.

We're all familiar by now with the many and varied problems associated with each of these liquid refreshments, not
the least of which are the empty calories or the potentially
harmful additives in sodas and sugar-free drinks. I switched
to drinking water almost exclusively years ago when I realized
that the alternatives were highly caloric. It was a personal
choice; I decided I'd rather save my calories for something
like chocolate mousse.

If you did nothing more than substitute water for these
liquids in your diet, you could easily lose ten to fifteen pounds
over the next year. If you fall into the over 75 percent of the

population that is at least 20 percent overweight, that may be reason enough to switch to water.

If your local tap water is good and clean, there is probably no need to buy bottled water. The tap water in our area tastes terrible so we drink bottled water, which, compared to any of the other liquids mentioned above, is inexpensive and readily available. With ice and a slice of lemon, we find it preferable to designer waters like Perrier and Calistoga.

If you're used to drinking highly flavored or stimulating liquids, water may seem boring at first. But after drinking water for a change, you'll wonder how you ever drank some of those yucky-sweet sodas and carbonated or caffeinated beverages we as a nation have become addicted to. Also, you'll be amazed at the reduction of glass and aluminum cans you have to worry about recycling.

Certainly if you have kids, one of the biggest favors you can do them is to keep them away from carbonated sodas. Someday they'll thank you.

*Hint:* Remember, coffee and caffeinated and carbonated drinks are addictive, so you'll need to brace yourself for the physical and psychological hazards accordingly. Even if you're not a heavy coffee drinker, quitting cold turkey can sometimes cause severe withdrawal symptoms, including migraine headaches, depression, and nausea. Start by cutting back by half for the first week, then by a quarter the second week. By the third week you should be able to quit altogether without adverse effects.

# 61.   Eat a Muffin

✍

Several years ago, after routine blood tests, both Gibbs and I found we had elevated cholesterol levels. After doing some research, we decided to significantly reduce our consumption of red meat. And, we got on the oat bran wagon.

We replaced our weekend eggs-and-bacon breakfasts with blueberry oat bran pancakes and maple syrup (but no butter). Also, Gibbs started experimenting with oat bran muffin recipes, and ultimately developed his own delicious, low-fat version, shown below. We started eating oat bran muffins in place of breads. Within a few months we had lowered our cholesterol levels to within acceptable ranges and, as an added benefit, we both lost weight.

Every week or so we make up a double batch of muffins—about two dozen. With all the ingredients on hand it takes roughly ten minutes to mix the batter, and another fifteen minutes or so to bake them. (This exceeds my ten-minute rule [#57] but, since it makes a two-week supply, I can justify it.)

These muffins are great with fruit or cereal for breakfast, with salads or soups for lunch, as a low-calorie, high-fiber between-meal snack, or even to keep the wolves from the door at bedtime. They're so delicious it seems amazing that they are also good for you. We expect to hear any day now that the cholesterol scare was a hoax, and that oat bran causes dancing deliriums in mice, or some such thing. In the meantime we continue to enjoy this simple, healthy treat.

## Gibbs's Oat Bran Muffins

*2¼ cups of oat bran (not bran flakes)*
*1 tbsp baking powder*
*¼ cup sugar or maple syrup*
*2 tbsp chopped almonds*
*handful of raisins or blueberries*
*¼ cup shredded coconut (optional)*
*1¼ cup nonfat milk*
*whites of two eggs, or one large egg if you're not concerned about cholesterol*
*2 large overripe bananas*

Combine all dry ingredients in a mixing bowl. Blend all other ingredients into a puree and mix thoroughly with the dry ingredients.

Fill muffin tins, allowing some room for mix to rise. If you use blueberries, it's easier if you add them by hand to the filled muffin tin.

Bake at 450°F until top of muffins are brown (about 15 minutes). Makes approximately one dozen muffins.

As soon as they're cool, we bag them and put them in the freezer. Whenever we want one, we pop it in the microwave oven for 30 seconds on high.

# 62. Pack Your Own Lunch

∽

This idea came about as a measure of self-defense against business lunches and the "I'll just grab a quick bite" method of solving the perennial question of what to do for lunch.

If, like me, you love to eat and tend to go overboard when ordering food in a restaurant, there is only one solution to business lunches: don't do them. This may put a crimp in your business style—though there are alternatives—but it will do wonders for your waistline and your budget.

(The alternatives to business lunches are business breakfasts—where you can get by with ordering fresh orange juice or a slice of melon, or a "Let's do Perrier" mid-afternoon or before-dinner meeting. The other alternative is to practice moderation when ordering from a menu, but since I have so little self-discipline when it comes to food, I don't know how to tell you how to do that.)

Packing your own lunch offers several advantages over eating in restaurants, or grabbing a quick bite. First, you have control over what you eat. You can pack your own fresh fruits or vegetables or sandwich makings, and not have to worry about being at the mercy of the empty-calorie, highly processed foods of most food vendors.

Second, you can control the amount you eat. How often have you been overwhelmed by the sheer quantity of food on the plate a waiter puts in front of you? And how many times have you eaten it all because a doggie bag wasn't feasible, and you couldn't stand to let it go to waste? Just make sure you pack your lunch *after* you have your breakfast, when you're not feeling hungry.

Third, there's no question that packing your lunch is less expensive than restaurant or food vendor meals.

You might argue that packing your own lunch is just one more thing to add to the list of things you have to do each day. But if you plan for it on your computerized shopping list (#4), and get into the routine of it, the actual preparation time is minimal. Any way you slice it, making your own lunch has to take less time than it takes to get to a restaurant, stand in line for a table, place your order, wait for it to arrive, eat it, wait for the bill, argue with your luncheon date about who's going to pay for it, calculate the tip, pay the bill, wait for the receipt, and make your way back to the office.

When you're planning what to pack in your lunch, don't forget an apple. The apple is almost a perfect food. Not only is it full of vitamin C and other vitamins, minerals, and nutrients your body needs, it's also high in fiber and has no fat. The pectin in apples can soothe overstressed stomachs, and it's a passable substitute for after-meal brushing. An apple or even two for lunch on Monday is an excellent antidote to a weekend of overeating. Besides all this, the apple comes in its own packaging, travels well, and keeps indefinitely. What could be simpler?

## 63. Beware Exercise Equipment, Fire Your Personal Trainer, and Go Take a Walk

*∽*

There's a wonderful scene in the movie *Alice* where a fashionable yuppie has to reschedule her appointment with her personal trainer, who can't come for his appointment until after her session with her Rolfer, which has to be rescheduled so she can meet with her chiropractor. After that, she can go to the club for her massage and shiatsu lessons, which she plans to do following her Nautilus routine, but before the Swede walks on her back.

This is only a slight exaggeration of the rigorous physical exercise regimen many of us have set up for ourselves. Does all this go-go exercise do us any good? It might if we stuck with it, but the road to flab is paved with good intentions. The average number of times a new exercycle is used is 7.2, then it either sits in the corner of the room, cluttering up your life and making you feel guilty, or it goes into the next garage sale. Every day this expensive equipment—or the health club membership—goes unused, the guilt level rises, which only increases the stress in our lives.

We've become so addicted to compulsive, competitive behavior that we've even extended it to exercise, which, theoretically, we do for relaxation, and to improve and maintain our health. Now is the perfect time to get off the high-tech equipment sports treadmill and go take a walk.

Walking requires no fancy equipment, no new clothes, no club membership, and it's the best exercise you can get. Studies at the National Institute of Health and the Department of Physical Education of the U.S. Marines have shown beyond question that a thirty-minute walk every day, or even only three times a week, provides all the aerobic exercise anyone needs to maintain good health. Not only does a good, brisk walk energize the heart and lungs and respiratory system, but it clears the head and soothes the soul. It provides an excellent opportunity to get in touch with nature every day, to listen to the birds, to savor the seasons, to give a friendly nod to neighbors, to walk your dog, or to have a quiet few moments on your own just to treasure and enjoy.

Try it for one month. Get up half an hour earlier and go for a walk, in good weather or bad. If you don't like to walk alone, set up a buddy system with your mate or a good friend. Or have your kids join you on your daily walks. This is a good way to teach your children the importance of regular exercise. Once you've done it for a month, commit to it for six months.

After you've walked regularly for six months, the chances are good you'll stick with it for life.

There are few things you can do that will be better for your soul, and nothing you can do that will be easier, less stressful, and more beneficial for your body.

## 64. Get Up an Hour Earlier

The best hour of the day is the hour just before the time you are currently getting up. If you're like most people, you schedule your wake-up hour so that you have just enough time to get dressed, grab a bite of breakfast, take a quick peek at the headlines or the morning news, maybe help get the kids off to school, and get to work by eight-thirty or nine o'clock. There's not much time in there for lollygagging.

Imagine how nice it would be if you had a whole extra hour in the morning to do some things you've been wanting to do, like taking a walk (#63), or establishing your own morning ritual (#67), or just to have enough time for a leisurely breakfast with your family.

Adding an extra hour to your day, especially if you use it to do something other than work, is a very effective way to relieve stress and to give yourself the feeling of having much more time throughout the day. Studies have shown that we need less sleep as we advance in years. It could be that extra hour in the morning would do you a lot more good if you were awake and enjoying it, rather than trying to catch up on sleep you don't really need.

If you've never had an opportunity to enjoy that quiet hour before dawn, I urge you to start doing so tomorrow. You'll be amazed at the richness, peace, and simplicity it can add to your life.

# 65.  Be in Bed by Nine
## One Night a Week

$\infty$

A friend suggested this idea to me several years ago. It appealed to me immensely, and Gibbs and I incorporated it into our simplicity program. We made Friday night our night to be in bed by nine. Not only does it provide a satisfying end to a busy work week, but it gives us a head start on having a relaxing weekend. We find ourselves looking forward all week to our quiet, early-to-bed Friday evening.

If you've cut back on your go-go entertainment (#23), you may be staying home on Friday night anyway, so this would be a good night to start with. Sunday is also a good night for being in bed by nine, since there is usually so little happening on Sunday evenings, and the extra sleep could give you a good jump start on your busy week ahead.

Whatever night you choose, this investment in your sleep will provide you with an excellent return. You'll be more refreshed than on nights when you stay up late, and the added energy will make you more efficient at work and at play.

Since I secretly love to sleep, it took me a while to figure out why I hadn't thought of this on my own. It finally dawned on me that, because I have a heavy dose of the Protestant work ethic, I felt there was something almost decadent about going to bed early unless I wasn't feeling well. Many former yuppies I've talked to have had that same reaction.

But there is an amazing thing that happens when you begin to simplify your life: A lot of those once valued but often restricting beliefs—like the Protestant work ethic, idle hands are the devil's workshop, don't put off till tomorrow what you can do today, the early bird gets the worm—start to have less influence on you. You begin to realize it's okay to relax, and to do nothing, and even to go to bed early just for the ease of it.

# 66. Throw Out Everything But the Aspirin

Several years ago we were in New York City on a business trip in the middle of winter, and I came down with a doozie of a cold. I didn't have time to run to a pharmacy to stock up on my usual supply of cold medicine. All I had with me was aspirin, so that's what I took to get me through. The cold lasted three days, then it was gone. Period.

I couldn't believe it. My colds have *always* lasted ten days to two weeks. Always. But then, I've always taken cold medicines. I began to wonder if there was a connection here. Did my colds last longer because I used cold remedies?

Next time I got a cold I resisted the temptation to turn to my usual cold relievers. I took only aspirin instead. Once again, the cold lasted only a few days.

I've discussed this idea with literally dozens of friends and associates, and many of them have started using aspirin in place of cold medicines with the same positive results I had. In addition to its use as a pain reliever, aspirin is now thought to prevent heart attacks in men, reduce the risk of certain types of strokes, reduce mortality among heart attack patients, reduce fevers, stop aches and inflammation, prevent gum disease, prevent high blood pressure in pregnant women, and prevent the recurrence of migraines.

I am the first to admit that this brief history does not constitute a scientific study of this phenomenon. But I was pleased to see a recent news item which supports my findings. According to this report, medical experts have told a House subcommittee in Washington that antihistamines, found in most over-the-counter cold medicines, are ineffective and pose unnecessary health and safety risks. They are urging the Food and Drug Administration (FDA) to withdraw antihistamines from cold medications.

In another recent report, the FDA declared flatly that hundreds of ingredients in over-the-counter medications simply don't work.

Perhaps it's time to approach your medicine cabinet with a heavy hand. Think seriously about getting rid of everything but the aspirin. That means throwing out the eye drops, ear salves, heartburn relievers, stomach coatings, hemorrhoidal preparations, and all the other products, including prescription drugs like sleeping pills and tranquilizers, that we Americans spend billions of dollars a year on.

If your eyes are bloodshot, instead of using Visine, which only masks the symptoms, figure out what is causing your eyes to be bloodshot; then stop doing it. If you've got heartburn, lay off the pepperoni pizza, or get out of that stressful job.

There are no doubt dozens of medications we could do without if we just changed the way we live, so that the problems go away and eliminate the symptoms.

## 67. Create Your Own Rituals

The type of ritual I'm referring to here is any special thing you can do on a regular basis that you look forward to, and that you think about with a happy heart.

I have a friend who has developed a special ritual for getting up in the morning. She wakes up a few minutes before daybreak and makes herself a special cup of tea, just the way she likes it with milk and honey. Then, winter or summer, rain or shine, she takes her tea and the huge comforter from her bed out to her screened porch. There, wrapped in her toastie blanket, she sips her tea and watches the sights and listens to the sounds of dawn. She never lets anything interfere with this quiet, sacred time. She knows that even if the rest of the day turns hectic, she'll have one memory of something being exactly the way she likes it.

It's possible that you've been working so hard and moving so fast that you haven't taken the time to incorporate some personalized moments into your day. If that's the case, take some time right now to think about a few special rituals you could create either on your own or with your family that would make each day memorable. And then start doing them.

## 68.  Learn to Laugh

*~*

Probably the best-known study of the effects of laughter on our lives and on our health is Norman Cousins's, described in his book, *Anatomy of an Illness.*

Mr. Cousins suffered from a rare connective tissue disease which left him completely debilitated. Finding no cure or respite through modern medical treatment, he decided to heal himself with laughter. He went to bed, fortified with every humorous movie and book he could get his hands on. It worked. His cure was remarkable, though little understood, or indeed explored, by the traditional medical community.

As children, we laugh naturally, but we gradually lose that skill as we become adults. It seems as we've moved faster and faster on the fast track, we've moved further and further away from our natural ability to laugh and have fun. Happily, laughter, like riding a bike, is a skill that can be easily relearned.

We are fortunate in our community to have an internationally known laughter therapist, Dr. Annette Goodheart, who offers a set of audio and video tapes on laughter, and who teaches courses and seminars around the world on how to laugh. She's been teaching these classes for over fifteen years, and they are always fully booked.

Laughter therapy is becoming more popular as practitioners learn the many benefits of this skill. If there are no classes in your community where you can learn how to laugh again, write for information on Dr. Goodheart's program—it may be offered in your area. (See below.)

Or think about the kinds of things that make you laugh, such as your favorite writers or comedians or cartoonists. Then stock up on books or tapes that you know will make you laugh, and watch or listen to them regularly, especially in times of stress. Or pick up one of those audio tapes that consists of solid laughter. Perhaps you have friends who make you laugh. If so, arrange to spend more time with them.

Laughter reduces stress, relieves tension, and soothes the angry heart. Just imagine how much simpler your life would be if you learned to respond to stressful situations with laughter rather than with frustration, or anger, or resentment.

For a brochure describing Dr. Goodheart's audio and video tapes, or for information regarding her seminars, write: Annette Goodheart, Ph.D., 635 N. Alisos St., Santa Barbara, CA 93103. (805) 966-0025.

# 69. Learn Yoga

〜

$Y$oga is another technique, either by itself or in combination with meditation, that will help you simplify your life.

The principles of hatha (physical) yoga have been practiced for centuries because of the increased vitality, reduced fatigue, improved efficiency, enhanced concentration, and the serenity and peace of mind they generate. Yoga can be learned by people of all ages. It will strengthen, firm, tone, and shape your body, in addition to quieting your mind.

I had the good fortune years ago to study yoga with a yoga adept. I have used yoga consistently over the years for the physical, mental, and psychic benefits it provides. Once you have learned a sufficient number of the basic positions, they are easy to maintain and practice throughout your life. If you find from time to time you can't fit them all into your schedule, completing just a few of the stretching positions, combined with the proper yoga breathing, will produce obvious positive results.

Yoga is easy to learn, either through books and video tapes, which are readily available, or through class or private instruction, which is offered in most communities.

The combination of the yoga positions and the yoga breathing, by their very nature, will help you to slow down your hectic pace.

# 70. Learn to Meditate

All my life, though I have been attracted to the idea of meditation, I have resisted actually doing it. I was seldom able to sit still long enough. Now that I've simplified my life, meditation has become an important part of my regular routine. Many people have just the opposite experience: once they have learned to meditate, they find they gradually begin to simplify their lives. Whether you simplify first, and then learn to meditate, or start meditating, and begin to simplify, or even start both processes at the same time, you'll find meditation an effective way to maintain a simple life.

This is not to say that learning to meditate is easy, nor are the results necessarily immediate. But both the physical and psychological benefits of a sustained meditation program are well known and well documented. They include a much greater ability to deal with the everyday problems we all face, and a calmness and serenity that result from few other disciplines. Most people also find that meditation produces more energy, more restful sleep, an increased ability to concentrate, and an overall feeling of well-being.

There are many excellent books and tapes available which you can use to learn how to meditate. Some easy and effective methods are described in the little book, *How to Meditate,* by Lawrence LeShan. (Available in paperback from Bantam Books.)

Learning to meditate will give you a new understanding of your life, and will help you get clear on exactly how you want to live it.

# 71. Slow Down to the Posted Speed Limit

∾

I was taught to drive in my youth by a professional race car driver. This may or may not have anything to do with the fact that I've always driven fast. I considered this an asset when I got onto the fast track, where it seemed as though everyone else was moving, both on foot and on wheels, at breakneck speeds. I was several years into our simplicity program before I realized that, while I had slowed down in almost every other area of my life, I was still driving as though I were on a race course.

I decided to change my driving style; I've learned to drive more slowly. Doing so has given me a whole new appreciation for driving, since I now have the opportunity to see and hear and feel more when I'm behind the wheel. And I'm more patient with other drivers, which has reduced the stress of driving. Paradoxically, it seems that slowing my driving speed has given me more time; more time to think, more time to reflect, and more time to enjoy life.

Once you slow down your driving pace, you'll no longer have to wonder why the driver in front of you is always traveling slower than you are.

*S i x*

# Your Personal Life

## 72.  Clean Up Your Relationships

$\backsim$

Creating a simple life isn't always simple. Some steps, like stopping the junk mail or throwing out everything but the aspirin, are easy and can be accomplished in a matter of minutes. Others, like moving to a smaller home or cleaning up your relationships, can take much longer and be among the most difficult things you ever have to do.

I'm referring to an impossible marriage or a relationship that isn't going anywhere, and that is causing you stress or pain. If you're in such a relationship, and you've tried to fix it and you can't, get out. If you can't come to that decision on your own, then get help. Talk to a therapist, or join a support group of people who are committed to your happiness and well-being. If you can't find such a group, then form one of your own. Meeting on a regular basis with people who are going through similar problems, and who are committed to growth, can provide a powerful impetus for you to get out of a dysfunctional relationship.

Cleaning up relationships applies to friends, too. Perhaps it's time to think about moving on from a friendship that no longer works for you. Ending a friendship, unlike ending a marriage, doesn't necessarily require a major confrontation or discussion. Depending on your history together, sometimes it's easier to retreat and simply fade out of someone else's life.

When you think about it, the *getting out* of a difficult relationship can be relatively easy. It is the *deciding* to get out that is often the difficult part. No other thing you could possibly do will simplify your life as quickly or as completely as getting out of a relationship that isn't working.

# 73.  Just Be Yourself

~

Have you ever stopped to think about how much energy you spend—and how much you complicate your life—by pretending to be someone other than who you are? We all do it. It's part of being human, and it was also a big part of the fast-paced life-style of the 1980s.

A good exercise is to sit down and go through all the major areas of your life and decide how each would be different if the only person you had to impress was you. Would you have a different career? What kind of house would you live in? Would you drive a different car? How would you dress? How would you spend your spare time? Would you be married to the person you're married to? Would you have the same friends?

Often we assume various layers of pretense not so much out of our own needs, but because of someone else's. How often are we untrue to ourselves because of the pressures of our family, the demands of our mate, the entreaties of our children? If your life-style reflects someone else's idea of how your life should be, take a few moments to imagine how much simpler it would be if you dropped the pretense and learned to just be yourself.

## 74.  Trust Your Intuition

⌒

Have you ever found yourself getting into a situation that you just *knew* was not right for you? There were no doubt all kinds of "reasons" you could put down on paper that pointed toward going ahead with it, but there was something about it that just didn't feel good. If you listened to your intuition, you were probably glad later; if you didn't, you were probably sorry.

All of us come equipped with a still, small voice inside. Unfortunately, our life-styles have become so fast-paced and hectic that many of us have forgotten how to listen to it.

For years, whenever I was faced with a major decision, I would make a list of all the pros and cons, and then make my decision accordingly and, I always thought, logically. Oftentimes, logic had nothing to do with it. One of the things I've learned by slowing down is that, if I'm listening to my intuition, I don't have to make a list, I just *know* what I should do.

I have a friend who, when he can't decide between course A or course B, simply decides on one or the other—it doesn't matter which one—*then* he listens for the small voice which tells him whether he's happy with that decision. He has made a special point of teaching this method to his kids so they can get an early start on learning to trust their intuition.

Uncluttering your life (#1), learning to say no (#84), spending one day a month in solitude (#77), making an annual retreat (#79) and many of the other ideas in this book will contribute to slowing down your pace, and help you get in touch with your intuition. Learning to trust it will help keep your life in balance.

## 75. If It's Not Easy, Don't Do It

$\backsim$

One of the many positive changes to come out of our simplification program is that I've finally learned that if something is difficult, it's better not to do it.

Many of us grew up with the misguided belief that if something is not going right, a business transaction, a partnership, or any kind of endeavor, all we had to do was work harder at it, and somehow we could solve it. Holding on to that belief has kept millions of people in difficult life choices, and has created a lot of unhappiness that could be avoided. Obviously, there is a difference between hard work that produces wonderful and satisfying results, and hard work that you just know is never going to get you anywhere.

You can't fit a square peg into a round hole. It takes courage to realize that something you've been working on, perhaps for a long time, just isn't right and to walk away from it. When I look back on my life I can see that the things that have worked out well were, for the most part, relatively easy; and the things that didn't work out well were, for the most part, difficult; they were simply not meant to be. I've learned that if it's not working, it's best just to move on, and to put my energies elsewhere.

Think how simple your life would be if you eliminated the difficult things—the things that probably weren't meant to be anyway—and concentrated on doing what was easy.

## 76. Stop Trying to Change People

∽

I have a good friend who got into an awful mess a few years back from which she is still trying to extricate herself. But, in fact, she hasn't been trying nearly as hard as I have. I've spent a lot of frustrating time and energy over the years attempting to get her to see how she could change her life for the better. The solutions to her problems were so obvious—at least to me! The bottom line is that, though she pays lip service to wanting to change, she is really not all that interested.

One of the things that has become clear to me since I've started to slow down is that people do what they want to do. Understanding that has made it possible for me to see the fine line between being supportive and getting in the way. When it comes right down to it, we can't change other people. They change when they're good and ready. Ultimately, we all have to get out of our own predicaments. Most often what people really want is a supportive ear. This includes kids and spouses.

Now I just listen. Boy, has that simplified my life. And it has freed up a lot of energy to spend in more enjoyable and more productive pursuits.

## 77. Spend One Day a Month in Solitude

~

If you already spend a fair amount of time alone, or if you've made sufficient changes in your life so that you are out from under the pressures that once made it so complicated, you may already be getting all the solitude you need.

But if your days are full of family, friends, traffic, noise, demands, requests, pressures, deadlines, schedules, and an endless parade of people, you may want to think about spending a day or possibly a weekend each month by yourself, completely away from the everyday distractions that complicate your life.

Spending a day in solitude can mean doing anything from taking a hike up a mountain trail, to sitting quietly on a park bench. It can mean a day spent wandering through art museums or art galleries, or a day browsing in the stacks at your local library. While it doesn't necessarily mean getting away from people, it definitely means getting away from people you know who are likely to make demands on you.

Spending time away from the constant barrage of pressures we face can get us back in touch with what is real, and can help to alleviate the tensions of everyday life. After all, freeing ourselves from the pressures of modern living is a major part of what simplifying is all about.

*Hint:* If you're not in the habit of taking time for yourself, you may need to explain to your mate and/or family members what you plan to do and your desire to spend time alone. It's important that those close to you understand your need for solitude so they won't feel left out or rejected.

## 78. Teach Your Kids the Joy of Solitude

∽

As anyone who has children knows, the pressures on kids today are enormous. Alcohol, drugs of every variety, sex, AIDS, gangs, guns, and violence, not to mention the constant stimulus and often ear-shattering intrusions from inane television, tempestuous movies, rock music, rap singers, coffeehouses, computer games, and video arcades. How can a young person find peace of mind today, learn to get in touch with his own feelings, or find out what is important to *him*?

One way is for kids to learn at an early age how to seek out quiet time on their own. As you are learning to spend some time in solitude, teach your kids to do the same. Take them on nature hikes or on camping trips away from the continuous jangle of urban living. Make a ritual of watching a beautiful sunset with them.

Or teach them how to spend a quiet afternoon at home. Set up a regular time in their week where they can be away from the unremitting influence of their peers, as well as away from the pandemonium of the electronic age. Fortify them with good books (but no TV) and thoughtful meditative exercises they can do, so they get in the habit of personal reflection, and of seeking answers within their own hearts.

Once your children learn the joy of solitude, it'll be a gift they can carry with them throughout their lives. And, imagine how much simpler your life will be when your children, in learning to enjoy their own solitude, learn to appreciate your desire for solitude as well.

# 79. Do a Retreat
## Once a Year

*ᘒ*

If you find it difficult to schedule some regular time for solitude, consider doing an annual retreat. I have found few things as good for the soul as slipping off on my own for three or four days to get away not only from the material clutter we all face, but from the emotional, psychic, and social clutter as well.

It's surprisingly easy to do. It doesn't have to be connected to any type of religious organization. A spa or resort hotel-type retreat can be very effective. But going off on your own to contemplate your life doesn't have to be expensive. One of the most refreshing retreats I've done recently was a camping trip in the mountains. It was a much welcomed opportunity to get in touch with nature as well as with my psyche. It is amazing what a couple of days surrounded by the beauty and peace and quiet of nature can do for your perspective.

Also, there are dozens of small and often elegant retreat houses that offer simple but comfortable accommodations for three or four nights at very reasonable rates. Many of these are former monasteries or convents that have been converted into nondenominational retreat centers. Their directors are committed to providing a quiet setting for personal and spiritual growth.

*Sanctuaries*, by Jack and Marcia Kelly (published by Bell Tower in both an East Coast and West Coast edition) is an excellent source of information on lodgings, monasteries, and retreat houses around the country.

## 80.  Keep a Journal

Keeping a journal is another effective way to stay in touch with how you want to live your life.

A journal can be as loose or as structured as you wish to make it. It can include random reflections and ideas about the world and your place in it, or it can be a formal method of keeping a daily record of your thoughts and feelings as a means toward spiritual growth. It can be something you write in every day, or you can use it sporadically as the mood and the need arise. It can be a dream journal, an idea journal, a diet journal, a creativity journal, an anger journal, or a health journal. It can be full of thoughts you want to share with others, or as private as you want to make it.

Many local community college and adult education programs offer courses in journal writing. Being involved in a journal-writing class is an excellent way to work with other people who are learning how to use this technique effectively in their lives, and to share ideas on new and different approaches that could work for you.

Or just pick up a pen and a notebook and develop your own journal-writing system to help you keep in touch with what's important to you.

# 81.  Do One Thing
## at a Time

W e're all familiar with the image of the modern American yuppie barreling down the highway in his BMW while talking on the car phone to his office and pulling an urgent memo off the car fax. He's in the process of closing a major deal with the executive sitting in the front seat next to him, assuming he can get to the sales presentation meeting at his client's office across town on time.

Or the young executive who's having a relaxing weekend at home in front of the TV with her family. She's changing the baby's diaper and talking to her boss long distance, while keeping her mother-in-law on call waiting. As soon as she's off the phone(s), she'll be wrapping up the game of Go Fish with her three-year-old so the kids can finish their snack before the ten dinner guests arrive for the business meeting she's hosting for her husband.

We each could tell our own version of this "gotta do it all" madness that has pervaded our lives. Do we really get more done by trying to do everything at once? Maybe. Does it *really* matter? Probably not. Are we happier at this frenetic pace?

Most definitely not. Can we do anything about it? Yes. Just as we gradually learned to do ten things at once, we can gradually learn to do one thing at a time.

Start with a list. Not the HAVE TO DO TODAY list you have in your Day Runner, but a *new* list of the things that really matter. Cut the list in half, then pick the most important thing, and do it. Then, and only then, go down the list, doing each thing, one at a time. As much as possible, allow no distractions, no interruptions. After the first couple of weeks, consider it a major accomplishment if you are able to cut in half again the number of things you feel you *have* to do each day.

With a little discipline and regular self-checks, you can learn to do one thing at a time. And do it better. And be happier doing it.

## 82.  Do Nothing

Do nothing. It sounds so easy. Then I think back to my frenetic life-style of a couple of years ago, before I decided to simplify. I had to-do lists a mile long, nonstop appointments, and phone calls around the clock. Every moment of my day was scheduled, even my sleep time. And I remembered how long it took for me to get to a point where I could actually *do nothing*. It took a while. It's more difficult than it sounds.

If you're not in the habit of doing nothing, how do you start? Start with an hour. Maybe a lunch hour, or an hour at the end of your workday, or perhaps with the extra hour you have once you start getting up an hour earlier (#64).

If you start with your lunch hour, go to a quiet place and just sit. This is not the reading a book, or the talking with friends, or the working on your knitting kind of doing nothing. This is not about meditation. The idea is to just *be* with whatever is going on in your head without having to *do* anything about it.

Another good way to learn to do nothing is to stay in your office or your home, surrounded by all the things you should be doing, and do nothing. If you've not done this before, it may take several tries at it to get past the guilt or the almost uncontrollable urge to start doing something.

Gradually, you can start increasing the time you do nothing, until you build up to at least a half day or a full day once a month, or more if possible. Once you've learned to do nothing, you'll be amazed at the clarity it will bring to your life, or to whatever project you're working on. It's unbelievably refreshing.

Now, at the very least, I have one or two days a month where I do nothing. Few things will put a hectic, over-scheduled life-style into perspective faster than learning this skill. I urge you to get started, and do nothing.

# 83. Take Time to
# Watch the Sunset

～

Sunset has always been one of my favorite times of day. Before I simplified my life, I was frequently too busy to enjoy it. Now that my world is simpler, I almost never miss what is regularly one of the most spectacular shows on earth.

There's something so captivating about the setting sun, especially when weather and atmospheric conditions help to create dramatic cloud formations and brilliant colors that give your whole world a different hue. Seen in the light of the setting sun, our problems seem minor, even if only for a few moments.

The wonderful thing about sunset, and much the same can be said for sunrise, is that it happens every day, and even if the sunset itself is not spectacular, it marks the beginning of the end of another day. It's a great time to pause and take notice. Teach your kids to enjoy the beauty of sunrises and sunsets, too. It's a very inexpensive show and it's a whole lot better for them than television.

# 84. Just Say No

One of the things I promised myself when we decided to simplify our lives was to reduce my social commitments to people beyond the circle of my immediate family and friends. I've finally reached a point where, if someone asks me to do something I don't want to do or spend an evening with people I don't have any interest in being with, I simply say no. Thank you, but no.

My weekdays are devoted, for the most part, to my work, and, unavoidably, there are deadlines and obligations I have to meet. But my evenings and weekends are my own. They have become sacred, and learning to say no to things I don't want to do—especially those things I have always felt I *should* do—has kept them inviolate.

If you have a problem saying no, go back and read *When I Say No, I Feel Guilty,* by Manuel J. Smith. This classic best-seller from the 1970s will give you the verbal tools you need to reduce your commitments and make your time your own again.

## 85. If You Can't Say No, Prevaricate

⎰

Have you ever found yourself trapped at a social gathering you didn't want to attend in the first place because you were caught off guard when the hostess invited you? The truth is you didn't really *want* to go, but you didn't have any other plans, *and* you didn't have an excuse ready. It's happened to most of us.

I have a friend who for years just couldn't say no. Sally is a strong, dynamic woman who runs a successful business and has never had a problem managing a staff of twenty people, dealing assertively with suppliers, or meeting on an equal footing with corporate executives. But when it came to her social life, she'd always been a pushover. She knew it, but she couldn't bear to hurt people's feelings.

However, she recently found herself fidgeting through yet another dinner party. She realized that if she'd been prepared with a socially acceptable excuse when Martha had called to invite her, she'd be at home at that moment cozying up on the sofa with a good book. She decided right there, in the middle of Martha's Canary Islands cassoulet, that she'd never again say yes when she wanted to say no.

So she's learned to prevaricate. She drew up a list of all-purpose excuses which she keeps by her home and office phones. Now, when people call with invitations to gatherings she has no interest in, she's prepared. She has also developed the habit of keeping a couple of excuses on the tip of her tongue to ward off acquaintances she might run into on the street or in the grocery checkout line. She's finally reconciled to the fact that just because she may like someone, she doesn't have to give up her free time to be with them, unless she wants to.

She's learned that a simple excuse is the best: "Thanks, Martha, but I've got plans for Saturday night." And she's also learned not to add, "Maybe next time," because she knows the Marthas of the world will take her at her word.

Needless to say, her social life is dwindling rapidly, but she has more free time than she's ever had to do the things that really matter to her.

## 86. Resign from Any Organizations Whose Meetings You Dread

*ᵔ*

While I've never been much of a joiner, Gibbs went through a stage in his life when he'd join any group that invited him. One of the things he did when we started to simplify was to resign from the groups where he found his heart was no longer in it.

It's amazing how quickly memberships—and the accompanying obligations and guilts—can pile up. The financial drain—with countless dues and assessments and overpriced rubber-chicken dinners deadened by Worst Speech Ever contests—is one thing. But the frustration of working with often disorganized and fanatical amateurs, or trying desperately to make small talk with people whose only connection to your life is through a single, narrowly focused interest, can be emotionally and psychologically debilitating.

Here is his advice for getting out. Take all your membership cards (you may be appalled at how many there are). Make two stacks. The smaller, maybe nonexistent, pile consists of organizations that meet at least two of three criteria:

1. Membership is a professional imperative.
2. You actually look forward to their meetings.
3. You never find yourself apologizing for being a member.
Resign from all the rest. Or if you can't bring yourself to resign, just let your memberships quietly lapse. You'll find you've reclaimed a significant chunk of your free time.

## 87. Learn to Reinterpret the Past

∽

Do you ever find yourself reliving some upsetting event or circumstance of your life, feeling you just can't seem to get over it? This could be anything from an altercation with a co-worker to the dissolution of your marriage. It could have happened years ago, or only yesterday. You keep thinking about it, wishing you had done things differently. It haunts you, but agonizing over it doesn't seem to help.

One of the things I've been able to do as a result of slowing down the pace of my life is to stop reliving the past. I've come to realize that, when you get right down to it, there are no mistakes; there are no wrong decisions. I've gotten into the habit of interpreting the events of my life—whether apparently "good" or "bad"—as powerful circumstances that, no matter what the temporary outcome, will ultimately get me where I want to go.

Constantly reliving past events only complicates your life. Reinterpreting them as positive steps forward, and then moving on, will keep things simple.

## 88. Change Your Expectations

The 1980s created sometimes unrealistic goals and expectations that we all felt we could or should live up to. It was taken for granted that we would strive for the biggest houses, the fastest cars, the best jobs, the highest paychecks, the most promising futures, the happiest marriages, the most organized households, the brightest kids in the best schools, the latest fashions, and all the space-age gadgets and toys money could buy. Many people have worked harder and harder and feel they haven't achieved all those expectations. Many people have exceeded their expectations, but it hasn't made them happy.

We have an acquaintance who is stuck in his expectations. He's got the big house, the big car, the club memberships, and the high-powered career, but he's miserable. He doesn't like what he does for a living, but he can't imagine giving it up because it's the job that makes it possible for him to keep the big house, the big car, and the big life-style that he feels he's "earned" and is entitled to.

Much of our own simplification program, in fact, revolved

around changing our expectations. For Gibbs and me, and a lot of other people, the big life-style wasn't as advertised. When we moved across country so we could get away from the four-hour commute and live where we worked (#51), we had to change our expectations about our career goals. We wondered at the time if we had lowered them, but the extra four hours that the move added to our day, and the tremendous improvement in the quality of that time, more than made up for any loss in terms of career advancement. And, as it turned out, both of us experienced career changes that are now much more satisfying, though very different, from our original expectations.

If you feel you haven't achieved all those goals, or if you exceeded them and you still aren't happy, maybe it's time to admit that the life of the superachiever isn't necessarily what it was cracked up to be. Hanging on to the expectations of the 1980s is a surefire way to complicate your life. Letting go of them, and establishing your own priorities, will greatly simplify your life.

## 89. Review Your Life Regularly to Keep It Simple

$\backsim$

Maintaining a simple life requires a certain amount of vigilance. It is not realistic to go through the steps to simplify your life and then think it will automatically stay simple. First of all, many of us have been in the habit of consuming and expanding for some years now, and old habits die hard. Second, our culture is not structured to readily accommodate those who choose to simplify. There are constant messages from the media, our families, our friends, and the Joneses urging us to buy this new gadget or try that new toy or, in one way or another, get back on the fast track. Most of these messages seem irresistible. Some are valid; some are not. It's your choice.

We have friends who decided to simplify their eating habits. They were both dedicated gourmet chefs and owned practically every piece of cooking equipment known to man. When they went through the uncluttering routine in their kitchen (#1), they got rid of, among other things, the wine-making apparatus, the electric tortilla press, the combination capuccino/espresso brewer/milk steamer, the pasta maker, and the institution-sized mixer with 42 attachments. They spent many months rejoicing in their newfound liberation from cooking-equipment catalogs.

Then, before they knew what had happened, they woke up one day to realize that they had replaced the wine gear with a juicer, the pasta maker and tortilla press with an electric breadmaker, and the 42-attachment mixer with a seed-sprouting contraption that took up half their deck space.

Simple? Not exactly, and it shows you what can happen when you're not paying attention.

*Seven*

# Special Issues
# for Women

In the movie *Tootsie,* Dustin Hoffman plays an actor who impersonates a female actress in order to get an acting job. He has just come home from a shopping spree where he has purchased all the accouterments he needs for his role as a woman: wigs, hair rollers, makeup, nail polish, jewelry, shoes, handbags, etc. As he is putting on his wig and makeup, he comments to his roommate that he never realized how much time and energy and money women have to spend just to make themselves presentable. Boy, isn't that the truth?

There is no doubt about it, women in our culture are high-maintenance. I decided to take a cold hard look at the routine I've always gone through to be presentable. I came up with some specific things women can do to get to low-maintenance, and I've included them in this separate section, written just for women. Men, for the most part, are already low-maintenance.

# 90. Ten Minutes to Drop-Dead Gorgeous

∽

I've always marveled at how Gibbs could get dressed and look totally put together in less than half the time it took me to get ready for the same event. When we started simplifying our lives, I made it my personal goal to go from a standing start to drop-dead gorgeous in ten minutes or less. (I've got the ten minutes down pat; I'm still working on the drop-dead part.)

I started with my hair style. For most women the time-consuming part of getting dressed is the hair we've been brainwashed into believing has to be not only shampooed, but conditioned, color rinsed, moussed, spritzed, gelled, blow-dried, extended, enhanced, straightened, or curled, and then sprayed before we can go out the front door.

Men have hair styles that make it possible for them to wash their hair, run a comb through it, and go. Women can do that too. Years ago a hairdresser told me that every woman has at least one flattering low-maintenance easy-care hair style that is natural for her hair type and facial structure. It took some experimentation, but I found an easy-care hair style that works for me. Now, rather than the twenty' to thirty minutes it used to take, my hair is clean and ready-to-go in five or six minutes.

Second, I changed my skin-cleansing habits. For years I was unable to pass a cosmetics counter without stocking up on the latest eight-step day-time-night-time-cleanser-moisturizer-scrub-softener-pore reducer-skin enhancer-line eliminator program for my sensitive skin. Fortunately, I recently was stranded on a deserted island without my usual array of skin products. All I had was a sponge, water, and a natural skin cream. After three weeks on this routine my skin had never looked better.

Now, all I use is a sponge and water for cleansing and a few drops of light moisturizer. I can't tell you what a relief it is not only to have a system that is easy and that works, but to be rid of all those half-used jars of goop that for years have cluttered up my drawers and countertops.

Another thing you can do is rethink your use of makeup. Have you ever seen a face that was improved by the tons of makeup cosmetic manufacturers would have us wear—all with the purpose of making us look like we're not wearing makeup? Ask the men in your life. Most will tell you they prefer women with a natural look and a smile.

While you're at it, be sure to include your daughters in

your natural looks program. Just imagine the hassles you could save them—and the positive self-esteem you could build—if they never became enchanted with the beauty-in-a-jar myth.

You may have to change your expectations (#88) to get to low-maintenance, but once you do, you'll wonder how you ever put up with your old routine.

## 91. Kick Off Your High Heels— and Keep Them Off

Few of the dictates of fashion have been more universally limiting and damaging to women than high-heeled shoes. Any podiatrist will tell you that women who regularly wear high heels suffer not only from deformed, bunioned, and callused feet, but from myriad other maladies, including calf, knee, and back problems. And yet, women continue to wear heels, all in the name of fashion.

Isn't it fortunate that current styles allow at least some room for individuality, and that it's possible to wear comfortable, low-heeled or flat-heeled shoes and still make a fashion statement? Yes, it's true that many men find high heels sexy. (That, after all, is why we put ourselves through the torture and inconvenience of heels.) But if you really want to simplify your life, and you're still wearing high heels because the men around you find women in heels attractive, maybe it's time to change the people you spend time with.

Aside from the discomfort, having high heels in your closet raises the complexity of your wardrobe to another level. Think how simple it would be if all the shoes in your closet were the same heel height. That's one of the primary reasons men's wardrobes are inherently simpler than women's: They can wear any number of different shoes, in total comfort, with the same suit or pair of slacks without having to worry about the length of the pant leg.

After you've been away from high-heeled shoes for a while, few things will look more pathetic than a woman mincing down the street in high heels. And you'll know that if her feet aren't hurting her now, they soon will be.

# 92. Take Off Your Plastic Nails and Throw Out the Nail Polish
~

One of the most complicating and time-consuming aspects of the high-tech dress-for-success mode of the 1980s was the highly polished, brightly colored, fake nails craze. When you stop to think about it, it's hard to imagine any cosmetic procedure we've ever put ourselves through that takes more time, costs more money, does more damage to ourselves with toxic fumes and the potential for nail fungus and other problems, and creates more havoc for the environment for less benefit to anyone than fake and/or highly polished nails.

Obviously, spending several hours each week surrounded by noxious fumes while having acrylic nails cemented layer by layer to your fingertips is not compatible with the simple life. Thank goodness, the vampire look is out. If, like me and millions of other women, you have indulged in this practice, it may be time to start developing an appreciation for the simple beauty of neatly filed, closely trimmed, unpainted nails. Just imagine never again having to go through the gyrations of pulling on a pair of nylon stockings after having just touched up your nail polish.

## 93.  Stop Carrying a Purse the Size of the QE2

If you want to simplify your fashion statement, your purse should be the most inconspicuous item you have. Preferably it should be invisible.

If you feel you must carry a purse, make it a very small one with a shoulder strap, so you can keep your hands free, and just big enough to hold an ID, some money, and your lipstick. What else do you really need for getting back and forth to work or going out for an evening? Any other items you think you can't live without can be kept in the glove compartment of your car and/or stowed in your desk drawer at the office.

Of course, the slacks and skirts and jackets of your simple wardrobe (#22) will have pockets, and you can get by on most outings by stashing some cash and possibly your lipstick there.

If you've never experienced the freedom of not having to lug around a huge purse full of items you don't need and seldom use—a so-called handbag that in almost every instance detracts from whatever you're wearing—now is a good time to start.

# 94. Minimize Your Accessories

If there is one variable that can make or break a fashion statement for women, it's accessories. Once again, men have it easy: All they have to worry about is a tie, possibly a tie pin, a watch, a briefcase, and shoes (which, because they are almost always the same color and height, aren't, strictly speaking, an accessory). Women have to deal with earrings, necklaces, bracelets, brooches, watches, scarves, ties, belts, glasses, handbags, a briefcase, occasionally a hat, stockings, and shoes of every conceivable color and height.

Because the variety of accessories is unlimited, and because the appropriate combination of these items is an art form that few women have mastered, most of us have a problem getting it right, particularly when it comes to shoes and purses. How many times have you seen an otherwise wonderfully combined outfit ruined by shoes of the wrong height, or a handbag that simply doesn't work with the rest of the ensemble? Gucci and Louis Vuitton and other "initialed" bags are the worst offenders. They seldom go with *anything*.

The classic fashion statements that have endured the test of time have always been the simplest. Getting rid of your handbag and kicking off your high heels will go a long way toward simplifying your look. Cutting back your jewelry to a couple of simple but elegant pairs of earrings, and eliminating most of the rest of the accessories, will make the job even easier.

*Eight*

# Hard-Core
# Simplicity

## 95.  Rent Rather Than Own

⌒

Over the past fifty years we've been brainwashed into believing that owning our own home is the only way to go. In
a recent survey conducted by the National Association of
Realtors, 87 percent of the respondents said that owning their
own home was the most important element in fulfilling the
"American dream." Home ownership is valued more than a
happy marriage, an interesting job, high pay, or even having
a lot of money.

Considering the high cost of home ownership these days,
maybe it is time to reconsider that philosophy.

We have friends who, like us, have recently made some
major changes in their lives. They sold their home, got rid of
their cars and most of their stuff, quit their jobs, and spent two
years traveling around the world. They took the equity they
had built up in their home, and used it to generate income to
support their greatly reduced life-style.

When they came back from their travels, they initially
considered buying another, smaller home. But they decided
to rent an apartment instead. Not only can they now rent a

comfortable apartment for much less than it would cost to own comparable space, they want the freedom of not owning. Should they decide to take off and do some more traveling, they don't want to be trapped by a slow market and not be able to sell when they're ready to go.

But, to their surprise, the biggest reason for not owning a home is the emotional and psychological freedom it gives them. Contrary to what they had believed all these years, home ownership had become a burden rather than a security. If your home is costing you more time, energy and money than you're willing to pay, consider renting. It could greatly simplify your life.

# 96.   Get Rid of Your Cars

$\infty$

We have friends who live in San Francisco. Several years ago they sold their cars because they were just too much trouble. In a city like San Francisco, parking is always a problem as well as a major expense. And they didn't really need even one car, let alone two of them. They live close enough to their offices so they can both walk to work. They love the forced exercise and the fresh air. They also love not having to fight big-city traffic. In a pinch or in inclement weather, they can catch a bus.

Now, rather than running all over town, they do all their shopping within walking distance of their home. The money they save on gas, parking, insurance, taxes, registration fees, and maintenance they can use to rent a car if they want to get away for the weekend or if they need a car for some other short-term purpose. After years of being psychologically dependent on cars, they feel a tremendous sense of freedom in not having to worry about the problems of owning a car. Now that they don't have the "convenience" of a car, they spend a lot less time running around on unnecessary jaunts, and they can spend that time doing things they really want to do.

Obviously, if you live in the suburbs and work in the city, and if public transportation is unreliable or nonexistent, giving up your car probably wouldn't make a whole lot of sense. But if you could rearrange your life so that you didn't *need* a car, it could be a major step in simplifying your life.

# 97. Get Rid of Your Phone

$\backsim$

As a teenager, I loved the telephone. It always rang with such anticipation. As an adult, I look on the phone as a necessary inconvenience. However, now that I've developed the ability to not answer a ringing phone and to use the answering machine to monitor phone calls, having a phone in the house is at least tolerable. But I have a friend who came to look on the phone as a major intrusion in her life. She disconnected it entirely a couple of years ago and says she wouldn't have it any other way.

She is in sales and consequently spends most of her day talking on the phone. The last thing she wants to do at home in the evening and on the weekends is spend more time on the phone. She is able to conduct whatever personal phone business she needs to during the day, and her family and friends know that if they want to talk to her, they have to call her at the office. (It helps to have your own business; or a tolerant boss.)

Obviously this technique would not work for everyone. If you have children at home or aging parents who may need to reach out and touch you at a moment's notice, disconnecting the phone might create more problems than it would solve. But think about it. If your life-style is such that going without a phone at home wouldn't be inconvenient and, in fact, would create a sanctuary of peace and quiet, doing away with the telephone in your life could go a long way toward simplifying it.

## 98. Stop Making the Bed

*If it's good enough to get out of, it's good enough to get into.*

—Aunt Myrna, 1953

*If an unmade bed is good enough for Ralph Lauren, it's good enough for me.*

—The author, 1993

There's no question housekeeping practices have become less rigid in the past forty years. Just look at the ads for bed linens. A few years back Ralph Lauren started making a very appealing case for the unmade bed, with all the sheets, dust ruffles, pillows, duvets, spreads, and coverlets that abound in the confusion of the unmade beds in his ads. In the perfection-personified *Leave It to Beaver* household of the fifties, Mrs. Cleaver—and no doubt your mother and mine—would never have *thought* of leaving a bed unmade. And Aunt

Myrna's philosophy was thought, by our family anyway, to be close to heresy.

But now, fortunately, times have changed. Who cares if the bed is left unmade? And who is going to see it? A good friend of mine, who is a firm believer in the unmade bed, has what I think is a wonderful response to anyone who might comment on the disarray of her bed: "Oh, we're just airing the linens."

I've adopted that philosophy totally. Not only is it simpler, but now, when I get out of bed in the morning and know I don't have to spend ten minutes making up the darn thing, it gives me the delight of feeling as though I'm getting away with a little something. It's a treat I can carry with me throughout the day. And besides, why would anyone spend all that money buying linens from a guy named Ralph, and then cover them up?

## 99. Get Rid of All the Extras

༺

When I started college, I threw out all my old emery boards and, in what seemed like an extravagance on my student budget, decided to go for broke and purchased a stainless nail file that was guaranteed to last a lifetime.

I was fond of that little file. I carried it back and forth across the country and around several continents for fifteen years.

Once I started generating some discretionary income, I splurged and bought half a dozen more stainless nail files. I wanted one in my handbag, one in my desk, one in the glove compartment, one in the nightstand, etc.

But then a curious thing happened. When I had only one nail file, I always knew where it was. As soon as I had several, I could never find a nail file when I needed one. Over the years, I've discovered that same phenomenon applies to many things.

For example, a person with one watch knows what time it is, but someone with two watches is never quite sure. And what's worse, he's become a collector. Now, not only does he have to deal with the maintenance and upkeep of the collection, but he also has to keep track of where each item in the collection is at any given moment. In no time at all, having extra sets of things can get very complicated. I long ago got rid of the extra nail files, and more recently I've gotten rid of the extra eyeglasses, sunglasses, fountain pens, umbrellas, pocket knives, hammers, and all kinds of specialized tools, even the extra computers. It's made my life so much simpler.

# 100. Build a *Very* Simple Wardrobe

*ᵔ*

If you're *very* serious about simplicity, here is another fashion option you might want to consider.

A wealthy Wall Street financier is reputed to have developed the simplest wardrobe of all: he has half a dozen copies of one exquisitely tailored black three-piece suit, a couple of identical white shirts and silk ties, and a couple of pairs of black shoes. That's it. Year in and year out that's all he ever wears. His reasoning is that he has enough decisions to make each day without having to worry about what to wear too.

Think about it. This, or your own variation of this idea, could *really* simplify your life.

# Inner
# Simplicity

## 100 Ways
## to Regain Peace and
## Nourish Your Soul

*Elaine St. James*

SMITHMARK

*To Sam Vaughan and to Wolcott Gibbs, Jr.*

*In memory of*
*Phil Babcock*
*1946–1994*

# Acknowledgments

M Y  S I N C E R E S T  T H A N K S  to Marcia Burtt, Catha Paquette, and Pat Rushton for taking their valuable time to read the manuscript, and for their thoughtful comments and helpful ideas.

My deep appreciation to Marisa Kennedy Miller, Jackie Powers, Meg Torbert, Carolyn Howe, Himilce Novas, Dave Sowle, Joe Phillips, Chris Wahlborg, Tiffany Miller, Penny Davies, Frances Halpern, Vera Cole, Chris Souders, Helen Free, Zig Knoll, and Nancy Marschak for rooting, inciting, boosting, exhorting, prodding, promoting, egging, and cheering me onward.

My eternal gratitude to Judy Babcock, Phil Babcock, Jim Cummings, Bev Brennan, and Claudia Bratten for all the inner stuff.

A special thanks to Benjamin Sawyer, Margot Collin, Ken Warfield, Doris Mooney, and all the other reference librarians at the Santa Barbara Public Library who have been so generous with their time and energy, and to all the members of Toastmasters Club No. 5 and Unity Toastmasters for holding still long enough.

I am much obliged to my agent, Jane Dystel, and to my editor, Leslie Wells, and to Laurie Abkemeier, Carol Perfumo, and Samantha Miller for their assistance, encouragement and support, and to Victor Weaver, Marcy Goot, and Brian DeFiore for getting it right.

I am indebted to Anne McCormick and Sam Vaughan for their inspiration and wisdom, and to my husband Wolcott Gibbs, Jr., for everything.

# Contents

## Three: More difficult things to think about doing

## Five: Some fun stuff

# Six: The real stuff

# Inner Simplicity

# Operating Instructions
# for Inner Simplicity:
## *Read carefully*

A FEW YEARS back my husband, Gibbs, and I began the process of simplifying our lives. We'd finally started to realize that we weren't going to be able to do *everything* we'd been trying to do. So we sat down and figured out what we could do and, more importantly, decided what we really *wanted* to do. Then we started, through simplifying, to arrange our lives so we would have the time and energy to do those things that really mattered to us and, for the most part, to let go of all the rest.

We got rid of the clutter in our lives, moved out of our big house into a small condominium, and began what turned out to be a delightful and liberating adventure, which I wrote about in my book, *Simplify Your Life: 100 Ways to Slow Down and Enjoy the Things That Really Matter.*

That process concentrated mostly on the external, or *outer* areas of our lives, such as our household, our finances, our careers, our social lives, and many of the routines of our general lifestyle. The things we did to simplify went a long way toward contributing to happier, healthier, more satisfying lives for both of us. In the bargain, we freed up somewhere between twenty and thirty hours each week to do the things we really wanted to do.

Simplifying the outer aspects of my life gave me the opportunity to discover that there were many areas of my *inner* life that I could simplify as well.

I began to see that there were old conflicts I could now resolve, limiting habit patterns I could change, and new routines I could establish.

I felt that by starting to look within I could simplify my life even more—and increase my physical, mental, and spiritual well-being in the process.

And so I began to explore ways to establish inner simplicity.

What exactly *is* inner simplicity? I've found there is no single answer to that question. It means different things to different people.

For me, inner simplicity means tuning in to what, in my opinion, is the best this world has to offer, such as the love of family and friends, the wonders of nature, and the serenity and clarity that come from silence and quiet contemplation.

It means getting in touch with our creativity and latching on to synchronicity, and figuring out what we need to do to heal ourselves of the things that ail us.

For me, inner simplicity means creating joy in our lives, and remembering to stay connected with that joy every moment of the day.

It means meeting life's challenges, conquering our fears, and letting go of the hurt and the traumas that keep us from being the best we can be.

Inner simplicity means getting rid of the extraneous things—such as worry and anger and judgment—that get in the way of having peace and tranquility in our lives.

It means exploring other levels of consciousness—both the known and the unknown, because I've found that by expanding those levels we can enhance our awareness of how best to live the life we do know.

It also means connecting with a power that is larger than ourselves, whether we think of it as God, a supreme being, or simply the energy of the universe. For some of us, inner simplicity means finding a *middle ground* between the excesses of our outer lives in recent years and the impracticality for most of us of moving to Walden Pond. And so it also means creating an appropriate balance between our inner and our outer lives.

When I thought about it, I realized that my search for inner simplicity had actually started many years ago when I reached the age of reason, which for me was eighteen. It was then I first began to question the beliefs of my childhood (#45).

I spent the next fifteen years exploring various avenues of inner growth, including numerous attempts at learning to meditate (#98), searching for my teacher (#36), working with affirmations (#28) and visualizations (#29), experimenting with diet (#78), studying yoga (#96), practicing deep breathing techniques (#96), exploring various levels of consciousness (#97), and doing lots and lots of reading (#16).

Then, in the mid-seventies, I hopped on the fast track and, for the next fifteen years, with the exception of a couple of forays into the interior regions, left the major part of my inner search on the back burner.

Then, when I'd made significant inroads in simplifying my outer life in the early nineties, and had gotten rid of a lot of the material clutter, the complexities, and the time demands that one collects along the way, I finally came back to taking another look at my inner life.

It was then I began to see that one of my primary motivations for simplifying my life had been to find the time to go within and nourish my soul.

And so I started with some of the things outlined in Chapter Six, such as spending time in solitude, learning to do nothing, tuning in to my intuition, and experimenting with various types of meditation. I wrote about these in *Simplify Your Life*, and I've expanded on them here, based on what I've learned since then.

As I continued, I began working seriously on what I think of as the hard stuff, which I've included in Chapter Four, such as forgiveness, letting go of anger, figuring out my big issue, and getting rid of thoughts that burn.

I tried to balance the heaviness of these things with the more lighthearted aspects of listening to subliminal tapes, casting the runes, chanting, dancing, and creating joy in my life, which I've included in Chapters Five and Six.

And I've continued to find ways to simplify my life, and keep it simple.

Frequently, people who are intrigued by the idea of simplifying but haven't quite gotten to the point of starting to do it yet, ask me, "What do you *do* with all the time you have now that you've simplified your life?"

*Inner Simplicity* provides some answers to that question. The things outlined in this book are, to some extent, the things I've been exploring since I simplified my outer life and have *had the time* to go within and connect with my inner self.

Obviously, the items included in *Inner Simplicity* are not all-inclusive. There are an unlimited number of other things one can do to achieve inner simplicity. And what appeals to one person may not appeal to the next.

It might be helpful to think of *Inner Simplicity* as a smorgasbord. It includes a variety of things to think about, experiment with, enjoy, reject, pursue, use, take with you, leave behind, or save for another time. There's no hurry, no deadline, no schedule. You can take all the time you need.

Establishing inner simplicity in your life will provide unlimited possibilities for personal growth. It will help you get in touch with how you want to live your life, and give you boundless energy to do it. It will help clear your head and give you a sense of direction and purpose you haven't had before. It will enhance your ability to love yourself and others, and help you create genuine pleasure in every moment of the day. It will give you a new zest for your life and new hope that things can be right in the world.

I urge you to approach inner simplicity as an exciting adventure, a delightful odyssey, a glorious pilgrimage, a wondrous search, a personal exploration, a natural unfolding, and a spiritual quest that has the potential to fill your heart, expand your mind, and lift your soul to new dimensions.

# One

# Things you'll
# *want* to do

# 1. Simplify your life

I F YOU'RE THINKING about achieving a level of inner simplicity, no doubt you've already taken steps to simplify other areas of your life. But if you haven't, you might think about how reducing the complexities of your life can contribute to your inner growth.

In my book, *Simplify Your Life,* I outline one hundred things my husband, Gibbs, and I did to rearrange all the areas of our lives—our household, our finances, our careers, our personal lives, our social lives—so we have the time and the energy to do the things that really matter to us. In the process of simplifying we uncovered somewhere between twenty and thirty hours each week to do those things.

As I look back, I see that it's not just having the *time,* it's the *quality* of the time that makes the difference for my inner explorations. I found it wasn't sufficient to cut my work schedule so I had the time to spend in peaceful solitude on Saturday afternoon (#93), if I spent that time worrying about the grocery shopping, or getting the lawn mowed, or what we were going to take to Jack's potluck dinner Saturday night because I hadn't been able to say no (#54) when he invited us.

You'll find it's much easier to enjoy the full benefits of your quiet time if you're able to reduce the distractions and the energy drains as well.

People often take up yoga or meditation to relieve the pressures of their lives, and to find inner peace. But frequently, unless they've made a conscious effort to make changes in other areas—such as reducing their workload or cutting back on their social obligations—their frenetic lifestyle gets in the way. The inner quest becomes difficult, and it falls by the wayside.

Spend some time thinking about the things you could do to make your life easier.

Simplifying will help create the peace and stability you need to launch into and continue your journey.

# 2. Spend time each day in nature

MANY CULTURES THROUGHOUT history have thought of nature as an integral and necessary part of their inner lives. Our society, for the most part, has lost contact with the restorative, healing, and inspirational power of the great outdoors.

Make spending time with nature an important part of your spiritual pursuits. If walking is included in your daily regimen, make sure that in addition to the exercise and fresh air benefits of being outdoors, you also connect on an inner level with the beauty of the sun and the sky and the earth.

Start each walk with a deep, invigorating breath of fresh air, and an appreciation of the weather, no matter what it's doing. Make a point of delighting in the trees and birds and flowers and plant life on your route. Let the glories of nature energize your body, heal your psyche, and uplift your spirit.

If you don't exercise outdoors, at the very least make certain you spend a few moments each day appreciating and drawing energy from nature. Plan to leave your house five minutes early tomorrow morning. Before you get into your car or hop on the train, use that time to notice the patterns of clouds in the sky or the dew on the grass. Or, take five minutes before you come into the house when you return from work, and simply acknowledge the closing of another day.

When weather permits, have your lunch outdoors on a park bench, or on the grass under the shade of a tree, and use the time to quietly commune with nature. If the air is clean, do some deep breathing to energize your body and your mind (#96).

Before you go to bed at night, get into the habit of simply opening the front door and stepping outside for a few minutes. Encourage your spouse and your children to join you. You can all enjoy a deep breath of fresh air, and get lost in a silent, meditative look at the night sky.

If you live in the city and are surrounded by tall buildings and concrete, make a special point of taking advantage of nearby parks or nature walks. Be sure your schedule includes weekend trips to places where nature's beauty has been allowed to flourish, and where you can use the power of the cosmos to get in touch with who you really are.

# 3. Connect with the sun

ALL THE ENLIGHTENED cultures of the past and many sages of the present recognize the role the sun plays in getting us in touch with our soul.

We know our bodies need sun in order to maximize the vitamins and minerals we get from our food. Yet, we now spend close to 90 percent of our time in artificial light.

Numerous studies have shown the debilitating effects on many people of the absence of adequate sunlight. Medical science has recently acknowledged the existence of SAD (seasonal affective disorder), and the need for sunlight for certain personality types.

One of the simplest ways to brighten your mood is to step into the sunlight.

Brief—definitely not extensive—exposure to the sun's rays is tremendously beneficial for our overall physical, mental, emotional health. But most importantly, linking with the sun increases our vitality and elevates our consciousness, thereby contributing to our inner growth.

Whenever you can, get ten to fifteen minutes of full exposure to the sun, either early in the morning or later in the afternoon. In winter, sit next to a sunny window to get a mini-sunbath.

Experiment with this. Connect with the sun every day for the next couple of weeks to see how beneficial it can be for expanding your inner awareness.

# 4. Create beauty in your life

BESIDES TAKING TIME to appreciate the restorative power of the beauty of nature, you'll find it helpful for your inner journey to make your personal environment as uplifting as possible.

This doesn't necessarily mean you have to run out and *purchase* something beautiful. More often, it means getting rid of a pile of clutter or a profusion of objects, each of which has lost its importance because it has become one of the crowd. A single vase on a shelf can have more value and significance to your life than when it's surrounded by a lot of other objects that detract from its singular beauty.

Or it can simply mean creating beautiful empty spaces. I have an artist friend who for years collected valuable objets d'art from other artists and from her travels around the world. Her home resembled a museum, and one practically had to conduct a tour of her living room in order to fully appreciate what each painting or piece of sculpture had to offer.

She recently made the decision to get rid of all of it. She looked around her home one day and realized she no longer knew what she thought because her mind was so distracted by *things*. Not only did they take up space, and not only did she have to worry about their getting broken or damaged, but she had to keep them dusted and lighted and insured. She created a beautiful, contemplative space by letting go of all the objects she had previously thought she couldn't be without.

Take a close look at the things you are surrounded with, both at home and in your workplace. Sometimes we can go for months or years without noticing, at least on a conscious level, some aspect of our environment that is less than pleasing.

Take whatever steps are necessary to make the places you spend your time in as inspiring, beautiful, and liberating for your spirit as possible.

# 5. Create simplicity, not austerity

WHEN I FIRST started to let go of some of the distractions I had unthinkingly allowed to accumulate
in my life and to look within, a friend said to me, "But I don't
want an austere life."

I said, "I don't either!"

She had the idea that we were going to give everything
away and go live in a hut in the wilderness.

I explained to her that getting rid of a lot of our stuff and
moving toward an inwardly simple life is not about deprivation or denying ourselves the things we want. It's about getting rid of the things that no longer contribute to the fullness
of our lives.

It's also about creating balance between our outer and
inner lives. One of the issues many of us are dealing with now
is coming back to our centers after having spent so much time
pursuing careers and creating fortunes in the outside world.

We've neglected the inner worlds, and our souls are craving some attention. Devoting more time and energy to the cultivation of our inner lives will help us create that balance and also enable us to live our outer lives more fully.

But living fully doesn't mean having it all, going everywhere, doing everything, and being all things to all people. Many of us are beginning to see that too much *is* too much. Doing too much and having too much get in the way of being able to enjoy the things we *do* want in our lives, and to simply be who we are.

Achieving a level of inner simplicity makes it possible to choose intelligently the things that are meaningful in our lives and that contribute to our happiness and our peace of mind.

It may ultimately mean doing fewer things and having less stuff, but that decision will come, not from self-denial, but from the wisdom that comes by taking the time to figure out what is important to us, and in letting go of all the rest.

# 6. Learn to enjoy the silence

IN ORDER TO hear what's happening on an inner level, we have to cut back as much as possible on the external racket. Start becoming aware of the continuously high noise levels you are subjected to every day.

It often begins with the nerve-jangling clamor of the alarm clock, the buzz of an electric toothbrush, or the blast of a hair dryer. This is followed by the drone of the latest news report or the babble of morning talk shows. Then comes the revving of car engines, and the honking of horns in rush hour traffic.

Our days are often filled with the nine-to-five sounds of ringing telephones and office equipment, not to mention the countless interruptions of coworkers, customers, and bosses. Even if you work at home, there can be a constant din from which there is seldom any respite.

On weekends there's the often ear-shattering roar of

lawn mowers or leaf blowers. How can we possibly hear ourselves think?

Often we can't. We're stressed by all the noise in our
day-to-day lives—frequently without even being aware of it.
At the same time, we're so used to it that it's hard for us to
imagine being without it.

As you begin to go within, you'll want to eliminate as
much of the outer commotion as possible so you can hear
your inner voice.

There may be some noises you won't have any control
over—such as traffic or the festivities of neighbors. But you
can start by creating as much quiet in your own space as possible.

Learn to wake up without an alarm. Go into your right
brain mode (#30) as you're about to fall asleep, and simply
visualize yourself waking up at whatever time you choose.

Try going without the TV or stereo for periods of time.
Also, leave your Walkman at home when you're walking or
exercising, and keep your radio and tape player off, especially
when you're driving. Bask in the silence, and use that time to
simply be with the moment rather than letting those forms of
entertainment distract you from your inner life.

Turn off your phone. Let your answering machine silently pick up messages, which you can listen to at your convenience.

Arrange a formal retreat (#95) or a private weekend of solitude at home (#93) so you can start tuning in to the joy of silence.

If you haven't been used to it, silence may seem strange at first, but you'll gradually come to treasure it. Eventually you'll find it indispensable for your inner search.

# 7. Have a family meal in silence

A S A PERSONAL or family ritual, have a meal in silence from time to time. Often the pressures of daily life can make meals a stressful routine. Or we can get so caught up in all the events of the day that we forget to take the time to enjoy our food. The tendency is to hurry through dinner so we can then dash off to the evening's activities.

Sit down with all the family members and discuss how you could approach having a meal in silence. Imagine everyone coming to the table with reverence, and sitting quietly for a few moments while you all connect with each other on an inner level. It's amazing how much you can hear when no one is saying anything.

Rather than mindlessly diving into the food, you could each genuinely but silently express your own gratitude for the meal, and accept on an inner as well as a physical level the benefits of the sustenance it will provide. Then make a point of being aware of the food, and of savoring each bite. So often we rush through meals, talking a mile a minute, and later don't even remember what we ate, or how it tasted.

Obviously there would be no TV or radios or stereos playing in the background. And no reading. Simply contented eating and a true familial connection.

If you have young children, a regular practice of having meals in silence could be an important lesson of family union, and instill in them at an early age an appreciation of the real value of food in their lives.

# 8. Figure out what you need to do to get well

T HERE IS MUCH evidence to indicate that at some level we all have the power to heal ourselves.

Slowing down and learning to look within often makes it possible for us to tap into our own healing powers or, at the very least, find the appropriate healing practice we should follow.

I experienced this firsthand several years ago when I injured my back in a river rafting trip. The range of healing choices available today is mind-boggling. I had lots of people suggesting lots of different methods of treatment.

Fortunately, I'd spent the previous couple of years simplifying my life and had started, for possibly the first time ever, to listen to my inner voice. After a six-month process of trial and error, I connected with the ancient healing technique of acupuncture that virtually healed my back in a couple of weeks.

This is not to say you should ignore the options of modern medicine, some of which can provide almost miraculous cures for what ails us. But, whenever possible, take the time to *listen*.

Consider *all* the options. If you've got an ailment or an injury from which you are not recovering, look into self-healing or alternative methods of healing and repair, such as visualization and positive imagery, especially if traditional medical treatments you've been using aren't working. Standard medical practices tend to focus on symptoms and disease rather than on health and wellness. Often the cure is worse than the illness.

I know listening to an inner voice isn't always easy. I spent six months virtually flat on my back in continual pain and discomfort, essentially incapacitated and unable to live a normal life. And, in the first six months or so, nothing I did seemed to help.

Even though my problem wasn't life-threatening, it was frightening and discouraging to feel there was no end in sight. The temptation was strong to take what seemed at the time to be the easy way out, and pursue what could ultimately have been a disastrous course of surgical treatment. In the past, I might very well have done that. Now I waited, and listened.

In time the appropriate solution for my situation came. We each know exactly what we need to do to heal ourselves. If the circumstances are appropriate, make it your personal quest to spend time in solitude or quiet contemplation until your intuition guides you to the proper course of treatment or self-healing.

# 9. Get in touch with your creativity

W E ' R E  A L L  B O R N with a deep core of creativity. Some fortunate few are able to connect with that core at an early age. Others of us spend years longing, oftentimes unconsciously, to tap into it. Many of us go through life denying that it exists. We live with the belief that we are not creative.

Often there are explanations we can point to that justify our seeming lack of creativity. Possibly it was stifled through some childhood trauma, or by real or imagined criticisms from our mentors. Maybe it was simply starved by the absence of encouragement when we needed it.

Like many people, I grew up believing I wasn't creative. At some level I recognized that this denial excused me from having to *try* to be creative. I also recognized that *saying* I wasn't creative kept me from *being* creative.

At another level, however, I wanted to explore the artistic possibilities. Over the years I've enrolled in dozens of art and drawing classes, hoping to learn to draw and paint. Over and over again I would drop out of these classes after just a few sessions because I was embarrassed to be the only one—or so it always seemed to me—who couldn't draw. Perhaps you've done this, too.

Julia Cameron, in her wonderful book *The Artist's Way* says this is analogous to dropping out of a French class because we can't immediately speak French. But this is a common occurrence. Many of us have come to believe that if we weren't born with talent, we'll never be able to develop it.

High on the list of major benefits I've received from inner simplicity has been the ability to get in touch with my artistic side. Some months after I'd started meditating (#98) and almost immediately after I'd completed some serious work on forgiveness (#70), I was able to start painting.

And because I'd started to learn through meditation that it's all right to just *be*, I felt okay with just being a *bad* painter. That got me to the point of being an okay painter.

For many of us, the ability to tap into our creativity comes only after we have slowed down to the point where we can take the *time* to get centered. Learning to *be* and learning to be creative are two sides of the same coin. Now that you have the time, your inner search can open you up to both.

# 10. Latch on to synchronicity

W E'VE ALL HAD days where everything just seems to go right. We hit the traffic at the opportune moment, and drive straight to the office without delays. We pull into the parking lot just as a convenient parking space opens up for us. The people we've been trying to reach all week suddenly call or appear, and we're able to wrap up our business with them with unusual efficiency. Our iced tea is cold and our soup is hot. The money comes out of nowhere for a project we want to start. Everything is in sync.

Since I've begun taking steps to simplify my life—both outer and inner—I've found synchronicity operates in all areas, and much more frequently than it did when my life was complicated. Over and over again, as soon as I've become clear on what it is I want, the circumstances I need to get it are miraculously available to me.

As I look back, I realize that before I slowed down, the

messages and the possibilities for these synchronicities had always been there, but often I was too busy to pay attention to them, or didn't believe them when I heard them.

This is not to say that *everything* is now a piece of cake for me. But I've learned that if things aren't going well, I need to slow down and listen. When I get back into sync, things start to flow again.

Reducing your pace and looking within will help you make your life work the way you want it to. It will also expand your time and energy so that synchronicity becomes a natural and joyous part of your life.

If you like the idea of latching on to synchronicity, perhaps it's time to make a formal declaration to yourself and the universe that this is what you want. It's amazing what can happen when we simply declare ourselves in the game.

# 11. Slow down

I WAS SURPRISED to discover that simplifying my life didn't automatically mean that I'd slowed down, too. The speed of life on the fast track permeates every area of our lives. Hurrying becomes a *habit*. Even after we've simplified many of our daily routines, if we're still surrounded by fast-moving people and phones that never stop ringing, slowing down can take a major effort.

Start by thinking about how you can slow down your morning routine. Getting up even half an hour earlier so you won't have to rush out the door will make a big difference in the pace of your entire day.

Take the time to *sit down* for your morning meal. Eat in a leisurely manner so you can feast on each bite. Eliminate the distractions of the radio, TV, and morning paper. Simply enjoy eating.

Make the gathering, preparation, and consumption of

food a conscious part of your inner quest, especially if you have lunch or dinner in fast-paced restaurants away from the peace and quiet you have established in your home. In fact, as much as possible, avoid fast-paced restaurants for your mid-day meal. Have your lunch on a park bench in the sun or sitting on the grass in the shade.

Plan to leave home in plenty of time so you don't arrive at the office panting at the start of your workday. If possible, walk to work, or take the bus or some other form of public transportation so you won't have to compete in rush hour traffic. If you do drive, make a point of staying within the posted speed limit. Learn to appreciate moving with purpose at a leisurely pace.

Place Post-it notes around your home or office to remind yourself to *slow down*. Over and over I found that rushing through a project meant getting it wrong and losing time in the end by having to do it over, either partially or completely. Take your time and do it right in the first place, and *enjoy the process* as you go along.

Make a concerted effort to examine all the areas of your life, and figure out where you can slow down. If you've simplified a lot of your daily and weekly routines, you now have more time. Use some of it to reduce your overall *pace* of life so you can derive more pleasure from each thing you do throughout the day.

Slowing down will help you keep in touch with how you feel about what you're doing, and make it easier to connect with your inner self.

# 12. Learn to receive

Y EARS AGO I studied hatha yoga with a wise woman who taught the art of *receiving*. We learned to take the time necessary to complete each yoga position, and then to take the time it took to *receive* the benefits of it. It was an invaluable lesson, and one we can incorporate into every area of our lives.

Get in the habit of *receiving* the benefits of the things you do. When you come in from your walk, take a few moments to *absorb* the contribution the exercise and the fresh air have made to your day and to your life.

When you finish a meal, sit still for a moment and be *conscious* of the benefits the food brings to your body.

When someone pays you a compliment, instead of shrugging it off, accept it fully into your being, even revel in it. When you do something thoughtful for someone else, enjoy not only the pleasure they may derive from it, but the satisfaction it gives *you* to perform a good deed.

When you complete a project, take some time to *ac-*

*knowledge* your accomplishment before you rush off to begin the next one.

So many extraordinary things happen to us throughout the day and throughout our lives. We often either ignore them or make light of them as though they were unimportant. They *are* important. Take the time to notice them.

The little things may take only a moment or two to acknowledge. All you have to do is stop for a couple of minutes, and *receive*. You'll know when you've taken it in completely, and when it's time to move on.

For the bigger things, like the completion of a work transaction or the achievement of a major goal, schedule whatever time you need to totally embrace the contribution you have made and *receive* the benefits of it.

Now that you've simplified your life, you have the *time* to assimilate into your being the synchronicities, the beauty, the love, the joys, and the work of your day. As they happen, let their beneficence pour over you and penetrate every fiber of your being.

In a very real sense, these daily events make you what you are. Indulge yourself. Enjoy them. Receive all the amity they have to offer.

# 13. Be realistic

W HEN WE FIRST made the decision to start simplifying our lifestyle, Gibbs and I sat down and made
a list of our priorities. Our first list included twenty to thirty
things we wanted to concentrate on.

As we moved along in our plan to simplify, we began to
see that even after we had taken some major steps to free up
our time and energy, there was no way we'd be able to do *everything* on our list.

So we cut back and ended up, at least for starters, with
four or five things that were most important to us: our marriage, our writing careers, spending time with family and special friends, and pursuing our personal hobbies of reading and
exploring cultural pursuits.

In one respect that doesn't seem like much—at least not
compared to what we *thought* we wanted to do, or compared
to what many of us have been *trying* to do. But if you've got a
spouse, and children, and a career, and certain responsibilities
you *can't* get out of, three to four priorities is about all you

get. There's really not a whole lot of time for anything else, especially if you want to include quality inner time as well.

Recognize that inner pursuits take time, too. And to get the maximum benefit from going within, that time should be free of the distractions and the complications we often allow our lives to be full of.

So as you start to make changes in your life and in your schedule, be realistic. Attempt to strike a balance between your outer and your inner goals, and keep in mind you may not be able to do *everything* you think you want to do.

# 14. Figure out what you *don't* want in your life

IN ADDITION TO figuring out what your priorities are, it is also helpful to figure out what you *don't* want in your life anymore. This is a subtle distinction, but it's an important one to make.

We allow a lot of mental, emotional, and psychological clutter to accumulate in our minds and our lives, blocking our access to inner peace.

This clutter includes doing things we don't want to do but continue to do, either because we said we'd do them or feel we *should*.

It includes spending time with people we no longer want to spend time with because we've outgrown the relationship or because they don't contribute to our inner growth.

It includes doing work we aren't happy doing.

It includes trying to do too many things, even if a lot of them are things we do want to do.

It includes not doing enough of the things we want to do. It includes engaging in idle gossip and meaningless chatter that drains our energy and leaves us feeling grungy.

An amazing amount of the clutter includes fuming over past events we can't change, or being distracted by future events that may never happen. It includes judgment (#65), and harboring thoughts that burn (#62).

As you move toward developing harmony in your life, you'll find a lot of this stuff will fall by the wayside. Some things, however, will require an effort on your part to make sure they are eliminated.

You might want to sit down with your journal (#31) in the next few days and make a list of the things that are getting in the way of your inner progress. Then set up a plan to get rid of them.

# 15. Enjoy each moment

ONE OF THE ultimate objectives of attaining inner simplicity is learning to live happily in the present moment. Keep in mind that life is a continuous succession of present moments. Most of us spend an inordinate number of our moments regretting the past, or fidgeting in the present, or worrying about the future. We miss a lot of life that way.

Worry and regret and being anxious are *habits* that keep us locked in old patterns. But these habits can be eliminated once we've become aware of them.

If you find such habits are getting in the way of being happy, think about what you can do to change them. It sounds simplistic to say it, but you can get into the *habit* of enjoying your life. Setting up a calendar and a box of stars is one way to approach building this habit (#61).

Another way to choose to enjoy each moment is to start taking responsibility for your life (#68). If you're not happy in your present circumstances, you have no one but yourself to blame. Make whatever changes you need to make so that you *are* happy.

Going within will automatically bring you to a level of enjoyment of your day-to-day life that you may not have experienced before. Making the conscious effort to enjoy each moment will make your inner quest that much easier.

# 16. Take time to read

THERE ARE THOSE who say that once we get far enough in our inner journey, we'll know everything we need to know from a deep awareness of our own experience.

In the meantime, for those of us who are still plodding along, the appropriate books are an invaluable source of information, inspiration, courage, insight, advice, and confirmation that we're headed the right way.

Keep a suitable selection of books on your bookshelves, by your desk, in the glove compartment of your car, next to your favorite easy chair, and anywhere else you find yourself on a regular basis.

Whenever you start to worry, or feel sorry for yourself, or feel lonely or depressed, or find that you're judging others, or thinking negatively, or feeling anger or resentment, pull out a relevant book.

The list of soul-nourishing literature is almost endless. At the back of this book I've included a list of some of the works I've found helpful.

# 17. But don't read in bed

ALL MY LIFE I've read in bed until lights out, so I know this will sound like heresy to those who love to read themselves to sleep. But once I started to explore other levels of awareness, I found that reading just before sleep was a major distraction.

When I thought about it, I realized that often I was simply too sleepy to adequately absorb what I was reading, and frequently I'd have to go back the next day and spend time reading the same material over again. Or I'd fall asleep in the middle of reading about someone else's life drama, and would end up tossing and turning with wild and fantastical dreams that didn't contribute to my sleep or my life.

My friend Margaret mentioned to me recently that she'd been having nightmares. Since I'd just begun to explore my own dreams, I asked her if she had changed her bedtime routine. She assured me she hadn't; she was reading until she fell asleep, as she had always done.

It turned out that her favorite aunt had recently sent her

a huge box of detective stories that she was clearing out and thought Margaret would enjoy. The problem was that Margaret did enjoy them, which is why it took her some time to figure out that reading them just before sleep was having a negative impact on her dreams.

For a while, I made a practice of keeping only uplifting or spiritually oriented reading material on my nightstand. But after experimenting, I've found it's better to fall asleep consciously than under the influence of someone else's psyche, no matter how elevated it might be. This is especially important if you're exploring your sleep consciousness (#97).

I've gotten into the habit of having a few moments of quiet reflection or possibly even a brief meditation just before going to sleep. This has contributed significantly to my inner simplicity.

For the next few weeks, try going to sleep without reading in bed. You'll notice a big difference in your moods, in your intuitiveness, and in your level of awareness. You're also much more likely to get a good night's sleep.

# 18. Sleep a lot

SLEEP IS A vital part of your inner growth, especially in the early stages. There is a lot going on at the sleep level of consciousness that we are only just beginning to understand. Many spiritual retreat programs include naps, rest time, and/or sleep as a major part of the daily regimen.

If you've been moving quickly on the fast track in recent years, you may desperately need sleep to restore your body and your mind, not to mention your psyche. If you've simplified your life, you'll have time now to sleep and still do many of the other things you may want to do.

So sleep in whenever you can. Go to bed early every night for as long as you need to. Sleep throughout the weekends. Take naps whenever possible. Relish sleep. Luxuriate in it. Grow in it. Expand in it. You need it.

Two

Easy things to
*think* about doing

# 19. Have weekend retreats at home

I F  Y O U ' R E  W O R K I N G on establishing a level of inner simplicity, few things you can do will give you a better boost than a formal retreat (#95). But if you're not quite ready to do that, or you can't take the time now, arranging your own retreat at home might be the next best thing.

Obviously, having a weekend retreat at home will be easier if you're single or if your spouse and/or children are either away for the weekend or receptive to the idea of your taking some time on your own.

Set aside your normal weekend routine. Plan to start your quiet time by dinner on Friday evening and carry it through Sunday evening. Unplug the phone, and tell your family and friends that you won't be available until Monday morning. Plan not to answer the door.

Turn off your TV and your radio; put newspapers and magazines away, but make certain you have a supply of appropriate reading materials (#16). Take your watch off so you are not concerned with time. Wear loose-fitting comfortable clothes. Avoid the type of food and drink or other substances that will lower your energy.

Do whatever you need to do to your space to make it as pleasant and as conducive to quiet reflection as possible. Air out the rooms; bring in fresh flowers; provide candles or incense or essential oils. Have everything you might want at hand so you won't have to dash out into the world.

Spend your time in silent reflection. Meditate. Do yoga or gentle stretching. Practice deep breathing (#96). Write in your journal (#31). Create your inner affirmations (#28) and visualizations (#29), and start practicing them. Watch sunrises and sunsets. Take a mini-sunbath to keep your mind and spirits elevated. Spend time in nature. Stroll in the early morning or evening, away from people and traffic. Sit quietly, not thinking, just being with the moment. Ask for guidance and be open to whatever messages come to you from the universe.

Go to bed early and get up with the sun, or even earlier. If you rarely get to experience the joy of the birth of a new day, this is a good time to start.

Prepare your meals with love and awareness. Eat in silence without reading or any other distractions; make a point of savoring each bite.

Make a commitment to yourself not to worry or to engage in negative thinking during this time. If necessary, use the bean system (#63) to become aware of your thought patterns. If you feel lonely or frightened, write about your feelings in your journal.

This is the time to reconnect with your soul. Enjoy it.

# 20. Consider a family
# retreat

IF YOUR FAMILY is amenable, consider spending a
silent, meditative weekend retreat at home together. This
can be a very powerful and effective way to strengthen the
family bond.

If you haven't already established a pattern of regular
times of solitude with your family, a retreat—even a quiet,
contemplative afternoon together—would be a good way to
start.

# 21. Remember, growth isn't always a family affair

ONCE YOU START to look within and experience new insights about the world and your place in it, it'll be only natural that you'll want to share them with your family.

Consider yourself fortunate if the other members of your household are ready at the same time you are to explore the inner realms. It's much more likely that you'll be ready, but your spouse and your children won't be. Be prepared for this possibility, and don't make an issue of it. They'll come along when the time is right. Or they may not.

If you find yourself in this position, spend some time sincerely listening to your inner voice (#92). Figure out how you can move forward on your quest without alienating your family. Your task will be to arrange your life so you can continue your inner explorations without making anyone else feel uncomfortable or threatened.

How you proceed will depend to some extent on the level of communication that has already been established. Go slowly, and don't be attached to having them join you. It may be that the most you can hope for is their understanding and acceptance.

If you can't get even that for the moment, learn to keep your own counsel (#72), and don't make anyone else wrong in the process. Learning to deal with the reactions of the people close to you could be a major part of your growth. Your biggest challenge may be to accept the situation as it is, and continue on your way.

# 22. Don't get caught in the righteousness of your path

WHILE I'M FORTUNATE that Gibbs has been totally supportive of the inner explorations I have pursued in recent years, his methods of connecting with the soul have been quite different from mine. Happily, we've been able to establish a relationship in which we can each follow our own inclinations, respect each other's choices, and share with each other what we're learning.

But no matter how comfortable we are with our diverse paths, part of me wishes we were both on the same path. Namely mine, of course.

Recently, we took our own private retreat together at a favorite spot of ours in the mountains. He did his thing, and I did mine. After several days of quiet contemplation we found ourselves sitting side by side. I was reading about zen meditation; he was reading a biography of Napoleon.

Finally, I decided to ask him a question that had been

on my mind since I had begun this process of looking within.

So I turned to him and said, "Do you think I'm more evolved because I'm doing all this searching? Or are you more evolved because you aren't?"

He pondered this for a quiet moment, then said, "Maybe we're both evolved, but we're just expressing it in different ways."

I had to acknowledge the wisdom of this response. And it gave me the chance to see that at some subtle level I had been feeling smug about the rectitude of my inner work.

As we discussed it further, I also had to consider the fact that being *evolved* had nothing to do with it—we're both simply doing our own thing. It's so easy to fall into the trap of thinking that the inner quest is somehow superior to the activities of the everyday world. But inner seeking is just inner seeking. There's nothing inherently better about it. Outer explorations are just as necessary and just as valuable. The inner stuff often *seems* more important to those who are in the midst of it because many of us have spent so much more time recently in the marketplace and so little time cultivating our own souls. When our lives are in balance, there is no distinction between the outer and the inner.

This is a good lesson for me to remember. And remember. And remember.

I share it here in case you might need to remember it at some point, too.

# 23. Form a support group

THE INNER SEARCH requires a lot of time alone when you may well be doing things differently from the way you've been doing them. It's possible many of the things you'll be doing will be different from what most people you know are doing. You'll no doubt be having new insights and revelations about your life and your purpose. Sometimes it'll be exhilarating; sometimes it might well be terrifying.

And sometimes it will seem as though nothing at all is happening. You may find it helpful to be in touch with people who have some conception of what you're going through, and who have been there themselves.

Recently I spent several years in a group of three women and two men who were committed to inner growth. Our weekly meetings provided a safe setting where we could freely discuss the changes we were experiencing on a metaphysical level. The progress we made together not only elevated the energy of the group, but contributed to each of us individually.

Keep your eyes open and put feelers out for people who might have similar goals and interests to your own. These need not be people you know or are currently friends with. People who don't know you are sometimes more likely to be objective when it comes to evaluating your situation and your progress.

If you haven't experienced the tremendous benefits that can come from participating in a small group of people who are dedicated to each other's growth, I urge you to think about how this might enhance your inner work. You may have already discovered that the people you most want to spend time with are those who are working at the inner levels, too.

Eventually, it's likely you'll have to step into the void on your own, but until you reach that point, surrounding yourself with like-minded people can help you create an atmosphere for real spiritual transformation.

# 24. Create a positive structure for your group

W HEN WE FIRST set up our inner group, we found it helpful to agree on some guidelines for how our meetings would be structured.

We decided to meet at the same time and at the same place every week, and we each committed to the group and to each other for at least six months. We felt we would need at least that much time to establish a real bond of trust, and to get a feel for how effective these meetings would actually be.

As it turned out, the process was so helpful for each of us that we continued to meet weekly for several years, until a couple of the members moved out of the area.

In terms of format, we tried various approaches and decided what worked best was to allow each person half an hour or so to share whatever they felt was appropriate about their inner progress from the previous week, or about any new insights they might have come up with.

Then we took time for comments and suggestions from the other members before going on to the next person. We started the meeting with a different person each week.

We found that every now and then we needed to change the format of the meeting in order to adapt to the particular circumstances of the members. If one of us was at a critical juncture and required more time, other members would give up their time to the person who needed it most that week. We each knew we would get it back when our day of need came.

We decided not to bother with refreshments. We didn't want any outside distractions.

We also agreed that anything we discussed would be confidential.

We selected a meeting place where there were no spouses or children who might interrupt, and the host agreed to turn off the phone while our meetings were in progress.

If you're putting together a group of people who are dedicated to inner development, take some time in the beginning to arrange a format that will work for the members and for the group as a whole. Then be open to changing the structure as the group evolves.

# 25. Have some fun while you're at it

EVERY NOW AND then, we changed the format of our inner group meeting entirely. Once, one member brought blankets and food, piled us all into his Jeep, and drove us to the top of a local mountain peak. We had a very high-energy meeting in the cool night air as a beautiful full moon rose over the valley.

Another time we drove down to the beach and romped through the crashing breakers in the dark of night. Then we built a fire on the beach, and had a group meditation.

Once we arranged to spend a day on a wilderness adventure course. We confronted our own fears or limitations with rock climbing, rappeling, tree climbing, and nature hikes.

All these things were done with the intention of elevating our consciousness so we could team up with each other and with our higher selves through nature. We created a special bond individually and as a group that immeasurably helped our future work together.

Connecting with a group of like-minded people on an inner level can provide many benefits, not the least of which is to remind ourselves that our inner search can be fun as well as challenging.

# 26. Monitor the obvious distractions

IF YOU'RE MOVING toward inner simplicity, you're probably already cutting back on many of the diversions that may previously have occupied a lot of your time, such as television, movies, videos, noisy bars, and crowded restaurants.

You may find that the entertainment aspects of the inner realms are not only much more satisfying, but they leave you feeling refreshed and rejuvenated, whereas many of the more popular gratifications deplete your energy and often bring you down.

This is not to say that any of these amusements are unacceptable in themselves, or that you want to eliminate them entirely. But if you think about it, you can figure out which activities you might have partaken of in the past, that now no longer contribute to your well-being or your peace of mind.

And, if you think about it some more, you can come up with activities—sometimes seemingly insignificant ones—

that can fill your soul. A while back I was washing some grapes for lunch. I looked at that bunch of big, red, luscious grapes and saw how exquisitely beautiful they were. It was almost as though I'd never seen a grape before. I held them up and turned them this way and that and marveled at the gradations of color and how they appeared to change shape as the light hit them.

I stood for some minutes, totally absorbed in the essence of those grapes. And in those few moments I sensed my whole awareness expanding. I felt full to the brim, and I hadn't even eaten the grapes yet! I'm sure I got more sustenance from looking at those grapes than from any of the movies I've seen in recent years.

You may think spending an evening watching a bunch of grapes is not your thing. But if you're looking to feed your spirit, it might be preferable to watching people machine-gun each other into oblivion. If grapes don't do it for you, think about sunsets, sunrises, moonrises, moonsets, stargazing, or simply staying home and playing Scrabble with your kids.

You may also find yourself going through periods of time when nothing is coming through on the inner channels. That's when you can do something like casting a rune (#86), or dancing (#91), or chanting (#90), or laughing (#59), or possibly crying (#84).

# 27. Create your own sanctuary

IT WILL BE important for your inner pursuits to have a space you can call your own. It could be your own room, or even a small corner of a room. It will be somewhere you can go and not be disturbed.

This will be where you'll meditate, contemplate, do nothing, think, read, heal yourself, enjoy the silence, and do your journal writing. You can do your affirmations and visualizations here. You can keep your discipline calendar and your box of stars here (#61). You can review your day here (#41). It'll be a very functional space. Do whatever you need to do to make it special and sacred.

I have a huge cozy armchair in a corner by a window. I can sit comfortably for reading, and straight and alert for meditating. I keep a stack of my favorite books by the chair.

I have a tape player nearby where I can listen to my subliminal tapes or to music that I find uplifting—though usually I just enjoy the silence. I know I can go there at any time to clear my energy, or to work out a problem, or to just sit quietly and BE. Gibbs knows not to interrupt me when I'm there.

If you've never had the luxury of a place where you can go on a regular basis to get away from the daily routine of your life and be alone, don't waste another moment. This space will be essential for your spiritual growth.

# 28. Use affirmations

A N AFFIRMATION IS a mental or verbal declaration to yourself and to the universe about how you
want your life to be. Words and thoughts are powerful things.
Your life as it is right now is a physical manifestation of all
your thoughts, both positive and negative.

Positive affirmations are an effective tool for clearing the
negativity out of our minds and our lives, and for propelling
us along in our efforts to create our lives exactly the way we
want them to be.

I've used affirmations for years in my personal and business life. Anyone who has used them consistently knows how
effective they can be in helping us to achieve what we want in
our lives. But I was well into my inner search before it dawned
on me that affirmations could be effective there as well.

Take some time in the next few days, either on your own
or with an appropriate book, to come up with a personal statement that expresses the thing or things you most want in your
life right now—peace, tranquility, simplicity, wisdom, en-

lightenment, omniscience, spiritual growth, whatever.

Make your affirmation a positive statement that declares to yourself and to the universe that you have this thing or quality in your life right now, such as "I live a simple, peaceful life."

It doesn't matter if the statements you affirm are not true yet. Repetition of an affirmation, combined with *belief* and *imagination,* enhances the ability of your subconscious mind to bring about the reality you affirm.

Use a section of your journal to record these affirmations for your daily use. Get into the habit of actively thinking about and repeating selected ones to yourself throughout the day. Use Post-it notes or whatever means works as a reminder until the habit of working with your affirmations for your inner growth is firmly established.

Then be prepared to change and/or adapt your affirmations as your life changes, and you gradually begin to become the things you affirm yourself to be.

I've included several books in the Reading List that are helpful for understanding, creating, and using both affirmations and visualizations.

# 29. Use visualizations

**H**AND IN HAND with affirmations go visualizations. In addition to verbalizing to yourself both silently and out loud the inner qualities you want to develop, creating a powerful mental image that projects how you want your life to be focuses your attention on that outcome and helps bring it into your life.

Numerous studies in recent years have shown how effective visualization can be for healing, personal growth, and empowerment. Like affirmations, visualizations are just as potent for our spiritual journey.

Spend some quiet time in your sanctuary thinking about how you would look and feel to yourself if you had the inner qualities of love, compassion, joy, gratitude, understanding, patience, tolerance, acceptance, or whatever attributes you seek.

Pick one trait, such as compassion, and step into it each morning as part of your daily routine. Make this a habit. In your mind's eye, actually *see* yourself having this quality.

*Imagine* how you would look and how you would feel if you had compassion. Check with yourself throughout the day to make sure this feeling of compassion is still with you. Do this until you've absorbed this quality. Then move on to the next one.

We are continually bombarded with negative messages that can easily deflect us from our search for inner peace. Developing the ability to counteract that negativity with positive mental images will go a long way toward keeping you on track.

# 30. Use your right brain mode

MUCH RESEARCH HAS been done in recent years on the various levels of the mind, particularly the right brain mode, or the alpha level of consciousness, where we can tap into our creativity, get in touch with our intuition, enhance our thinking processes, and improve our performance in sports and other activities, among many other things. This is the level of the mind where artists, writers, and all great thinkers get their ideas. It is where we all work on problem solving and the creation of new perceptions and understandings.

Years ago I took a Silva Mind Control Seminar in which we learned how to create a "workshop" in our mind at the alpha level. We simply relaxed into the right brain mode and, using our imagination, created a space in our mind's eye where we could go to work on problems of any type at the alpha level.

We learned to clear up headaches, find lost objects, and even get rid of infestations of ants! (Anyone who has tried these methods knows how effective they can be. Skeptics can continue to use Raid.)

The theory is that any information we need to do the work we want to do is available to us. We simply have to get into the practice of tapping into it.

You may already be using these techniques in your life. If so, think about how you might use them for your inner endeavors.

One of the things I did almost unconsciously when I started to go within was turn my workshop into an "inner sanctum." Now I do almost all my inner work there. It's where I listen, heal, create affirmations, enhance visualizations, and do my serious thinking, among many other things.

If you're not familiar with right brain techniques, you might want to check out some books that outline detailed methods for accessing other levels of consciousness. Several are suggested in the Reading List.

Going into the alpha level is very easy to do. One technique is simply to sit down, close your eyes, relax, and take a couple of deep breaths. Breathe quietly for a few minutes. You might find it helpful initially to count backward slowly from ten to one. You'll begin to recognize a slight shift in your level of awareness, and you'll know you're in the right brain mode. Being effective there happens by *intention* and *imagination*.

After you've done this a few times, you'll recognize the *feel* of the space and how to get there, and you can come and go at will. It is a safe and very powerful place for your inner operations.

# 31. Expand your journal

I HAVE USED a journal on and off over the years for recording dreams and for writing about personal issues as well as to help me sort through difficult or complicated situations.

Since I simplified my life and have started my inner search, I've expanded my idea about what a journal can be. It has actually branched into a spiritual workbook. I've found it an invaluable tool for keeping track of my thoughts and feelings, and for recording the progress of my quest.

Now, in addition to sections for dreams and journal writing, I have space for recording affirmations and visualizations, since these change on a regular basis as I adapt them to my needs.

I have a section for recording rune readings (#86), since this is such an effective way to stay in touch with and develop my intuition. It's been helpful to be able to refer back to see how the runes have guided me in the past on a question that may keep coming up.

I also have a section for special issues I may be dealing with from time to time, such as forgiveness or negative thinking. And, perhaps most importantly, I make room to record unusual experiences and perceptions that come from my meditations and from quiet times of doing nothing. Even though we may have greatly simplified our lives and reduced much of the outside stimuli that assault us on a daily basis, it's amazing how quickly we can forget important insights that can help us in our growth. So not only does a journal serve as a device for working on solutions to problems as they arise, but it also serves as a reliable memory.

I'm careful not to become a slave to a journal, however, and I don't feel I have to use it every single day. It's simply there as an ally when I need it.

If you think a journal would be helpful to you on your odyssey, come up with a format that works for you.

I use a six-by-nine-inch spiral-bound notebook and tabulate it for dreams, runes, or whatever, depending on my needs. I find this size is easy to keep on a bookshelf with other books, and is a convenient size to travel with. It is also less forbidding than a larger notebook, and therefore easier to dispose of when it has served its purpose. Thus, it doesn't ultimately become one more thing to clutter up my life.

# 32. Ask for help if you need it

I GREW UP on the plains of Kansas and was imbued from an early age with a strong belief in rugged individualism and going it alone in the true spirit of the pioneer.

When I found myself in the fiasco that was my first marriage (#81), it never occurred to me to ask anyone for help. I figured I'd gotten myself into this mess and somehow I'd get myself out. Eventually, I did. But if I'd known then what I know now about asking for help, I'd have gotten out a lot sooner, and with a lot less trauma. In fact, I'd never have gotten into it in the first place!

My friend Judy grew up with what those of us who know and love her refer to as a strong sense of entitlement. Her childhood training was just the opposite of mine. She has no hesitation about asking anyone anywhere for help. And the absolutely amazing thing to me is that she always gets whatever help she needs.

I've picked up some valuable lessons watching her over the years. First of all, I've learned that it's okay to need help; it's nothing to be ashamed of. Secondly, I've learned that most people are willing to help someone who simply asks for it.

In addition, I've learned to be careful whom I ask for help. There's no point in going to an auto mechanic if you're having a coronary.

Also, I've learned to distinguish between an everyday, garden-variety upset that a friend or a support group could help with and major distress that requires a professional (#47).

I also make a point of avoiding the person who insists on helping whether I need it or not. I used to be that type before I simplified my life, so I'm familiar with that energy!

If, like me, you're one of those who's never been comfortable asking for help, maybe it's time to rethink your attachment to the pioneer spirit. We're all human, and we all need a little assistance from time to time.

Developing the ability to ask for help when you need it will often provide clarity to your life, and enable you to move through life's lessons much more quickly.

# 33. Ask for help from the universe

AS LONG AS you're asking for help, you might as well ask for help from the universe. You never know what might happen.

A while back I found myself in a particularly confusing and distressful situation. I'd had a counseling session or two for this particular issue. I'd discussed it with friends and family. But I was at an impasse. I simply couldn't seem to get beyond it.

I was driving to an appointment one morning when the seeming enormity of this problem overwhelmed me. I pulled to the side of the road, stopped the car, and turned off the engine. I threw up my hands and yelled to whoever was "out there" that might be paying attention, "Okay! I give up! I need some clarity and some relief on this one. Help!"

I pounded the steering wheel furiously several times for emphasis. I sat there silently for a few moments, feeling completely drained. Eventually, I started up the car and went to my meeting.

A short time later I noticed I was feeling a tremendous sense of release from this problem. As the day wore on, I began to get an understanding about it that I simply hadn't been able to come to before. I couldn't even quite put it into words; I just knew that I had passed through the worst of it, and that I'd soon be able to put it behind me.

Obviously, this is nothing new. We've all had similar experiences. Some might call this prayer and say God was listening. Others would call it a higher power. Still others would say it was my higher self responding to my desperation. I like to think of it as the power of the universe.

Call it what you will, there is an energy available to us. All we have to do is ask for it. And we don't have to wait until things get desperate. We can use it as a regular part of our everyday lives, for guidance, for inspiration, for getting in touch with our true selves.

I've learned that the more I call upon this help, the more it's available to me. I have a sense that, as I continue to utilize it in my life, my comprehension of it will expand as well. Enlarging our concept of the power that's available to us, and using it regularly in our daily lives, can only enhance our inner growth.

# 34. Figure out what others have to teach you

EVERY NOW AND then, you'll find yourself con-nected with someone who just drives you up the wall. There may be any number of reasons you can't get away from this person for the time being.

Or maybe you've gotten away, but you run into them from time to time, and they zap your energy. Soon you find yourself spending inordinate amounts of time grumbling to yourself about all the things they do that make you nuts.

Or maybe you don't see them at all anymore, but you still spend a lot of time grousing about the way they are, or fuming over something you think they did to you in the past. Usually, this is someone you once had a close relationship with.

When this kind of thing happens, you can be certain this person is in your life or in your mind for a reason: there is something you need to learn from them before you can put the relationship to rest.

For starters, sit down and spend some time *thinking* about what it is this person does that gets on your nerves. Make a list of the qualities or habits or behavior patterns that bother you. Then look objectively at your own personality. Maybe you have some of these same qualities, and you want, at some level, to get rid of them.

Or maybe you already have made changes in these areas, and it's disturbing to you to think that you were once like that. Often, once you get clear exactly what it is that bothers you, it's easier to let go of it.

Possibly this person actually did hurt you, perhaps intentionally. If you just can't seem to find it in your heart to forgive them yet (#70), force yourself to sit down again and make a list of all the people *you* may have harmed, either accidentally or on purpose.

It's even possible you've hurt *this* person in some way. Look at that same dark space you were coming from when those things happened and realize that, though you have moved away from that place, the person you're dealing with may still be operating in the dark.

Perhaps what this person has to teach you is how far you've come, and that in order to move on you've got to develop some compassion, for them and for yourself. When it comes right down to it, it would appear we're all in this to-gether.

At some intuitive level we all know why we're in the situations we're in. The objective is to reach a point where we can understand what those reasons are, make whatever changes we need to make, and then move on.

# 35. Use the events of the day to bring you back

ONE OF THE benefits that comes from slowing down our lives is the ability to get back in touch with who we really are and what we're doing here. It's tremendously liberating to make that connection, but often, because of the demands of our work schedule and the complexities of family and social obligations, we keep forgetting.

Get into the habit of using the events of your day to remind yourself of the inner realizations you are starting to get a sense of during your quiet times, and to remind yourself to connect with your soul. You can use any circumstance or happening of the day to bring yourself back to the inner you.

When you wake up in the morning, remember. When you brush your teeth, remember. When the water boils for tea, remember.

When the phone rings, remember. When you are stopped at a stoplight, remember. When you sit down to a meal, remember.

When you get upset, remember. When you have a headache, remember. When the kids are cranky, remember.

When you get into bed at night, remember. When you fall asleep, remember.

# 36. Find a teacher

T HERE ARE THOSE who say that when you're
ready to step onto your spiritual path, a teacher will appear to show you the way. This may be true, but it hasn't
been my experience yet.

But even though I haven't found that special relationship, I've found that the search for it is part of the journey,
and it can be a great adventure.

If you're thinking you might like to find some guidance
as you go along, one way is through books.

One book in particular that I found very helpful in outlining the plethora of teachings available today is *The Spiritual Seeker's Guide*, by Steven S. Sadleir. It's an excellent
reference for the major spiritual paths, metaphysical initia-
tions, teachers, masters, and movements of the world. It describes not only the teachings and the teachers and tells you
where to get more information, but it places each in a historical context, going back to 8000 B.C.

What a review like this provides, in addition to practical

information regarding areas you might want to explore—or avoid—is the realization that all true spiritual teachings attempt to lead ultimately to the same thing: an understanding of the mysteries of the universe and the role we each play in it.

Obviously some teachings do it better than others. And some have gotten corrupted along the way. It also becomes clear that no path is the best path, or the only path, and that there is something for everyone.

Needless to say, a book of this type has its limitations: it can't include everything. But it can give you a start. Then you'll find one thing leads to another. You meet people in one place who can lead you to other people and other teachings, which then can lead you to where you really want to go.

Or you can just listen (#92). This is harder for the more impatient among us, but ultimately it's what we all have to do anyway. Our intuitive guide, if we can simply sit still long enough to hear it, will always lead us in the right direction.

Once you've begun the inner search, your teachers may change fairly rapidly as you go along, or at least your understanding of them will. I've also learned that being too attached to a teacher can potentially hinder your process. The right teachers can provide many valuable teachings, but they can't live your life for you. Ultimately, we all have to be responsible for our own growth.

# 37. But don't get too attached

I HAD THE good fortune when I started the first leg of my inner journey years ago to be associated with several loving and helpful mentors who gave me a different perspective of the spiritual path than the one I'd acquired from the religion of my childhood.

They didn't have all the answers, but they provided what I needed at that time in my life. They broadened my horizons, then sent me on my way. In the long run, that may be the most we can expect from a good teacher.

In the process of looking for a teacher, I also did a lot of exploration on my own. If I heard about a mind-expanding technique or a guru who sounded interesting, I would check it out. Some were legitimate, others not. All were instructive. And, in one way or another, they were all part of the journey.

At one point in my youth I heard about a young "master" who was giving "knowledge" to anyone who wanted it badly enough to pin him down for it. As it happened, he had made a trip from India and was temporarily based in Houston.

On a whim I took a week of unpaid vacation, got into a van with half a dozen other seekers, and headed south. The Astrodome was filled with all manner of people looking for the answer. Many of them didn't know what the question was.

But after waiting days and days, those of us who wanted it got knowledge, an ancient meditative technique that was revealed to us in small dark rooms by thin guys wearing white robes. It was supposed to help us achieve cosmic consciousness. I didn't know what that was, but I figured since they were passing it out, I'd take some.

Several months later word spread that one of the more comely devotees had been impregnated by the pudgy little guru. Eventually this charlatan was sent back to India.

I left the fold at that point, and it took me years to admit publicly that I'd been so naive as to fall for that impostor. But advancing years have led me to see the benefits of that experience. After all, I got to go to Houston, where I'd never been before, and I picked up an interesting and effective meditative technique that I used on and off over the years.

I didn't achieve cosmic consciousness as promised but,

all things considered, it was not a bad teaching. And, contrary to what I wanted to believe then, I've since learned that enlightenment rarely happens overnight—and probably only very rarely in the Houston Astrodome.

The point is, if you stumble in your search for enlightenment, don't be afraid to pick yourself up, dust yourself off, and start all over again. And just keep listening. If I'd been listening back then, I'd never have gotten into the van.

# 38. Ignore the skeptics

A S YOU START to go within and begin to make some changes in the way you look at life and how you spend your time, you may begin to hear teasing remarks from family and friends who haven't yet begun to explore the inner levels. For the most part, they mean no harm. Simply smile, and ignore them.

Don't let this be a difficult thing for you. *You* know the changes that are taking place in your own mind and heart and soul. And even though you may not have entirely figured out the mysteries of the universe, don't let others who don't have a clue distract you. The only thing you have to answer to is your own growth.

If you find yourself in situations where people are needling you a bit, there are a number of things you can do.

If possible, avoid them. A good friend of mine used to spend time with a couple she knew. The husband could seldom pass up the opportunity to poke fun at anyone who ventured to explore anything he considered off the beaten path.

Even though my friend recognized that his comments were without malice, his closed-mindedness became limiting for her. She gradually stopped seeing them.

If that's not feasible, keep your sense of humor. Make a lighthearted comment to diffuse any heavy energy. You can also ignore them, or just listen, and figure out what these people have to teach you.

Above all, keep your own counsel (#72), and remember there may have been a time in the not too distant past when you were a skeptic, too.

# 39. Establish a routine

I'VE FOUND IT most helpful to have a regular routine for my inner activities.

Now that I've simplified my life, I find it easy to get up at the crack of dawn, or even earlier. In that quiet time I can do yoga and stretching, write in my journal, do some deep breathing, work on affirmations and visualizations, meditate, or have some quiet time to just sit and think.

Then I usually take a brisk walk with Gibbs and our little dog, Piper, before I come back to have breakfast and begin my workday.

Depending on the type of work I'm doing, I've found it beneficial to take a brief meditative break around noon to clear my head, and maybe do some more stretching and deep breathing.

I also try to make a point of reconnecting with nature in the middle of the day, either by having lunch outdoors on a park bench, or by taking a brief stroll after I eat.

I used to have another meditation just before bedtime,

but found I'd often sleep right through it. I've discovered it is much more effective to meditate at the end of my workday, just before dinner. In addition to whatever happens at an inner level, it also clears my head and my psyche for a relaxing evening. Then I take a few minutes before I go to bed to review my day (#41).

I keep this agenda flexible, and it changes from time to time as my patterns change. But having a routine makes it easier to keep in touch with my inner work, and I find I can go with the flow of the schedule. At the end of the workday, for example, my mind and my body are accustomed to a meditation, and I can just ease into it gently with no struggle.

As you expand your awareness and the level of the inner simplicity you want to achieve, think about arranging a convenient routine to make it easier for your inner efforts to fall into place.

# 40. Break your routine
## once in a while

EVEN THOUGH IT'S helpful to have a daily routine, getting too attached to it can limit your growth. I've
found it tremendously beneficial to completely break the pattern from time to time.

Every now and then, I stop meditating for a couple of
days, possibly even a week. I also stop or cut back on the other
inner practices I've been developing.

Partly what breaking the routine does is create some confusion and some insecurity in our psyche. This is beneficial
because it forces us to *think* about what we're doing. It gives
us a chance to take a close look at whether these activities are
contributing to our inner growth, or if they're just something
else we feel we *have* to do.

Rituals and habits are important, but if we forget why
we're doing them, or if they've lost meaning because at some
level we've moved beyond them, then they become one more

meaningless ceremony that isn't adding anything positive to our lives.

Breaking the routine also keeps us open to trying new things. What works for you today may not necessarily work for you next month, or next year.

Like all growth, inner growth is a process. Once we've learned to crawl, then we can learn to walk, and then we can learn to run. Breaking the routine from time to time insures that we won't get stuck in the crawling. Also, it helps to remind us that the things we do to make up the routine are simply tools for our inner expansion. Don't mistake the tools for the growth.

# 41. Review your day

ANOTHER PRACTICE THAT might be help-ful in your inner search is taking a few minutes each evening just before bedtime to review your day.

Go to your sanctuary (#27), and start by sitting quietly for a few moments to let the vibes from the day settle down. Take a couple of long, slow, deep breaths, and consciously relax your body. Have the *intention* of getting rid of any wor-ries or concerns. If you're tuned in, you can actually *feel* any negative energy slowly dissipate.

Then do a quick review of your day, and take particular notice of any issue you may want to deal with. Do what you can to to bring a level of understanding to this, either by sim-ply thinking it through or perhaps by working at the alpha level (#30). Then release it to the universe. Sometimes I've found just letting go of a dilemma brings a clarity that will help me address it later from a more enlightened point of view.

You can sit there for a few blissful moments and be

grateful for your day, and perhaps jot some notes in your journal. You can contemplate, do some deep breathing, or prepare for your dream explorations. If you're developing any new practices you want to incorporate into your life—or getting rid of any bad habits—have your calendar and box of stars handy so you can chart your progress (#61).

Basically, these few minutes at the end of the day give you a chance to slow down, unwind, enjoy the silence, and tap into any messages from the universe that might assist you as you go along. Not only will it help you stay on course for the things you want to accomplish at an inner level, but clearing away any mental, emotional, or psychic clutter will make it easier for you to get a good night's sleep.

When you spend time reviewing your life on a daily basis, you'll see that each day presents an opportunity to live your life exactly the way you want to. Imagine yourself moving into the best you can be, and then living each subsequent day from that perspective. With time, you'll get better and better at doing this.

# 42. Smile a lot

IF YOU'VE STARTED to slow down and simplify your life, if you're spending time in nature and have surrounded yourself with beauty, if you've latched on to synchronicity and tuned into your creativity, and if you've learned to enjoy each moment, you're probably already smiling a lot.

In fact, you may find yourself absolutely grinning from time to time for no apparent reason.

And, once you start doing some of the harder stuff in the next couple of chapters, you may well find yourself positively ecstatic.

Once you free yourself from anger (#66), or worry (#64), or negative thinking (#63), your life will be so much simpler.

Once you learn to detach (#49), overcome your fears (#50), and learn to say no (#54), your load will be so much lighter. Your heart and mind and soul will be free. Things will somehow start to make sense. It'll happen spontaneously. There's nothing to be done about it. Don't question it. Don't doubt it. Don't apologize for it. Don't gloat. It just happens. Enjoy it. And keep on smiling.

# Three

# More difficult things to think about doing

# 43. Be selective about current events

W HEN GIBBS AND I decided to simplify our lives, one of the first things we did was to cancel most of our magazine and newspaper subscriptions. We also eliminated TV news.

Our purpose at that time was twofold: We wanted to create more time for the type of reading and thinking we really liked to do, and we wanted to cut back on the amount of physical, emotional, and psychological clutter that came into the house and into our lives.

In reviewing the benefits of our media blackout program, the most valuable without question was drastically cutting our exposure to the psychic and emotional drain of what passes for news. At the same time we reduced the stress of worrying about war, famine, earthquakes, crime, political corruption, the erosion of the dollar, and the seeming decline of our civilization.

As you start to go within, you might want to think about cutting back on the amount of time you spend keeping up with current events. Few things can disrupt your inner tranquility faster than a jolt of bad news, especially when you're just starting out on your journey. The worst part is that until we're tuned in to our inner selves, we're often not even aware of the adverse impact tuning in to the apparent problems of the world can have on us.

After years of allowing myself to manipulated by the negativity of newsmongers, I found it was tremendously empowering to be able to pull the plug and to create the space for positive messages instead.

There'll always be people and organizations hawking bad news. And there'll always be people who are addicted to it, even though they may not be aware of it. But if you're embarking on a spiritual journey, it's very likely that your desire for real growth will become greater than your need to be constantly in the know.

At the very least, you might want to be selective about the type and the amount of news you allow yourself to be confronted with. Eliminating even some of the psychic clutter of bad news will greatly facilitate your inner quest.

# 44. Reduce your need to be in the know

F OR YEARS MY friend Sue has limited her exposure to the daily news. Frequently people ask her how she responds when someone asks her what she thinks about the latest current event.

She tells them she tries not to think about current events. It has taken her many years to get to the point where she could admit publicly that the latest news is simply not a major interest of hers. She's also learned not to let other people make her feel guilty because *they* choose to spend their time tracking some hot news story.

If what's happening in the news is your passion, then you'll obviously want to stay informed. But if you're keeping up with the news just so you can appear to be in the know when someone who's doing the same thing asks you about it, perhaps you need to do a priority check (#13). Do you really want to spend your time and energy immersing yourself in bad news so you can seem knowledgeable to someone you probably don't even care about?

If you do want to keep in touch with what's happening in the world, it's not necessary to spend hours with the newspaper or in front of the television to do so. Gibbs is a travel writer, and we frequently find ourselves in remote parts of the world for extended periods of time without any connection to the outside world. We've found spending a few minutes perusing a news magazine often provides more information than we want about what has happened in the world in our absence.

Rather than spending hours with a newspaper, you can keep up with world events by scanning the headlines. If you come across a subject that interests you, you can easily explore it further. Often, news reports are packed with misinformation or noninformation anyway, so while we think we might be learning something by spending time reading or watching the news, often we're simply absorbing empty filler.

It's a matter of how you want to spend your time. Once you've begun to explore new possibilities on the inner levels, there's a good chance you'll find these much more satisfying and productive than keeping up with what passes for news.

# 45. Rethink the beliefs
# of your childhood

THE NUMBER OF people who have abandoned the religion of their childhood is legion. Many people are able to leave and never look back. Others leave, but are often consumed with guilt for doing so.

Some people spend years feeling angry and bitter about the restrictive, small-minded thinking they've spent their lives overcoming. And many continue to feel adversely affected—sometimes unconsciously—by the dogma and the belief systems that permeated their minds as children.

There are also those who never had a childhood religion to leave behind, and who still basically believe in nothing. And there are those who have allowed the predominant conclusion of pseudoscience—which says if we can't prove it, it doesn't exist—to rule their thinking.

If you're beginning to take a look at your life, this might be a good time to examine any feelings you may have about the teachings of your childhood that could be holding you back from questions you really want to explore.

All the great philosophers and thinkers of the world, from Plato to Monty Python, have wondered about the meaning of life. If nothing else, you'll be in good company.

As you start to slow down and enjoy the silence and the solitude, as you learn to listen and begin to trust your intuition, as you start to make the changes in your lifestyle and habit patterns that will enable you to connect with your own truth, you'll begin to experience a new way of looking at life and the world and your place in it.

The answers to the age-old questions may not come overnight. In fact, you may have to spend some time in the condition of not knowing. This can be unsettling if you've spent years thinking you knew the answers, or believing there were no questions.

But if you keep at it, the time will come when you'll form your own answers to the questions thinking people have asked from the beginning of time. And these answers will be based not on faith, not on dogma, but on a deep understanding of your own experience.

# 46. Rethink your current beliefs

WHILE YOU'RE RETHINKING the beliefs of your childhood, don't forget to examine your current beliefs, the ones you may have acquired after you let go of the beliefs of your childhood, the ones you moved into at the time of your midlife crisis, or even the ones you settled into last year, or possibly last week.

It'll be helpful to stay open to new interpretations of the world and how it might work. Often we get stuck in our current thinking because, like an old shoe, it's so comfortable. Move out of your comfort zone from time to time, and keep an open mind.

# 47. Get some counseling

I T'S FORTUNATE IN many ways that we're living in the age of the dysfunctional family. Even as recently as a few years ago, you were considered an anomaly if you sought professional counseling. Now, if you haven't been in therapy, people assume you're in denial. Take advantage of the times. If you have a problem that neither you, your friends, nor your support group can solve, don't waste another moment. Seek professional help.

Be prepared for the possibility that the first person you see won't have all the answers for you. When I got into counseling several years ago, I made a couple of false starts with inadequate or inappropriate though well-intentioned therapists. I was lucky: I found the right person on the third try. Don't hesitate to look around until you find a therapist you're compatible with. You can't get to the core issues without a basis of trust.

Compatibility isn't the only consideration. You also need someone who's competent and well trained. If you're having trouble finding the right therapist, ask your friends and associates if they know from their own experience who is good. Interview several before you make a decision. Trust your intuition as to which one will work best for you.

Also, don't be put off by the therapy jokes that say you'll have to spend the rest of your life on the couch. If you've found a competent therapist, you should be able to get to the heart of your issues in a couple of sessions.

If you don't get an "ah-ha!" or two fairly early on, think seriously about trying someone else. Once you have a clear understanding of the issues you have to deal with, then the real work begins, and it's not unreasonable to expect to work closely with a good therapist for six months to a year.

Most of us have some kinks that can be straightened out more speedily with professional help than if we attempt our own therapy. Though it may be frightening at first, working with someone who is professionally trained to deal with our wounds and defenses is an effective way to eliminate out-moded patterns that no longer work.

Therapy is one of the many tools we have available today to speed us on our way to understanding ourselves. If you feel you need therapy, don't put it off any longer. It can go a long way toward helping to free you up for the inner business you came here to complete.

# 48. But don't get stuck in therapy

WE'VE MADE INCREDIBLE progress in the fields of psychology and psychotherapy in the last twenty-five years. We've acquired new and valuable insights about the roles our addictions, our families, and our childhood histories have played in our lives and in our ultimate success and happiness.

In addition to competent therapists, there are recovery and twelve-step programs for every type of physical, psychological, and emotional problem imaginable.

These programs, along with many other personal therapies, have provided tremendous help and understanding for people who, in previous generations, simply had no answers and had to live out their lives in quiet suffering.

If you find that psychotherapy brings you to a new level of comprehension about an issue that may have been troubling you, take from it whatever works for you. Incorporate it into your life, and even revel in it for a time, if that seems appropriate.

Then move on.

The urge is strong to hang on for dear life to therapeutic observations that bring relief to our emotional and psychic wounds. Sometimes the relief is so great the tendency is to hang out in recovery much longer than necessary.

Try not to get stuck in therapy. Doing so can make it harder to move on to the position we all have to come to eventually, that of being responsible for our own lives.

# 49. Practice detaching

WHEN YOU FIND yourself in situations where your blood is boiling or your stomach is churning, try to get into the habit of stepping outside yourself and becoming the observer.

This is easier to do in the heat of the moment if you've practiced it before the battle gets started.

Whenever you find yourself going through a particularly difficult time, make a point of taking five or ten minutes at the end of the day to practice detaching.

Perhaps you've had an argument with a coworker, or a disagreement with your spouse. As soon as you have the opportunity, sit quietly and do some work at the alpha level (#30).

Imagine being back in that scene. See in your mind's eye the *inner you* stepping away from the fracas and simply observing what's going on. Run through the entire argument in your mind with the inner you not being part of it, simply watching from the sidelines.

If you do this consistently, not only will you find that it relieves some of the tension of the current problem you're dealing with, but it will become an automatic response you can fall into when you find yourself in the fray again.

Detaching releases the tension, diffuses the negative energy, and helps you to see the insignificance of this event in the whole scheme of things. It also gives you a chance to see what lessons you might need to learn from this encounter.

# 50. Do the things you fear

ONE OF THE great inhibitors of our lives is fear. If you suspect that fear has been holding you back from the things you want to do, there is something you can do about it.

Set aside a couple of hours in the next few days, or take some time right now, to make a list of all the things you would like to do but haven't done because you were afraid to. Be honest, and really think about this. No one else ever has to see this list but you.

What would your life be like if you left the town you grew up in to seek your fortune out in the real world, instead of staying home where everything is safe, cozy, and guaranteed? What would your life be like if you gave up the company job, and started your own business as you've always wanted to do?

What would your life be like if you quit the job you can't stand and went back to school to get trained in a field you really love? What would your life be like if you got out of a relationship that wasn't working, and created the space for one that would work for you?

You may be starting to realize that the things you *want* to do are the things you *should* be doing, even if the thought of doing them may be terrifying for you. They are things you came here to do and to experience and to be. Not doing them is holding you back from being the totally full and realized person you can be.

If you can't energize yourself to do the things you fear, there are many seminars you can take and retreats you can attend that will provide you with an opportunity to do some seemingly terrifying feats—like walking across a bed of burning coals, or climbing to the top of a telephone pole and jumping off—that serve as metaphors for the real-life fears we all have to face.

Few things will liberate you faster and move you more quickly along your inner path than doing the things you fear.

# 51. Share your fears with someone else

I SAID IN #50 that no one ever has to see the list of things you're afraid of, but in fact, sharing your list with others can be tremendously liberating.

For years my life was ruled by two major fears: the fear of public speaking, and the fear of spiders. I sometimes shudder to think of all the things I didn't do in my life because of these fears. I also shudder to think of all the things I did to keep from having to *admit* to anyone that I had these fears.

Several years ago I found myself in the position of having to confront my fear of public speaking. The publisher of my first book notified me that they were arranging an extensive media tour. I would be appearing before millions of people on national television and radio shows to promote the book. Yiiiiiiikes!

I realized that I'd have to do one of two things: either *admit* I had a fear of public speaking (this was unthinkable) or confront my fear and *do the tour* (this was inconceivable). As it turned out, I did both.

Fortunately, at the time I belonged to a tremendously empowering support group (#23). Because I had no choice, I admitted my fears to the group, and asked for help (#32). I didn't realize it at the time, but my battle was half over. Admitting the fear to these allies made it possible for me to start doing the things I had to do to overcome it.

With the help of my group, I was coached and trained and rehearsed. I traveled up and down the coast and spoke to every gathering that would hold still long enough.

By the time the tour came, I was ready. I did the tour, and thoroughly enjoyed the entire process. The combination of overcoming my fear and doing the tour was one of the most incredible experiences of my life. It was a major gift from the universe.

And a funny thing happened on the way to the tour: I discovered that, in the process, I'd also overcome my fear of spiders. I urge you to get out your list of fears and start passing it around. Who knows what might happen.

# 52. Practice dying

YEARS AGO A yoga teacher I studied with guided us through a meditation in which we confronted our own death. Coming, as many of us have, from a culture in which death was never discussed, much less thought about, I found this somewhat startling at first. But after I'd gone through the exercise a number of times, I began to appreciate the benefits it offered. I started to see death as simply a natural process, and nothing to be afraid of.

Several years later I found myself in the middle of a hurricane with six other people in a very small boat on a very large ocean. I lived for forty-eight hours in the certain belief that we wouldn't survive. When I thought about it later, I was amazed at how calm I felt. It seemed as though I'd done this many times before—which of course I had, through the practice of the dying meditation.

Many cultures throughout history have practiced dying as a ritual. It is a way to confront the fear of death in order to loosen its hold on us. Once you get into it, it can be quite liberating.

So practice dying. Do this as a meditation, and as an exercise in personal growth.

Set aside some time in the next week to imagine your own death. Lie down. Close your eyes. Imagine that you are dying. Where are your friends and family? What do you feel? What are they feeling? Is there anyone you have unfinished business with whom you need to talk to? What would you say to the people you will leave behind?

Then imagine that you are dead. Gone. The End.

This can be terrifying. Even if you envision that you're surrounded by people you love and who love you, there comes a point when you have to take that last step alone. Even though it's only an exercise, go with it. *Experience* that terror. It'll free you.

After you've gone through your first imaginary encounter with your own death, spend some time thinking about other ways you might die: alone in your car on a deserted stretch of highway, or in an airplane crash with hundreds of other people. Run through all kinds of possibilities.

Engaging in the practice of dying, if done with sincerity and as an inquiry into the phenomenon of death, will liberate you from any fear of death you might have, and free you from many other fears as well.

Just think how you could live your life with full abandon if your fear of death were no longer there to hold you back.

# 53. Release your attachment to possessions

O NE NIGHT, WHILE we were still living in the big house, a huge firestorm came through our area, and we had to evacuate.

Just before we left the house, we looked around and realized how much of the stuff we'd accumulated we could easily get along without.

That's not to say it wouldn't be a hassle if all our possessions got destroyed, and it's not to say that we wouldn't miss some of them. But we'd gotten to a point where we could enjoy our stuff while we had it, and at the same time we wouldn't be devastated if we lost it. That was a big step toward liberation for us.

As it happened, our house didn't burn down. But we saw the evacuation as a good exercise to go through, not only for the uncluttering we ultimately did to simplify our lives, but for releasing our attachment to possessions and achieving a level of inner contentment.

Look around your house and imagine you have thirty minutes to evacuate, and the only things you can take with you are what you can fit in the back of your car. What would you take? If you had to start all over again, how would you do it differently?

We don't have to wait for nature to intervene. We can take responsibility for our lives and begin right now, today, to get rid of the things, and our attachments to the things that get in the way of our inner peace.

When you get right down to it, it's surprising how little we need to be happy.

# 54. Just say no

WHEN I WAS a young girl growing up in Kansas, I would accept invitations to my friends' birthday parties. But when the day of the party arrived, I invariably didn't want to go. My mother would always say to me, "Oh, Elaine, just go. You know you always have a good time." So I would go, and mother was right: I always had a good time.

It took me *years* to figure out that I always had a good time because I'm the type of person who wouldn't spend four or five hours somewhere having a *bad* time. No doubt you're that type of person, too.

When your friend Jack catches you off guard and invites you to his potluck dinner on Saturday night, you agree to go because you didn't have anything *specific* planned *and* you didn't have an excuse ready. So you end up going.

And often you have a good time. But that doesn't necessarily mean that you wouldn't *rather* have been doing something else, like sitting at home contemplating the meaning of life, or just relaxing and doing nothing.

When Gibbs and I started to simplify our lives we took a look at all the things we did either because we said we'd do them—like going to Jack's potluck—or because we felt we *should* do them—like heading up the fund-raising committee for a group we belonged to—and we stopped doing them. It took us a while, but we finally learned to *just say no*.

When I suggested this to my friend, Peter, he said, "But if I start saying no to people, they'll stop asking me to join them."

When I pointed out that these were people he didn't want to go out with anyway, he said, "Yes, but I want them to *ask* me."

Obviously, you've got to reach the point where your desire to not go is stronger than your wish to be included.

As you begin to listen to your inner voice, you'll start to get a feel for the situations that keep you from being in touch with what you really want to do and who you really want to be. Then you can begin gracefully to avoid them.

You reach a point where you have to be firm, and simply say no those distractions. Your social life may go down the tubes, but this may be just what you need so you can work on your inner growth and create the time and the energy to do the things you really want to do.

# 55. Examine the costs of not saying no

FOR YEARS I deluded myself into believing things like Jack's potluck involved just a few hours on Saturday night, so it was no big deal. But if you really don't want to do it, it *can* be a big deal.

And it's not just the four or five hours you spend at Jack's that get lost by doing things you don't want to do; it's all the time *leading up* to it, and often the time and energy you spend *recovering* from it as well.

Let's say you've gotten your week simplified to a point where you can spend Saturday and Sunday simply having a quiet, contemplative time getting in touch with your creativity, and painting.

Saturday comes and you've got your canvas set up, and you start thinking about this potluck you really don't want to go to. Just *thinking* about it is an annoyance and an energy drain. Then you realize you don't have anything on hand for the salad Jack asked you to bring. So at some point you have to stop painting, clean up, and run out to the store to get the salad fixings; then you have to make the salad. Then you have to decide what to wear. Then you have to get ready. Then you have to go. You've already spent at least several hours, and you haven't even gotten there.

By the time the evening is over, you've eaten a little too much, and you've had too much to drink. You have some coffee to sober you up for the ride home, and then you don't sleep well Saturday night because of the caffeine.

You wake up Sunday feeling groggy because of the lack of sleep, and you have a headache because you drank too much. You feel lousy all day, and there goes the painting.

You've lost part of the day Saturday, all of Saturday evening, and a good deal of Sunday, because you didn't say no to something you didn't want to do in the first place.

As you begin to work on inner simplicity, you'll start to become aware of the number of things you do that you don't want to do. You'll begin to realize how much that detracts from the time you want to spend on your own growth. You may not be able to stop doing *everything* you don't want to do. But you'll get to the point where the next time Jack calls, you'll just say no.

# 56. Be honest with people

WHEN JACK CALLS, tell him the truth. Simply say, "You know, Jack, I appreciate your asking, but I really *don't* feel like having dinner out on Saturday night. I've been going out too much lately, and I'd really *rather* stay home and spend time with the kids."

If Jack is your friend, he'll understand, even if he might not be happy about it. If he's not your friend, it doesn't matter. If you have a hard time saying no, however, this will still be difficult for you. Practice. Role play, either on your own, or perhaps with your support group (#23).

Remember, you're taking responsibility for your life now, especially the time you need for your inner life. Take a close look at how much time you could save for yourself next week, if you started this week being honest with people by saying no to the things you don't really want to do.

Obviously, there are some social situations where a little white lie is simpler to deal with, not only for you but for the other party as well. But for family and friends with whom you're closely connected, it'll be much more liberating for both of you if you simply and honestly convey your feelings. How *much* you decide to disclose will depend on the circumstances.

You can apply this same philosophy of honesty to any situation you find yourself in. Own up to how you *really* feel about not doing something. If you express your feelings with sincerity, people will accept them.

# 57. Choose to ignore an insult

THERE IS A Chinese proverb that says it is better to ignore an insult than to have to respond to one. There is such wisdom here.

Think of the troubles you could avoid and the stress you could eliminate if you made the *decision* to ignore a slight offense or a minor defamation, or an unintentional snub—or even an intentional one. Our reactions to the situations of our life are elective, and *we* get to do the electing.

The next time someone is flip with you, fail to notice it. It's a choice. Or choose to laugh (#59). (But do this later, on your own.)

This is not to say you should become a rug and let everyone walk all over you. But you may well find as you continue along your path that it's much more exhilarating to keep your head clear for contemplating the big picture, and not to sweat the little stuff.

*Ignoring* an insult is a very effective way to keep from getting bogged down in someone else's negative energy, or even in your own.

# 58. Be patient

O NE OF THE exciting things about the culture and the times in which we live is that we can do almost anything we want to do. Our advancing technology makes it possible for us to have and do things that previous generations never dreamed of. We've gotten used to the instant gratification of our wants and desires. This makes being patient more challenging than it might be otherwise.

As we begin to go within and start to address the big issues (#73), as we learn to love (#100) and to forgive (#70), as we overcome our fears (#50) and learn to just say no (#54), it becomes easier to create happier, more fulfilling lives.

But there will still be hurdles to overcome. The technology is not yet available that would make it possible for us to conquer our demons overnight. The process of growth in any endeavor can often seem like one step forward and two steps backward.

Sometimes I'm disconcerted when I look at my list of things I've wanted to accomplish. Six months ago I may have checked forgiveness (#70) off my list, only to find now that it's back in my life again as an issue I have to deal with. It seems as though I have to start all over. But as I begin to examine it, I see how much the things I've previously done have helped.

Use your journal as an ongoing means of gauging how far you've come in terms of tackling some of your personal challenges.

Learn to be patient with yourself. Enjoy the process of inner growth for what it is—an ongoing opportunity to become the best we can become at all levels of our life.

Don't push the river. Just let it flow.

# 59. Laugh a lot

EVERY DAY FOR the next week, spend five or ten minutes laughing, first thing in the morning. Do this in your sanctuary, at your kitchen table, or wherever works for you. This won't be easy. We are not encouraged to laugh a lot in this culture. But if you do it, you'll be amazed at the insight it will give you.

You'll probably have to start by faking it. You may have to fake it all the way through. That's okay. Pretend you're an actor, laughing for a part. It's easier if you stand, or sit on the edge of a chair. After the first few times, your stomach muscles will ache a bit. It's nothing to worry about. Keep at it.

When you're finished laughing, sit quietly and *receive* (#12). Let your body and your psyche and your soul absorb the benefits of this. Then start your day.

It's very powerful to do this with someone else who is amenable, but don't let the absence of an available person keep you from laughing. It's just as effective to do it on your own. Don't start crying during the laughing. The crying comes later (#84).

When the week is up, or possibly even sooner, you'll see that it's possible for you to laugh at *anything;* that laughter is a choice. That's a very powerful tool to have when you're working on some of this harder stuff. It's a powerful tool to have, period.

As you move along in your quest, and as you encounter seemingly difficult situations, don't forget to use this tool. It will change your life.

Also, make a point of spending time with people who make you laugh. Rent funny videos. Read funny books. Laughing is so good for the soul.

Four

The
hard stuff

# 60. Realize the importance of self-discipline

T HERE'S NO GETTING around it: many of the
steps we must take to achieve inner simplicity require
self-discipline.

Recently, while trying to eliminate a particularly recalci-
trant habit, I remembered a system I developed when I was
eight years old that, more than anything I've ever done,
helped me build self-discipline. Just for fun, I tried it again to
see if it still worked. It did. So I'm passing the idea on to you
here, for whatever it's worth.

When I was in the third grade I woke up one day and
realized I was the only kid I knew who was still sucking my
thumb. I wanted desperately to stop, but after eight years the
habit was deeply ingrained. Nothing I did seemed to help.

Then I got the bright idea of giving up thumb-sucking
for Advent. So I rounded up a Lahey Mortuary calendar—the
kind with a pretty picture on the top half and the days of the

month in one-inch squares on the bottom half—and hung it on my wall next to my bed where I was forced to look at it every night. And I went out and got a box of stick-on gold stars.

My agreement with myself was that I'd get a gold star for every day I got through without sucking my thumb. By the time Advent was over I'd stopped the habit, and as an added benefit, I'd started building self-discipline.

Many times over the years I called on that same system for developing discipline, both for starting good habits and for getting rid of bad ones. Somewhere along the way I gave up the gold stars, but through the years I've used a one month time-frame to keep track of my progress in whatever discipline I'm trying to establish.

Rewards are also an important factor when you're dealing with habits—though if you're motivated enough, getting rid of the offending habit may be its own reward. Obviously, motivation is the key. The calendar and the stars are simply visual tools to help keep track of your progress, evaluate your success, and spur you on to the end of the month.

You may think gold stars are not sufficient reward for you at this point in your life, though they're probably cheaper and less fattening than one of your addictions. And this whole idea may sound childish and absurd to you, which it is. But it works. I strongly urge you to humor yourself here. Recapture some of your childhood enthusiasm and get excited about gold stars. Besides a couple of dollars for the box of stars, and possibly a bad habit, what have you got to lose?

# 61. Find a box of stars

S O HERE ARE some specific steps you can take to develop self-discipline:

1. Get your calendar and a box of stars.
2. Decide what discipline you want to work on. Let's say you want to eliminate your habit of worrying.
3. Check your motivation level. If you're not fully committed to breaking this habit, you're wasting your time.
4. Don't tell *anyone* what you're doing, or what the stars mean. This dissipates the energy. But do make a private coded note to yourself in the upper left hand corner of the calendar, so you can look back and evaluate your progress in each habit you've worked on.
5. Keep your calendar where you'll be certain to check it every day.
6. At the end of each day, take a look at your calendar and think about your day. If you were able to nip each worry in the bud as soon as you became aware of it, pull out a gold star and place it in the appropriate date box.

7. Always start on the first of the month and go through to the thirtieth. If by the end of the month you've got stars on each and every box, you're on your way. Studies have shown that it takes twenty-one days to change a habit pattern. If that's true, then three weeks would work as well. But a month is such a convenient block of time. You start on the first of the month, and end on the thirtieth, and there you are.

Also, if it's now the fifteenth of the month, and you've decided to break a bad habit, you still have roughly fifteen days to indulge yourself in the old one— or until you have to start on the new one.

If you don't have a star in *every* box, congratulate yourself for the stars you do have, but realize you'll have to start the process all over again next month until you have an entire month with stars on every day.

If you miss a few days in between, don't make the mistake of thinking, "Oh well, I'll just wait until the first of the next month and start again." No. No. No. That won't work. If you stop to wait for the first of next month after missing a couple of days, you're only kidding yourself. You need to do a motivation check.

Even if, by the end of the month, you don't have stars on every day, you're still working at it. Once you've got stars on *every single day,* then you've broken the back of your habit. (It recently took me three months of constant vigilance to eliminate a bad habit.)

8. Once you've achieved a level of self-discipline in one area, go to the next habit you want to work on. Soon, you'll have established a pattern of self-discipline you can easily apply to *any* area of your life.

# 62. Harbor no thought that will burn

I'VE ALWAYS THOUGHT of myself as a positive thinker. I grew up believing each of us can, for the most part, do anything we truly want to do. I've made it a practice to avoid people who include "can't" in their vocabulary.

Therefore it came as a great surprise to me to discover, once I had started to do some work on the inner levels, that even though I was a possibility thinker, it didn't necessarily mean I was always a *positive* thinker. In fact, from time to time over the years I'd engaged in less than congenial thinking.

It gradually began to dawn on me that I'd have to do a major overhaul of my thought patterns.

Letting go of negative thinking might seem to be a never-ending battle. Our thoughts define our universe, and if we've spent years operating out of negative thought patterns—sometimes seemingly successfully—there can be a part of us that doesn't want to give it up.

Perhaps you know the type of thinking I'm referring to: the huffing, and puffing, and steaming, and fuming over insignificant inanities that never in a lifetime are worth the emotion spent on them. It's not difficult to figure out the kinds of thoughts that are keeping you from having peace of mind, and from moving on to a higher level of being.

You can glom on to every tool in your arsenal to overcome negative thinking. Use affirmations and visualizations. Connect with nature. Do some deep breathing. Every time you have a negative thought, use it as a *reminder* to get back to positive thinking (#35). Develop self-discipline. Keep your energy up. Chant. Meditate. Use your journal, or your pillows (#66). Or ask for help from the universe (#33).

It may take a major effort, but it will be vital for progress on your inner path to become aware of the self-defeating mental grooves you function in, and to make the decision to change them.

# 63. Try a modified version of an ancient technique

I WAS AMUSED recently to hear the story of a sage who grappled centuries ago with the issue of negative thinking. As a young man this fellow realized that, if he allowed them to, his negative thoughts would completely control his life, and he'd never get to heaven. So he decided to do something about them.

He acquired two stacks of pebbles, one dark and one light, which he placed outside his hut. Every time he had a negative thought, he'd take a pebble from the dark stack and place it in a pile. When he had a good thought, he'd take a white pebble and place it in another pile.

In his youth, the dark pile was larger than the white pile. However, as he went on in life, the white pile began to completely overshadow the dark pile. By the time he was ready to depart this world at an advanced age, he had completely conquered his negative thinking. No doubt he went straight to heaven.

My first urge, on hearing this tale, was to call up our local gravel supply company and have them drop off a couple of tons of pebbles. But, on reflection, that seemed impractical. After thinking about it for a while, as an experiment—and because I believe we have to have some fun along the way—I came up with what I think is a suitable, slightly modified alternative: black beans.

Actually, any type of bean would work. Get two cups. Fill one with uncooked beans. Keep both cups on your desk, or wherever you spend the majority of your time. The absolute first moment you see a dark thought lurking around the edges of your mind: bam! you have to make a beeline to the full cup, take out a bean, and place it in the other cup.

At the end of the day, check your cup and do a tally, which you can keep track of on your discipline calendar, or anywhere that's handy. This exercise will give you an incredibly clear picture of the amount and the variety of the less-than-positive thinking you engage in.

Once you're aware of your thought patterns—either negative thinking, worrying, judging, or whatever—you can begin to control them, and replace them with the kind of thinking you'd rather concentrate on. By elevating your thoughts you elevate your consciousness and accelerate your inner growth.

# 64. Stop Worrying

WORRY, LIKE NEGATIVE thinking, is a habit. And, like negative thinking or any other habit, it can be broken once we become aware of it. But worry is sometimes so subtle and so insidious—and so pervasive in our society—that we can worry for years and not even be aware of it.

I learned this lesson a few years back when I had completed a major promotional project for a company I worked for. After months of long, hard, demanding hours and many sleepless nights when I would lie awake worrying if everything would be all right, the deadline was met and the project was finally completed. It was out of my hands; there was not a single thing more I could possibly do about it.

One night a few weeks later, before I had had a chance to start another project, I realized I was still waking in the middle of the night and lying there worrying—even though there was *nothing* at all to worry about. Perhaps this same thing has happened to you.

As I lay there, I had one of those lightbulb experiences we all have from time to time. I saw in a flash that I'd been moving through life from one worry to the next. I examined each of the circumstances as I could remember them, and it became clear that not only had there never been anything to worry about, but worrying had never served any useful function. It was totally wasted energy that kept me from experiencing the joy of the moment and from getting any real sense of accomplishment from my work.

If you're a worrier, think about using the black bean system (#63), or any other method that works for you, to become aware of of the extent of your habit. Then, if necessary, use the discipline calendar (#61) to eliminate worries from your life.

A worry-free life is incredibly liberating, and it will help you achieve inner peace.

# 65. Stop judging others

ONE OF THE problems that comes from being raised in a patriotic and chauvinistic culture like ours is that we are bred from birth to believe in our own superiority.

It's not only patriotism that instills this conviction. Our religions, our ethnic backgrounds, our educational and cultural training, and the media advertising we are exposed to all teach us, sometimes inadvertently, that we're supposed to be better than the next guy.

Often, we go through life believing it's natural to look down on someone else because of the way they dress, where they live, the work they do, the amount of money they have in the bank, and whether or not they use deodorant soap.

This pervades every area of our lives. We are bombarded daily with hundreds of judgments, many of which we're not even consciously aware of.

When we start to glimpse the possibility that we're here for reasons other than owning a house on two acres and a four-wheel drive vehicle, we get the opportunity to take a look at our judgments and to see how they get in the way of our inner growth.

Once you start to understand that *you're* here for some other purpose, then you have to make the connection that we're *all* here for some other purpose, even if we don't all realize it, and even if we don't know what that purpose is yet.

At some point we begin to get the picture that we're all in this together, and that we're each doing the best we can with what we've got. It's not our place to judge where someone else is on their path.

The process of learning to suspend our judgment about other people and situations can be a particularly arduous one because we have so much training to overcome. But, as with other habit patterns, overcoming it starts with the awareness of how judgmental we are in every area of our lives.

Once we begin to see how often we subtly dismiss others because they don't live up to our standards, we can slowly start to let go of our judgments and get back to trying to figure out what *we* came here to do. And then get on with it.

# 66. Get rid of your anger

EVERY MORNING FOR the next week before you start your day, go to your bedroom, close the door, and pile all your pillows in the center at the head of the bed. Kneel on the bed with the pillows in front of you. Bow gently to your inner self and to the universe. Then start beating the living daylights out of the pillows.

Do this as a spiritual exercise. Use either your fists, or another pillow, or a plastic baseball bat. Do it for five to ten minutes, or longer if that feels appropriate.

When the time is up, fall into a heap on the bed and breathe deeply until you catch your breath. When you've come back to your center, get up, kneel on the bed as before, and bow again to yourself and the universe. Then go about your day.

You won't believe the incredible feeling of lightness you'll have after doing this. There are so many messages waiting to come to us, but they can't easily move through the negativity of anger and the bad feelings we frequently carry with us.

Get in touch with how you deal with anger. Do you clam up? Do you harbor burning thoughts? Do you take your anger out on others? Whenever you find yourself reacting in these or any other counterproductive ways of denying anger, go to the pillows and beat the living daylights out of them for at least five minutes, or as long as it takes. Teach your kids to do this, too.

If you have any anger you've been carrying around, or if you even *suspect* that you might, this will be one of the most powerful and liberating things you can do.

You may have to replace your pillows frequently. But that's probably preferable to having to replace your stomach lining, or a heart valve.

# 67. Ask what's happening

WHEN YOU FIND yourself embroiled in any kind of less-than-joyous emotion, such as anger, or frustration, or impatience, or worry, or negative thinking, take a moment and simply ask yourself, "What's happening here?" Try to figure out what is taking you away from your center.

When you can say, "Ah, that's anger" or "That's worry," then you know what you're dealing with. You can figure out what you're angry about or worried about, and then work on it. Often, simply identifying what's happening will be enough to relieve your distress.

If you're angry, get to your pillows as soon as possible (#66). Or get some fresh air. Or connect with the sun (#3). Remember to do some deep breathing (#96), which is good for almost anything that ails you.

It's possible that you're simply tired, hungry, or thirsty, and that your body and psyche are responding accordingly. If you don't stop to notice what's happening, it's so easy to end up being tired *and* angry *and* frustrated all at the same time. Then you're completely miserable and you don't know why.

Try living your life in the belief that our *natural* state is pure joy. It's when we're truly happy that we're in touch with our souls. The pain and the suffering we feel through any negative emotion or experience is simply a way to tell us how *not* to live. When we learn to identify what's going on, we can make the changes we need to make to get back into our natural state.

# 68. Take responsibility for your life

THERE ARE THOSE who say that, metaphysically, we choose all the circumstances of our life—our parents, our health, our physical characteristics, our race, and our cultural and geographical orientation—before we are born, and that we come into this life knowing, at some level, that we have to use those circumstances for our inner growth.

I don't know whether this is true, though I like to believe it is. But I do know that if I see my life as my responsibility, then I can make the changes necessary to create what I want and need to be happy.

If I take the position that someone else—a supreme power or whatever—is in charge and will take care of everything, I could be stuck for ages in circumstances I'm not happy about and feel powerless to change them. I've learned that if there's something in my life that doesn't work, and I'm waiting for someone else to fix it, I'd better not be holding my breath.

Nowhere is this more applicable than in the inner realms. If you're already taking responsibility for the outer areas of your life, it will be easier to make the choices you need to make for your spiritual growth.

# 69. Accept the things you can't change

TAKING RESPONSIBILITY FOR your life also means accepting the things you can't change.

If you're short and want to be tall, or you're an endomorph and wish you were an ectomorph, if you were born with some impediment or acquired one along the way, or if you find yourself in any particular set of circumstances that are absolute, immutable, and irreversible, then you basically have two options. You can rant and rave and curse and indulge in remorse or guilt or self-pity. Or you can go with the hand you were dealt and play the game the best you can.

You can be open to the *possibility* that those who say we have chosen our circumstances are correct, and then set about figuring out what you can learn from your life by making the most of it.

When you look at the personal limitations someone like Helen Keller had to deal with, and the extent to which she overcame them—not to mention the tremendous contribution she made with her life—you can see that it *is* possible to cooperate with the inescapable.

Going within to find the meaning of our lives does not mean seeking to avoid the challenges our circumstances present. Rather it means finding the grace to learn how to live our lives to the fullest extent possible—whatever that is for us—and, in the acceptance, to move on to the highest level of growth we can.

# 70. Learn to forgive

WHEN I WAS growing up I had an older brother who beat up on me fairly regularly for the first thirteen years of my life. I got little respite until he left home at eighteen to become a Jesuit priest.

Once he was out of the house, my life settled down to what most people would call normal, and I began to forget about all those early traumas with the monster brother. Today we call it denial, but I went on about my life and created the fantasy that I had had a happy childhood, which, for the most part, I did.

But you can't just stuff those early childhood hurts and expect them to go away. At some time, at some level, you have to deal with them.

Many years later I went into counseling to talk about a business relationship that was troubling me, and ended up talking about my brother.

It took months of therapy and personal reflection to uncover the resentment I'd been carrying around with me all those years. When I finally recognized the extent of the trauma, I was certain I'd never be able to forgive him.

As I began to get in touch with my anger, I began to understand why certain patterns and circumstances had been repeated over and over again throughout my life. And gradually I began to see that holding on to that anger was keeping me from truly moving forward. I realized that if I wanted to get on with it, I'd *have* to forgive my brother.

It took me several more years and many quiet hours of contemplation, but finally I was able to pick up the phone, call him, and have it out with him. I was able, in my heart of hearts, to forgive him for all those years of mistreatment.

Soon after that phone call, I started painting, something I had always wanted to do but had never quite been able to get around to. The correlation was so direct there is no doubt in my mind that forgiveness was a key: one month I forgave my brother; the next month I started to tap into my creative core.

I urge you to stop right now and make a list of any people you might be harboring anger or resentment against. Then start working today on forgiveness. You may not be able to come to a position of forgiveness overnight. And you may not be able to do it alone. There are many seminars, books, and tapes available to help you. If necessary, get some counseling

(#47). Do whatever you need to do to get started learning to forgive.

Keep in mind that you don't have to learn forgiveness for the benefit of the person who may have wronged you, but for the liberation of your own soul.

# 71. Get out of relationships that don't support you

WE HUMANS, FOR the most part, still maintain our herd instincts. It's comforting to be one of the pack, and to have family, friends, and loved ones near by to help us grow, at least at the start of our journey.

But it sometimes happens that the people we are closest to don't really support us. Look around you, not just at your spouse and the family members you're involved with, but at all the relationships and associations you have in your life. The lack of support can be so subtle. We can hang out for years with someone we love and think of as a friend before we begin to realize that the relationship isn't really helping us and, in fact, has been holding us back.

It's easy to be deceived by the comfort a longtime relationship appears to offer you. There's a certain ease that comes with familiarity and from knowing each other's history, and from the history the two of you have built together, even when it's been tumultuous.

But there comes a time when you have to ask some hard questions: Does that person really love you, or are they hanging on to you because of their own lack or their own needs? They may *say* they love you, but do they make you *feel* loved? Are they really happy with you in your successes, or do they always manage to put you in the wrong? Do they love you enough to let you go on to bigger and better things, even if it means they get left behind?

Nonacceptance and subtle putdowns can be powerful deterrents to your growth. If you're not getting the love and support you need from the relationships in your life, it'll be much harder for you to achieve inner simplicity.

If you're moving on, sometimes there is really no choice but to leave behind those who may not be ready to move on with you.

Often you simply have to retreat with a smile, and gradually but *resolutely* reduce their presence in your life.

Realize that all the family ties and friendships in your life are there for a purpose, but they aren't necessarily meant to last forever. It takes a certain grace to recognize when the time for a disabling relationship is over and, even if the other person doesn't recognize it, to bow out and move on. You'll then have the time and energy to concentrate on loving, supportive relationships.

# 72. Keep your own counsel

I F  Y O U ' R E  J U S T  starting out on your journey, you'll
have to walk a fine line between sharing the joy of your
new discoveries with friends and family and being sidetracked
by the negative energy of those who don't understand what's
happening.

Learn to zip your lip. At the very least forgo the urge to
share each new glimpse of your inner world with everyone
around you.

Also resist the temptation to have everyone you know
hop on your wagon. We each have our own path to follow,
and what works for you may not be relevant to the next person. Recognize ahead of time that the inner path can be exciting and very fulfilling, but sometimes lonely.

There's also a difference between getting the help you
might need from friends (#32), or a support group (#23), or
from counseling (#47), and baring your soul about the progress you are making on your spiritual trek to everyone who
comes along.

For those who ask, explain in general terms that you're

doing some soul-searching, and are beginning to look at your life in ways you've never done before. If you're not in friendly territory, there is no benefit to being specific. Whatever you do, don't get defensive. Arguing with someone over the rightness of your path can only lower your energy and set you back. You don't have time for that. *For those who don't ask, say nothing.*

Also, be cautious about getting distracted by the inner search of new people you'll be meeting along the way. What they're doing or the teacher they're following may look interesting, but more often than not their path will not be your path. But it'll be so comforting to find others who are searching too, and who perhaps have found answers to some of your own questions, that the desire will be great to hang out with them perhaps longer than necessary.

Learning not to get sidetracked by the energy of others will be one of your greatest challenges. Learning to keep your own counsel will be your greatest defense.

# 73. Figure out your big issue

WHEN YOU GET right down to it, we all have at least one major issue—and possibly several minor ones—to work on in our lives. Some of us are better at keeping them under wraps than others, but no matter how hard we may work at denying them, even to ourselves, they're right there just waiting for us to deal with them.

In my experience, it's much easier to establish a level of inner simplicity once we recognize what our big issue is, start to work on it, and eventually, eliminate it completely.

My big issue has been anger. I spent so much time as a child being angry at my brother that it became a comfortable habit.

As I grew older and my circumstances changed, I still continued often to react to situations with anger because I was familiar with it, and knew how to operate out of that stance. Several people had pointed it out to me over the years, but I hadn't understood, mostly because, until I started to simplify my life, I'd never taken the *time* necessary to face the issue and deal with it.

Those who are metaphysically inclined say that the big issues in our lives are what we came here to work on and to experience, and that working on them makes it possible for us to move forward. That may be true. At the very least, learning to deal with what I see as my big issue has been tremendously liberating for me. Being able to move beyond it has created the space for a lot more joy. And it certainly has simplified my life.

If you don't know what your big issue is yet, spend some time figuring it out. If you can't do that on your own, ask those closest to you to help. (Often they're only too glad to do this!) The responses you get may surprise you, and you may not want to believe what you hear. It's possible they could be wrong; only you will know for sure.

You may have to do a lot of inner searching and possibly get some counseling before you can come to terms with it. But if you've got an unresolved major issue that has been running your life, such as being a victim, being in denial, being meek, aggressive, jealous, suspicious, vulnerable, or whatever, don't wait any longer to start to work on it. Doing so will free your heart, your mind, your body, and most importantly, your soul.

# 74. Get your finances
# under control

THE PATTERNS OF greed, overconsumption, and instant gratification that were prevalent in the 1980s created a lot of financial havoc that many people are still trying to recover from. The movements toward simplicity and spiritual growth seem to be among the leading trends of the 1990s, but it's difficult to concentrate on inner peace if you can't pay the rent.

Often it's the way we spend indiscriminately and the constant media pressure to buy that drains us emotionally as well as financially. We've been led to believe that whether or not we can afford it, there's no reason not to get it—whatever it is. Often we're impelled by advertising hype to part with our hard-earned dollars in exchange for items we don't even want, that end up cluttering up our lives and getting in the way of our personal growth.

If your financial life is suffering from the expansion of

the past decade, it may be time for you to make some drastic changes in the way you relate to money.

There are many books available today that can help you get back on track financially. One of the best, in my opinion, is *Your Money or Your Life* by Joe Dominguez and Vicki Robin. This book will give you a new way of thinking about the time you spend getting money versus how you spend it.

And of course, living simply, as outlined in my book *Simplify Your Life* will reduce your expenses automatically.

Once you establish financial tranquility in your life, inner tranquility will be a lot easier to come by.

# 75. Get your body in shape

FOR MOST OF us, inner progress is easier if we
maintain an optimum level of health and strength, not
only to withstand the rigors of our spiritual disciplines, but
also to help ward off the negative patterns we encounter in our
everyday lives.

But getting in shape and staying in shape is no easy feat
in this day of overeating, overdrinking, excessive dieting, junk
food, recreational drugs, mostly useless over-the-counter pal-
liatives, and often dangerous prescription remedies.

So where do you start? Remember moderation in all
things, then start with your eating habits. Food really *is* our
best medicine. If you don't already know what is the best eating program for your body type, do a little research (see Reading List), and a lot of listening to your body's response. Keep
not only your health but your energy level in mind when you
eat. One of the most destructive things we do to our bodies is
to overeat.

Adopt a healthful exercise program. If you've been running and/or exercising yourself into the ground, think about how little exercise we really need to maintain good health, and at how much damage the excessive exercise regimens of the 1980s actually did to our bodies.

Start a healthful exercise program such as walking, and a limbering program such as yoga or stretching. Studies have shown that it's the loss of elasticity in our muscles and the tightening of our joints that create the immobility of our advancing years. Do whatever you need to do to keep your body supple.

Make sure you're getting an adequate amount of sleep. Again, listen to your body. Arrange your routine so you get the sleep you need. Our bodies and our sleep schedules have often been put on the back burner in recent years, but sleep is an important and completely natural way to restore and maintain good health and high energy.

We know that stress is a major cause of illness in our culture. Make whatever changes are necessary to eliminate the tensions in your life. The classic, proven stress releaser is meditation. Simplifying your life, spending time in solitude, and taking your own private retreats are invaluable stress reducers, too. So are laughter (#59) and joy (#99). Make room for them in your life.

# 76. Keep your energy up

IN ADDITION TO maintaining good health, inner simplicity also demands a high level of energy. Low energy can bring with it a myriad of problems such as frustration, boredom, inertia, depression, and a sense of overwhelming futility, any one or all of which can make it impossible to move forward on your spiritual journey.

Start to become aware of the situations and people that drain your energy.

Look at noise sources such as radios, stereos, television, shoot-'em-up movies, traffic, and raucous gatherings. Eliminate these and other disrupting aural intrusions from your life, and notice how your energy goes up.

Do you sense that certain people leave you feeling listless and off-balance? On the surface, someone you spend time with may seem perfectly pleasant, but somehow you always feel worn out after they've gone, as if they took your energy with them. As much as possible, avoid them.

Allowing yourself to become tired, overworked, overly

hungry, or overexposed to sun and weather can drain your energy. So can idle gossip, personal confrontations, and so-called news reports.

Sometimes you can find yourself completely deprived of energy for no apparent reason. It's important at those times to examine what you've been doing, talking, or thinking about, or what you've been eating or drinking, so you can eliminate as much as possible not only the obvious energy drains but the subtle ones as well.

While you're becoming aware of what gets you down, keep your eyes and feelings open for the situations and the people and the happenings that raise your energy, lift your spirits, and make you feel terrific. Train yourself to actively avoid the energy drains, and to make a point of including the things that make you feel good.

The more negative energy you can rout out of your life, and the more positive energy you can bring into it, the easier it'll be to connect with your soul.

# 77. Let go of the addictions that hinder your progress

I HAVE A friend who began meditating several years ago. She immediately felt a connection between how her various addictions affected her level of awareness and, without batting an eye, let go of all the foods, drinks, and ingestible substances she had been overly attached to and that she felt were getting in the way of her inner growth.

She adopted a more or less vegetarian diet: stopped drinking alcohol, coffee, and other caffeinated drinks; eliminated processed foods and sugars from her diet because they brought her energy down. She feels she's made tremendous strides in achieving a level of inner growth she wouldn't have been able to make otherwise.

When I first started working seriously on inner growth, I was more inclined to use St. Augustine's approach: Oh God, please make me a saint, but not yet. There's a possibility I'd be much further along on my path toward inner freedom if I'd been able to give up chocolate mousse five years ago, but the elimination of addictions has been a much more gradual process for me.

Many people find, once they start meditating, contemplating, and going within, that the things they eat and drink affect the quietness of their minds. Often, if we're consuming the wrong stuff, it makes it difficult for us to be in touch with what's going on at the inner levels.

Deciding which of your cravings you want to eliminate and how quickly you want to do it is a personal choice, based on your own intuitive reaction to the things you eat and drink. If you're tuned in, you'll know what makes it harder for you to stay in touch with the inner you.

# 78. Figure out the right foods for you

S OME YEARS BACK I asked one of the teachers I'd met along the way to give me some advice on food. What I wanted was a computer printout that said now, and for the rest of your life, you can eat this and this and this. And you must avoid this and this and this. It would be so simple. With such a list, I'd never have to be concerned about what to eat, and I could just get on with my spiritual quest.

I was mildly annoyed when he said he couldn't do that. He suggested I learn to listen to how my body responded to what I ate, and figure out for myself the foods that would be best for me.

I was into immediate fixes at the time, so I moved from one supposedly miracle dietary plan to the next. After years of doing this, I've finally come to the conclusion that he was right. We each have different nutritional needs, not only at different times in our lives, but at different times throughout the year. Seldom is there one simple program that will always have all the answers for our particular needs.

If your body is not functioning at its best, if you regularly have headaches, muscle aches, stomach problems, or any number of other health issues, take a look at what you're eating and drinking that might be contributing to your discomfort.

A while back I started eating mostly raw vegetables, thinking it would be better for my health. After a few months I began having digestive problems and then muscle aches that developed into bursitis. I thought at first it was simply advancing years, but when I examined it further, I began to make the connection between my supposedly healthful new diet and the way I felt. I finally figured out that my body wasn't able to assimilate the nutrients from raw foods. I started lightly steaming the veggies and my problems cleared up practically overnight.

Of all the health books I've read over the years, one of the best in my opinion is *Perfect Health* by Deepak Chopra. This book is a very readable introduction to the ancient science of ayurveda. It provides a coherent explanation of various body types and explains why and how our food needs differ from person to person and from season to season. It is an excellent guide for maintaining health and balance in your dietary as well as in your physical and spiritual life.

When it comes to specifics, the best way to figure out what we should be eating is to listen. This takes time and patience, and experimentation. But the more you pay attention to your body's responses, the clearer will be the messages that help you decide what the optimum foods are for you.

# 79. Eliminate your old patterns

WHEN I FIRST started to simplify my life, I made the decision to reduce the time I spent in my office every day. Eventually I was able to arrange my work schedule so I could quit at five o'clock in the afternoon rather than at seven o'clock in the evening.

So almost immediately I had two extra hours each day, or a total of ten to twelve hours each week, during which I could pursue other interests. At first, this felt quite liberating. I could go for walks in the early evening, or sit quietly and meditate or do nothing, or just relax and watch the sunset.

But after a while, I noticed a strong inclination simply to stay at my desk and continue working until seven, as I'd done for many years.

I couldn't quite figure out what was happening. I'd already decided that I didn't *want* to stay and work; I wanted to play or do other things. But staying in the office was so *easy*. I was comfortable, and I knew what I had to do there. If I quit work early, not only would I have to *come up with something else to do,* but then I'd have to get my head and my mind and my body in gear and *do it.*

It took some serious contemplation of this tendency before I realized that it was my well-established pattern that was keeping me in the office. Working late had become a *habit* and as with all habits, it took some serious desire, discipline, and determination to change it.

Keep this in mind as you are beginning to explore the riches of the inner worlds. Often we allow our good intentions—to do some spiritual reading or take some quiet time to think or learn to simply enjoy the silence—to be overpowered by our outdated habits or by insignificant interruptions. Unless we recognize what's happening and make a concerted effort to establish new patterns, it's easy to stay stuck in the old ones.

Sometimes simply being aware that your old habits are resisting being changed is enough to help you move beyond them, though it may still take some effort. If you need more corrective measures, get out your calendar and your box of stars (#61).

# 80. Get comfortable
# with change

GROWTH BY DEFINITION requires change. And that change, as I discovered when I first tried to rearrange my work schedule, can be unsettling. If you've spent years with certain habits, beliefs, and ways of doing things, inner growth may cause some upheaval in your life. Don't be put off by that. Get comfortable with it. Welcome it. Change offers an exciting, often exhilarating way of getting in touch with your soul.

A few years back, when I was in the process of making some career changes, a counselor I was seeing strongly urged me to take a year off and do nothing. Do nothing for an entire year? That possibility and the changes it would bring about in my life were beyond my imagination. For someone like me who'd been moving so fast for so long, there was at some level the fear that if I stopped I'd keel over, or never be able to get going again.

It took many months and many hours of quiet reflection

before I was able to see the wisdom of that advice. Finally, I took the plunge and arranged my business life so that I could take off for an extended period of time. After spending umpteen years knowing *exactly* what I was going to do each day, to get up in the morning and not have a clue was unsettling to say the least. And for someone like me who is a creature of habit and who loves routine, having each day be totally different from the day before was like hanging from a precipice.

But that year of doing nothing was one of the most enlightening and productive years I've ever spent. Not only did I have the opportunity to do a lot of *soul* work and in many ways revolutionize my belief systems, but I was able to get in touch with my *life* work as well. It kept me living on the edge, and got me comfortable with the prospect of change.

I'm not suggesting that you take a year off, though if your life is feeling out of control, that might a good place to start.

But if you find yourself stuck in outdated habits and ways of operating that no longer serve you, spend some time thinking about how you might do things differently. True inner growth might well require that you experience new thoughts, new feelings, new sensations, new friendships, possibly even a new identity. Allow yourself to be vulnerable, and open yourself to change.

# 81. Learn to see the problems in your life as gifts

WHEN I WAS twenty-three I married a brilliant physician who, by his own diagnosis, was a manic-depressive paranoid schizophrenic with delusions of grandeur. I spent the next four years in hell. They were without question the most miserable years of my life.

Fortunately, I found the strength necessary to get out of that marriage. And also fortunately, I had a wise friend who pointed out to me at the time what a tremendously valuable lesson those years had been for my personal growth. I learned more about human nature and my own strengths and weaknesses than I could have from any other circumstance I can imagine.

As I look back on that marriage now, painful as it often still is to think about, I see that it was one of the greatest gifts the universe has given me. I'm tremendously grateful for that experience, and the positive contribution it made to my life.

If you still think of the mistakes of your life as disasters, I urge you, for the sake of your inner growth, to change the way you think about them. Sit down sometime in the next few days and list the situations, conditions, circumstances, and happenings that you've always seen as problems or negatives.

Take the first item on your list and look at the *benefits* you got from that situation. Look at the other problems you may have avoided because of it. Think of the ways your life is better because of what you learned.

For example, because my marriage was so disastrous, I got out of it much sooner than I would have otherwise, and was able to move on and create a happy and satisfying life for myself. I know many people who've had less than compatible marriages, but because their choices were only bad and not, like mine, *intolerable,* they stayed many years longer in unsatisfying relationships than they needed to.

Of course, I could wish that I'd married right in the first place, but since I didn't, I had two choices: moan about it for the rest of my life, or learn what I could from it, then move on.

Continue through your life and rethink every circumstance you have previously regarded as negative, and see how each one can be used as a step to your inner growth. Start living your life and rethinking your past as though there are no problems. There are only opportunities for enlightenment.

# 82. Develop gratitude

NOW THAT YOU'VE taken a look at how mistakes can be positive factors in your life, make a list of all the things you've done right, and all the things (in addition to your mistakes) you have to be grateful for.

Look at your family, your friends, your home, your car, your town, your health, your job—the list is endless. It may not all be perfect at the moment, but what isn't perfect you can change.

If you can't change it, you can get rid of it, or move on. At the very least—or perhaps the very most—you can, through counseling or meditation or introspection or help from a variety of sources, learn to live with it. We all have the opportunity at this time and in this place to make our lives exactly what we want them to be.

If gratitude doesn't come naturally to you, work at it. Post reminders around your home and your car and your office until feeling grateful becomes a habit. You can replace your worry habit (#64) with it.

Get in the habit of taking a few minutes at the end of each day to make a list of all the things that happened that day for which you can be grateful.

You'll find, if you haven't already, there's a self-expansion aspect of gratitude. Very possibly it's a little-known law of nature: the more gratitude you have, the more you have to be grateful for.

# 83. Take time to think

ONE OF THE frequent reactions I hear from people who've read *Simplify Your Life* has been "It's so obvious what I need to do to simplify. I could have figured out how to do it myself if I'd just *thought* about it."

They're absolutely right. The changes we need to make to our lives are the obvious ones. But we're often too busy to stop and *think* about what we need to do to bring them about. We've been so caught up in the stress and the pressures and the demands of our days that we've gotten out of the habit of thinking about our lives.

As you set out and continue along your path of inner simplicity, be sure to set aside time to think on a regular, even daily, basis. Get in the habit of spending a few minutes in the morning before you start your day thinking about how you want to be in your work and in your interactions with the people you come into contact with.

Then, at the end of the day, take a few minutes to think about how you did in relation to how you wanted to do.

Think about the things that may have kept you from enjoying your day, or from living it the way you'd like to. Then think about how you might do things differently tomorrow.

In addition to the daily evaluations, we need to set aside larger blocks of time to think about the big picture. Use some of your regularly scheduled times of solitude (#93) to really *think* about your inner life and your outer life, where you want to go with each, and what kinds of things you can do to get there.

Set aside time for weekend or longer retreats, and use the time to question your long-accepted assumptions or beliefs. There are few things as liberating as coming up with your own solutions to your own issues.

All the information we need to know about our lives and how to live them is available to us. Thinking is one of the tools we can use to tap into that information.

Inner peace rarely comes about automatically. We have to work at it. Thinking is a powerful tool for that work.

# 84. Cry a lot

CRYING A LOT is harder than laughing a lot (#59). Crying is discouraged in our culture even more than laughing is. But it's such a powerful tool for clearing out the stuff that gets in the way of our inner growth.

It's possible you need to cry and you're not aware of it. Or maybe you live much of your life on the brink of tears.

In either case, arrange your schedule so you can cry every day for the next week, or however long is necessary. You can do it in the same thirty days you're doing the laughing, or you can do it in the subsequent thirty days. Now that you've simplified your life, you'll have the time.

Allow thirty minutes for the crying; longer if possible. You'll need at least that much time to get the floodgates open. If you get a good cry going, don't stop just because the time is up. Cry to the end of the cry.

As with the laughing, you may need to fake it to begin with. The more drama you can put into it to start with, the better. You may go for several days with only fake tears.

That's all right. Eventually real tears will come. Keep at it until they do.

My friend Cindy recently went through a difficult divorce. She is a strong, mother-earth kind of woman who has spent many years letting everyone else cry on her shoulder. But when it came time for her own tears, she had difficulty in letting them flow.

Finally she started renting tearjerker videos. She would sit in front of the VCR with a box of Kleenex, crying her eyes out, initially over some plot line on celluloid, and eventually over her own life. It took her a couple of months to get through all her tears, but it allowed her to grieve and then released her so she could get on with her life.

We've been told for so long that it's not okay to cry. But it *is* okay. In fact, it's desirable. More than that, it's vital. The energy we've been using to hold back the tears is getting in the way of being who we truly are. Let that energy go, and cry. It'll free you.

# Five

# Some fun stuff

# 85. Consult a psychic

SOME PEOPLE WILL no doubt take exception to this suggestion. However, I know from my own experience that a good psychic can provide valuable insights and explanations for our dilemmas when we are unable to come up with them on our own.

Some years ago I found myself in a particularly difficult situation. I was under a lot of stress and simply wasn't able to sort out the problem and move on from it. A good friend called one day with the suggestion that I contact a psychic she knew.

I took her advice and scheduled a psychic reading. Not only did that reading provide a lot of answers for the current situation I was in, and thereby relieve me from a good deal of distress and anguish, but the psychic's comments about what led me to that circumstance, and the probable outcomes, were tremendously helpful in terms of the actions I took for the future.

Many times over the next year or so I read over the notes I kept from our session together, and was continually amazed at the insight and wisdom she had provided. Several times since then I have contacted her on other issues, and found her perceptiveness and clear vision a considerable contribution to my life.

Obviously, this is not to suggest we can turn our lives over to someone else's interpretation of our predicament, no matter how intuitive they are. One's response to a psychic reading should always be coupled with common sense and intelligence.

And now that I've simplified and have created the time to listen, I've made progress in the development of my own insight and intuition. I've reached a point where I can rely on my innate psychic abilities, which we all have—though I wouldn't hesitate to contact a psychic again should the circumstances warrant. I look at it as one more tool we can use to help us gain the insight we may need.

How do you find a good psychic? The same way you find a competent professional in any field: ask around. Interview a few, if necessary, until you find someone you can connect with.

The information we require to solve and understand our own problems is always available to us, but if for some reason we are unable to tap into it on our own, a competent psychic can be a valuable aid in the interim.

# 86. Cast a rune

ONE FASCINATING AND fun way to get in touch with your intuition is through runes. *The Book of Runes,* by Ralph Blum, can be purchased at most bookstores, along with a bag of twenty-five flat stones roughly the size of a quarter, each imprinted with an ancient Viking symbol. You can easily make your own runes, but you'll want to get Blum's book if casting the runes appeals to you.

Blum's text provides an inspired unconventional interpretation of an ancient alphabetic script that can be used as a contemporary oracle to assist what he calls the Witness Self in dealing with whatever life questions you may find yourself confronted with.

When I first started to experiment with these guides, I was astounded at the accuracy with which my issues were described, and at how appropriate the interpretations were for the situation I was addressing.

My initial thought was that the runes were simply so cleverly written that any one rune pulled could provide answers for any circumstance. Yet, as I look back—I've kept a rune section in my journal for this purpose—I've found a level of relevancy for each individual question that I haven't been able to chalk up simply to good writing. Somehow, the runes always provide just the insight I need at the moment.

I don't know why the runes work and, because they're so easy and so much fun, I really don't care. I've reached the point in my life where, if something works—or even only appears to work—I graciously accept whatever help it can provide.

The runes do not predict the future, nor provide specific advice for one to follow, though they are written with such wisdom that they *seem* to do all this. When you analyze the messages, you see it's your own intuition that pulls what you need from the rune reading for your particular problem at this particular time.

# 87. Check out subliminal tapes

S EVERAL YEARS AGO a friend gave me a subliminal audiotape for my birthday. It was called "Happiness
and Laughter" and, at her request and to humor her, I kept it
playing softly in an auto-reverse tape player that I kept on my
desk during my work day and in the main part of the house—
or wherever I happened to be—the rest of the time.

My husband Gibbs might accurately be described as a
skeptic. Recognizing this, I didn't bother to mention to him
that the peaceful sounds of nature we were hearing on the tape
were supposedly masking over a million messages per hour
that were recorded on the tape below the conscious level of
hearing.

One morning at breakfast, after about a week of constant
exposure to the subliminal messages on this tape, Gibbs said
to me, "You know, I feel so good. I've never been happier in
my life."

I began to suspect there might be something to subliminal programming. Over the next six months I experimented with more than half a dozen different subjects and brands of tapes.

I haven't explored all the possibilities, but the most effective subliminal tapes I've used are those produced by Alphasonics (35 Cuesta Road, Santa Fe, NM 87505, 1-800-937-2574). I have successfully used their "Stop Procrastination" to get started on the last three book projects I've completed. When it gets down to the wire I pop in "Peak Performance in Business" and am able to work with a level of concentration I haven't yet been able to tap into without the tape.

I played the "I Can Do Anything Tape" for an entire year while I was getting over my fear of public speaking (#51). "Deep Relaxation" got me to a point where I could sit still long enough to begin to learn to meditate. I want very much to try the "Stop Sugar Addiction" tape, but I'm not quite ready to give up Häagen-Dazs Chocolate Chocolate Chip ice cream yet.

In addition to the titles that will assist you in your outer life, there are half a dozen—such as "Joy of Life," "Loving and Feeling Loved," and "Healing Power"—that can help you get started on your inner work.

I don't know for certain how or why subliminal tapes work, but I have found them to be a fun and effective tool for tapping into the power of other levels of consciousness, and a delightful medium for continued growth and change.

# 88. Stop the world—you *can* get off

SOMETIMES WHEN THE pressures of the world get to be too much, leave it.

Sit quietly wherever you are, close your eyes, breathe deeply for a couple of minutes, and get centered.

Then *imagine* you're on the ceiling, or eight or ten feet above your head. See yourself down below, sitting there quietly, and examine how it feels to have stepped out of your life for a moment. Then go higher, above the rooftops, and look around the town or the countryside. Enjoy the view from this new perspective.

Keep moving higher until you can start to see the curve of the horizon. Everything is below you, except possibly the clouds. You can imagine the people and the traffic down there, you can even hear the faint hum of the collective noises, but you're not part of it for this moment.

Keep moving higher and higher until the earth is a tiny

globe. You are above it all. Free. Enjoy this freedom for as long as you can. Then, when you're ready, gradually return to earth and to your self. *Notice* how you feel and if things *seem* different. Even a slight change can be important for you. The more often you make these smaller changes in your consciousness, the more often you can make larger ones.

# 89. Write like mad

WHENEVER YOU FIND yourself in a dilemma you don't know how to get out of, or a life situation you simply don't understand, get out some paper and a pen— not your journal, because you're not going to save this or even read it again—and start writing furiously with the hand opposite to your handedness.

Write. Write. Write. Write. Write. Write until you get some relief.

If you're right-handed, writing with your left hand— even though it's harder to do—will help you access your right brain mode at an intuitive level. It will sometimes make it easier to get in touch with your true feelings than when you're using your left-brain analytical mode.

If you find it too difficult to write left-handed, simply write fast and furiously with your right hand, but don't stop to read or analyze what you've written. If you have trouble getting started writing, begin with the Gettysburg Address, and take off from there. Just keep writing until you start addressing the real issue.

Sometimes, when you are under a lot of stress, you're unable to hear messages through your normal channels. Writing like mad is an effective and relatively painless way to access your intuitive wisdom, and to uncover truths previously unknown to you.

# 90. Chant

CHANTING IS AN ancient and universal practice that has been used in most cultures and in all the major religions of the world as a powerful way to raise consciousness.

This is most effective when done with a group, but chanting can also be done individually to great benefit. Pick an uplifting, soul-expanding word or phrase, in English or any other language, that you respond to.

Sit quietly where you won't be disturbed, and where you won't disturb others. Start repeating your word or phrase out loud. Let a rhythm develop with it. Try several rhythms, until you find one you and your chant can flow with. Clap or sway with it if that feels right. Keep at it until you become one with it, thirty or forty minutes, or however long it takes. This is very uplifting.

Change your word or phrase from time to time. Discover the different properties of each. One might make you peaceful, another might make you happy. Another one might raise your energy. Use your journal to keep track of how you respond to each one.

Then, when you need to change your disposition, pull out the appropriate chant.

# 91. Dance

F IND A TIME and a place where you won't be disturbed for thirty to forty minutes, or even longer. Wear loose-fitting, comfortable clothes. Put on some music you truly connect with. It can be classical, rock, jazz, drums, whatever. Turn it up as loud as you dare, but not so loud you invade someone else's peace and quiet.

Stand in the middle of the room, close your eyes, and start to feel the music. Let it move through your entire body. Breathe with it. Move your head and arms and your upper body with it. Bend at the waist with it. Still standing in one place, move your feet with it, keeping your eyes closed, sway and gyrate with it, totally absorbing the music into your being.

Slowly open your eyes and start moving around the room with the music. Create your own dance. Whirl and twirl or rock and stomp. Do whatever you need to do to become one with the music. Be totally uninhibited, spontaneous, and ecstatic. It may take you a time or two before you can really let yourself go. Keep at it until that happens.

When the music ends, fall to the floor and lie on your back. Keep your eyes open and gradually, slowly, and with total awareness bring your consciousness back into your body. Stay there absorbing the silence until your breathing returns to normal. Then slowly stand up, and give a slight bow of gratitude to the music and the universe.

Do this every day for a couple of weeks and you will begin to feel incredibly uplifted, lighthearted, and joyous.

If you do this in a group, each person should dance on their own, aware of the others, but not dancing *with* anyone else. A shorter version of this dance is an incredibly enlivening way to begin your inner support group meeting. Or, every now and then, use the entire meeting time to dance.

# Six

# The real stuff

# 92. Learn to listen to your inner voice

IF YOU FEEL you're not naturally intuitive, or if you've lost touch with your inner voice, learning to listen will be a great aid in helping you achieve inner simplicity.

It will require time. It will require patience. It will require discipline. There will be times when you simply have to force yourself to sit still and listen.

Don't forget the listening part. When I first started to work on developing my intuition, I'd ask the questions, but incredibly, I didn't take the time to wait for the answers. Intuitive responses are often quite subtle, especially when we're first learning to tap into them. So unless we're paying close attention, we can easily miss them.

Also, the intuitive *insight* telling you to do something that's easy and that you want to do can be much different from an intuitive *warning* that is urging you to avoid something that might be harmful. Become familiar with how both your body and your mind respond to various situations, and learn to accurately interpret those responses.

Start with the smaller things. Should I turn right at the corner or left? Should I run that errand this afternoon or tomorrow? Should I take the umbrella today or not? Should I make this phone call now or later? There are dozens of times throughout the day when we can ask ourselves these small, seemingly insignificant questions. Every time you find yourself in one of these minor quandaries, ask. Then *listen*.

Use your journal to keep track of the results. If you took your umbrella, did it rain? If you made the call, did it turn out the way you wanted it to? Soon you'll begin to get a sense of what the right answer *feels* like beforehand.

When you've reached a level of certainty about that feeling with the little questions, start asking yourself the bigger ones.

Our explorations of the inner worlds often bring us into exciting and unfamiliar experiences and expose us to new ideas and ways of thinking. There may be times when our habitual methods of responding are no longer appropriate. Learning to interpret your intuitive signals will give you an effective means of examining the old and interpreting the new.

Elsewhere in the book, I've suggested things you might consider doing when your own messages aren't coming through, such as using the runes (#86), or contacting a psychic (#85), or writing like mad (#89). There are many other options as well, such as Tarot cards, the I Ching, using a pendulum, or working with a Ouija board.

If you consult other such oracles, make it a practice to check with yourself first. Then, as you get answers from other sources, check back to see how those answers feel compared to your own. Again, use your journal to help you keep track of these feelings.

The goal is to eventually become familiar with your own responses and begin to rely on them exclusively.

# 93. Learn to enjoy solitude

THERE ARE FEW things as powerful as solitude to help you get in touch with your inner self—especially when that solitude is accompanied by silence and the elimination of outside stimuli such as television, radio, newspapers, magazines, and other popular forms of escape.

If you haven't started already, begin to enjoy solitude. Get comfortable with being alone. This is time you can spend on your own thinking, reading elevating stuff, communing with nature, getting in touch with your intuition, smiling, laughing, crying, forgiving, and contemplating the questions of the universe.

This doesn't mean you need to move to a cave in the wilderness. Far from it. People and relationships are a vital part of both our inner and our outer growth. But we all need time to recharge every now and then, not only to nourish our spirit, but so that we have new energy to give to others.

If solitude feels threatening to you, start in small ways, perhaps with a lunch date with yourself in a quiet setting, such as a pew in an open but vacant chapel. Expand that to a Saturday afternoon alone, possibly in a secluded garden or some other place where you won't be disturbed. Then plan a private weekend retreat at home, or possibly in an organized retreat situation where everything but the inner search will be taken care of for you.

Be creative in coming up with ways you can spend time in solitude on a regular basis. I have a friend who for years spent his lunchtime in a deserted cemetery. It was the most convenient quiet place near his office he could find. He claims it got him comfortable not only with being alone, but also with the idea of death, a beneficial concept to have under your belt when you're examining the big issues of your life.

Solitude gives you the opportunity to confront your inner self in ways that few other endeavors can. Out of your times of solitude come serenity, peace of mind, and unparalleled opportunities to connect with your soul.

# 94. Do nothing

L EARNING TO DO nothing is another valuable
tool that will help you get in touch with your inner self. I
first learned to do nothing in an attempt to cure myself of the
habit of moving too fast, and of trying to do too many things
at the same time. And it worked. By *scheduling* time each
week to do nothing, I gradually began to get some understanding about where I wanted to go with my professional
life.

And as I continued to incorporate this practice into my
schedule, I was able to reach a new level of understanding in
terms of my inner life as well.

There are plenty of reasons why many of us have been
moving at breakneck speed in recent years. Oftentimes, they
have nothing to do with trying to accomplish a lot in a short
amount of time. Some of us have kept moving, either to prove
to ourselves that we're still alive, or in the unconscious fear
that if we stop, we'll have to take a close look at who we are.
That can be terrifying.

But learning to stop completely can be incredibly constructive. Doing nothing is different from meditating and from spending time in solitude, and in some respects, it is much more difficult. In our culture, anyway, it's usually a learned habit that has to be nurtured. Or sometimes Mother Nature mercifully intervenes by providing us with a convenient ailment that forces us to stop and do nothing.

Accept the fact that it's okay to do nothing. If you've begun to slow down, simplify your life, and go within, doing nothing will be much easier.

You can start by getting in the habit of doing nothing for two to three minutes at various times throughout the day. Simply stop whatever you're doing, sit quietly with your eyes open, your mind aware but not active, and just *be*. Doing some deep breathing (#96) will help.

Gradually increase the time. As you begin to spend more time doing nothing, be prepared for your body or your mind to balk. You'll get hungry or sleepy. You'll think of a dozen things you should be doing or that you think you'd rather be doing. Resist the temptation to give in to those feelings. Think of it as necessary and valuable time, which it is.

When you do this consistently, when you lean into it, when you start to delight in it, you'll find doing nothing one of the most productive inactivities you engage in.

# 95. Do a retreat

A FORMAL RETREAT can provide an effective
jump start for a program of inner simplicity.

A retreat can be as organized or as loosely structured as
you wish to make it. If you're just beginning to explore the
inner realms, you might wish to spend a few quiet days at a
retreat center where you can have time on your own to quietly
read and think about your life and where you want to go from
here.

In this type of setting, your schedule is completely your
own. You don't have to answer to anyone, and there are no
ceremonies to attend or rituals to perform, other than ones
you might choose. The accommodations vary, but usually a
simply furnished room is provided, along with meals—either
on your own or in a communal dining room. The general atmosphere is one of quiet reverence that allows for private reflection.

If you're practicing a certain type of meditation, or looking into a new teaching, or even energizing an old one, connecting with a formal retreat center that provides instruction or guidance in the teachings you've chosen to explore might be the way to go.

In this type of arrangement, there is normally a routine the participants are expected to follow as a group, usually with meals together, and with set times for instruction and group discussion, as well as scheduled quiet times during which to practice meditation techniques or other exercises.

Sometimes our expectations can get in the way of having a fruitful experience, so it's helpful to get as much information as possible ahead of time about the setting and particular demands of the routine. Or, at the very least, be willing to change your expectations if necessary. A friend of mine recently attended a four-day retreat to clarify some questions she had about a meditational technique she was learning. Her primary interest was in having a quiet setting, away from traffic and noise.

When she got there, she discovered her room was located directly above one of the major highways of the western world. She seriously considered leaving. But after thinking about it quietly, she decided to go with the flow. The weekend turned out to be incredibly beneficial for her, but completely different from what she had anticipated.

There is an interesting array of retreat experiences available today. If you don't have one in mind, see the reading list for some places to look into.

# 96. Check your breathing

ANCIENT YOGIC TEACHINGS say that if
you can control your breath, you can control your life.
Proper breathing can be an important tool for your inner
growth. It can clear your head, energize your body, raise your
energy, improve your outlook, elevate your mood, restore
your health, rejuvenate your psyche, and take you to other
levels of awareness.

Experiment with your breathing to see what a difference
correct breathing can make in your everyday life.

Yogic breathing involves the use of both the abdomen
and the diaphragm. If you're doing it right, the lungs are filled
with each inhalation and emptied with each exhalation, so
there is no residual air left in the lungs to get stale.

The first thing to do is *get in the habit* of sitting up
straight and standing up straight. The shoulders should be
relaxed and the stomach held in. No slouching towards nir-
vana here.

This also means continually being aware of your level of consciousness. If you're feeling logy, listless, lethargic, down, sleepy, or irritable, it's time to check your breathing.

You can do this by placing your hands lightly on your abdomen, with the fingertips touching. Keep your mouth closed and inhale through the nose, with the area just above the back of the throat actually drawing the breath in. If you exaggerate this step while getting the feel of it, you can hear and feel this as a slight rasp in the back of the throat. Once you're comfortable with the movement, normal breathing should be inaudible.

As you bring the breath in through the nose/throat, the abdomen expands and the bottom of the lungs start to fill with air, followed by the expansion of the rib cage, the top of the lungs, and the upper chest cavity. The fingertips should move apart slightly as the abdomen fills out.

Then gently pull the muscles of the abdomen inward to expel the breath up and out through the abdomen, the chest, and the nose in one smooth movement. The fingertips will come together again.

You can practice lying flat on your back until you get the hang of it. The entire movement for each breath should be fluid and easy. The idea is to have the process be automatic, while at the same time maintaining a level of consciousness with regard to the breath.

Make a point of connecting with your breath throughout the day. Use it to keep yourself on track. The study of hatha yoga is an excellent way to bring the incredible power of the breath into your everyday life.

# 97. Explore your sleep consciousness

ONE MORNING NOT long ago I found myself totally overcome by drowsiness after having had a restless sleep the night before. When I couldn't keep my eyes open any longer, I went to bed for a brief nap. I closed my eyes, and when I became conscious again, in what seemed like only a few moments, the "I" of me was outside of and hovering above my physical body. I saw and felt a whirling vortex emanating from the center of my chest.

Before I realized what was happening, the "I" of me was in the vortex. I sensed rather than heard a pop, and "I" was back in my body. When I looked at my watch, two hours had elapsed.

I didn't realize it then, but I'd had an out-of-body experience, commonly referred to as an OBE. Some researchers suggest we all leave our bodies on numerous occasions during sleep, though only a very small percentage of us remember these experiences. Others interpret OBEs as simply another level of dream consciousness. In either case, it would appear we all have the ability to have out-of-body experiences at will.

Why would we want to do this? Well, my own OBE was an incredibly thrilling adventure. It was one of the first times I've had the opportunity to actually *understand* how the "I" of me could be separate from my body, and different from what I'd always felt myself to be. I saw how that "I" of all of us could be eternal and immortal. But most importantly, it has totally expanded my concepts of and beliefs about my life and the possibilities of the universe.

If you've ever done any dream analysis, or taken the time to remember, record, and/or program and direct your dreams, you know that dreams can contribute fascinating and valuable information for our waking lives. Dreams often provide intuitive answers we haven't been able to get from any other source. If we allow them to, dreams can afford a much broader understanding of the greater context in which we live.

Recent research has shown it's possible to learn to control our dreams and to create what we want in our dream life, and then to *transfer* that learning to our waking lives. This offers incredible opportunities for our personal growth.

# 98. Explore meditation

MEDITATION IS ONE of the most powerful tools we have for self-expansion and inner growth. Through meditation we can reach levels of mental clarity that we cannot achieve through any other means. Meditation is a major pathway to the soul.

There are many, many ways to meditate. You can meditate on the inflow and outflow of the breath. You can meditate using a sacred word or phrase. You can meditate on the flame of a candle, or on the inner light at the center of your forehead.

You can meditate on the idea of love, or wisdom, or immortality, or any other concept. Or you can meditate by simply being aware of your thoughts as they pass through your mind. There are sitting, standing, walking, laughing, crying, dancing, and chanting meditations. There is living your life—every single moment of the day and night—as a meditation. And this is just for starters.

When I first came back to meditation a few years ago

after simplifying my life, I picked up a book on the subject, read through one of the suggested techniques, and sat down to meditate.

When I opened my eyes thirty minutes later, I found myself embraced by one of the most profound feelings of peace and serenity I'd ever known. I recognized in that moment that I'd been given a gift. I knew from my past attempts at meditating that it's not every day that meditation comes so easily, nor are the results so absolute.

It took many more months of regular, dedicated practice of meditation before I encountered even fleeting moments comparable to that initial experience. But I was hooked from that first day, and that was the gift.

Your acquaintance with meditation is no doubt entirely different from mine, or from anyone else's you know. We each bring a unique combination of body, mind, and spirit to the adventure of connecting with our inner selves.

If you haven't explored meditation, I urge you to consider it. Making meditation a regular part of your life will open you up to new and exciting possibilities for your inner growth.

If you don't know where to begin, start with one of the books on the Reading List, and branch out from there. Or connect with a teacher, or contact people you know who have had experience with meditation. If you start now, you will be amazed, when you look back six months or a year from now, at how far you've come and by how much your life has changed for the better. You'll also see how subtly you've been guided through the inner maze.

Meditation provides a natural unfolding of the process of inner exploration. Some of the rewards are immediate. Others take time, often years, to achieve. There is no substitute for simply doing it, and seeing what the rewards are for you.

# 99. Create joy in your life

A WHILE BACK Gibbs and our little dog, Piper, and I took a stroll down to the beach at sunset. It was one of those spectacular displays that casts a rosy glow, seemingly over the entire creation. There were a few wisps of white clouds in the sky, and as the sun sank lower on the horizon, the clouds became tinged with pink. Within a few moments, they had changed color entirely as they totally absorbed the brilliant hue of the sun. Venus began to be visible in the western sky.

We looked to the east, and saw the nearly full moon rising huge and golden. We sat and watched as the sky changed from one glorious shade to another. We were so enthralled with this exquisite display that we felt nearly full to overflowing with what I can only call unbounded joy.

The next day I found myself starting to succumb to a difficult moment in my work. Perhaps because this irksome note was in such contrast to the continued delight I had been feeling from the previous evening, and because that enjoyment had been so complete, I immediately recalled that sunset. Instantly the difficulty was overshadowed by the re-creation of the joy I'd experienced the night before. It wasn't that I was living in the past, but that I was somehow able to bring that joy to the present.

As the days and weeks passed, I found I was able to tap into that joy again and again, and to absorb it to the present moment. Even now, months later, I'm still getting mileage from that sunset.

We all have these moments in our lives. They are available to us in one degree or another every single day. We can find them in the smile of someone we love, or in the smile of someone we don't even know. We can find them in the hug of a child, in the presence of a friend, or the touch of a lover.

Think about the times in your life when you've been overcome with joy. It's in those moments that you're in love with yourself and everyone else. It's in those moments you believe you can conquer the world. It's in those moments that you dare to imagine how you want your life to be.

It's from that imagination and that belief and that love that we can and do create our lives.

Think about the things that bring you joy, then make a point of connecting with as many of them as possible, as often as possible.

# 100. Love a lot

LOVE IS THE most important thing in our lives. All the great masters, saints, and sages agree on this. But it seems to me that a lot has been lost in the translation of this teaching. It would appear that many of us have forgotten how to love, or never learned how to love to begin with.

This has always been a difficult issue for me, and I don't claim any expertise here. I've done well—or have been fortunate—when it comes to specific loves, such as my husband and family and friends. But something has always been missing for me when it comes to loving mankind, or the world at large. I believe I've learned one thing about love in recent years, which I'll share with you. For the rest, I'll refer you to the masters.

I've learned that in order to love others, we have to love ourselves first. How do we do that? By allowing ourselves to do things we love to do.

Like many of us, I grew up in a culture that fostered a belief that the most important thing was to get trained for a career so I could support myself and my family. It didn't matter whether or not I liked what I was doing, as long as it paid the mortgage. As a result, I spent years in jobs that drained my energy and starved my spirit.

One of the steps I took to simplify my life was to get to a point where I could do the things I love to do, not only in terms of my career, but in all areas of my life.

Obviously, this is a gradual process, and a lot of the steps I've outlined in this book helped, such as getting counseling, spending time in nature, and figuring out what I *didn't* want, among many others. But having at last found a career in writing and a fulfilling pastime in painting—both of which I love to do—has made all the difference in my ability to share love with the world at large, and to really *feel* that love for others.

If you're feeling weak in the love department, the first place to start is with yourself. Spend some time figuring out the things you love to do, and the things that make you happy. Then start doing them. Don't expect it to happen overnight. It may take you a while, and you might need to get some guidance along the way. Fortunately, there is a wealth of information available today to help you do this.

Many times we've been taught that doing what *we* love to do is selfish or narcissistic. But, in fact, before we can give love to others, we have to fill ourselves with love first.

# Reading List

## Meditation/Philosophy

Frost, S.F., Jr. *Basic Teachings of the Great Philosophers: Including Plato, Kant, Descartes, Spencer, Rousseau, Comte, Spinoza, Berkeley, Dewey, Santayana, Hegel, Leibnitz, Locke, Aristotle, Bacon.* New York: Anchor/Doubleday, 1942, 1962. Provides a fascinating historical perspective of how our understanding of the universe and a higher power has developed through the centuries, and continues to develop and unfold.

Hittleman, Richard. *Guide to Yoga Meditation: The Inner Source of Strength, Security, and Personal Peace.* New York: Bantam, 1969. A good beginning guide to hatha yoga and meditation.

Levine, Stephen. *A Gradual Awakening.* New York: Anchor/Doubleday, 1979. For those already familar with meditation and looking for new areas to explore.

Lindbergh, Anne Morrow. *Gift from the Sea.* New York: Vintage Books, 1978. A charming story of one woman's search for solitude and simplicity and the meaning of life.

Snow, Kimberly, Ph.D. *Keys to the Open Gate: A Woman's Spiritu-*

*ality Sourcebook.* Berkeley, CA: Conari Press, 1994. A collection of spiritual insights, meditations, and experiences from numerous classic and contemporary sources.

Strong, Mary. *Letters of the Scattered Brotherhood: A Twentieth-Century Classic for Those Seeking Serenity and Strength.* San Francisco: HarperCollins, 1991. This is a soothing companion to have in times of stress, anger, frustration, worry, loneliness—or any time. It offers page after page of practical guidance and inspiration about how to move beyond the distractions of the day and create inner peace.

## Retreats

Benson, John. *Transformative Adventures, Vacations & Retreats: An International Directory of 300+ Host Organizations.* Portland, OR: New Millennium Publishing, 1994.

Cooper, David A. *Silence, Simplicity, and Solitude: A Guide for Spiritual Retreat.* New York: Bell Tower, 1992. An exquisitely simple and readable description of how to prepare for and what to expect from a spiritual retreat.

Ram Dass. *Journey of Awakening: A Meditator's Guidebook.* New York: Bantam, 1990. A good general guide for launching a spiritual quest. Includes a directory of retreat centers and groups that teach meditation and provide retreat accommodations.

Sadleir, Steven S. *The Spiritual Seeker's Guide: The Complete Source for Religions and Spiritual Groups of the World.* Costa Mesa, CA: Allwon Publishing Co., 1992.

## Health/Exercise/Love/Healing

Anderson, Bob. *Stretching.* Bolinas, CA: Shelter Publications, 1980. Outlines various stretching programs for keeping your body limber.

Chopra, Deepak, M.D. *Perfect Health: The Complete Mind Body Guide.* New York: Harmony Books, 1990. An excellent program for physical, mental, and spiritual health.

Jonas, Steven, M.D., and Radetsky, Peter. *PaceWalking: The Balanced Way to Aerobic Health.* New York: Crown, 1988. A healthful alternative to running or jogging.

Siegel, Bernie S., M.D. *Love, Medicine & Miracles: Lessons Learned About Self-Healing from a Surgeon's Experience with Exceptional Patients.* New York: Perennial Library/Harper & Row, 1986.

————. *Peace, Love & Healing: Bodymind Communication & the Path of Self-Healing: An Exploration.* New York: Perennial Library/Harper & Row, 1989. As Bernie Siegel's books illustrate, we can and do heal ourselves.

## Creativity/Affirmations/Visualizations/ Exploring Other Levels of Consciousness

Cameron, Julia. *The Artist's Way: A Spiritual Path to Higher Creativity.* Los Angeles: Jeremy P. Tarcher, 1992. This program will free you to develop your own creative process.

Ferrucci, Piero. *What We May Be: Techniques for Psychological and Spiritual Growth through Psychosynthesis.* New York: Tarcher/ Perigee, 1982. Provides many easy mind-expanding techniques for exploring other levels of consciousness.

Gawain, Shakti. *Creative Visualization.* New York: Bantam, 1983. A beginning guide to affirmations and visualizations.

Silva, Jose, with Philip Miele. *The Silva Mind Control Method.* New York: Pocket Books, 1989. How to use affirmations, visualizations, and the alpha level of the mind to help you arrange your life exactly as you want it to be.

## Sleep/Dreams/Out-of-Body Experiences

Godwin, Malcolm. *The Lucid Dreamer: A Waking Guide for the Traveller Between Worlds.* New York: Simon & Schuster, 1994. A beautifully illustrated and written exploration of the world of dreams.

LaBerge, Stephen, Ph.D. Stanford University Sleep Research Center. *Lucid Dreaming: The Power of Being Awake & Aware in Your Dreams.* New York: Ballantine, 1985. Dr. LaBerge's work has brought much-needed understanding and insight to the study of dreaming.

Stack, Rick. *Out-of-Body Adventures: 30 Days to the Most Exciting Experience of Your Life.* Chicago: Contemporary Books, 1988. A straightforward, proven approach for anyone interested in exploring out-of-body experiences.

# Living the Simple Life

## A Guide to Scaling Down and Enjoying More

### ELAINE ST. JAMES

This book is dedicated to

everyone who wants to live a simpler life

# ACKNOWLEDGMENTS

I am deeply indebted to Catha Paquette for her perceptive and insightful reading of the manuscript.

I'd like to thank Marcia Burtt, Joe Phillips, and Pat Rushton for their advice and assistance throughout the process of writing this book.

I'm grateful for the continuing friendship and support of Judy Babcock, Phil Babcock, Himilce Novas, Tiffany Miller, Marisa Kennedy Miller, Jackie Powers, Carolyn Howe, Meg Torbert, Bev Brennan, Vera Cole, and Jamie O'Toole, and for the presence and guidance of Michael Russer, Stu Sherman, Bob Maloy, Don Foster, Michelle Gysan, Colleen McCarthy Evans, and Maryke White.

I'd like to thank my agent, Jane Dystel, and my publisher, Bob Miller, for helping me put this book together, and I especially appreciate the wisdom, direction, and encouragement of my editor, Laurie Abkemeier.

Many thanks to Cynthia Ferguson, Carlie Gnatzig, Erin Webreck, and all the other readers who gave me permission to use their comments in this book, and to everyone who wrote to share their excitement, their enthusiasm, and their ideas for living simpler lives.

I thank my husband, Wolcott Gibbs, Jr., for everything, most especially for helping me keep life simple.

# CONTENTS

# TWO    Getting Started

# THREE    The Things That Really Matter

## FOUR    Some Things to Think About

# FIVE    Getting Rid of Our Stuff

# SIX    Changing Our Consumer Habits

Contents    505

Contents   507

# Living the Simple Life

# AN OVERVIEW

I first made the decision to start living a simpler life in the summer of 1990. Prior to that time I had spent roughly twelve years as a real estate investor. I worked ten-hour days buying, refurbishing, managing, and selling investment properties.

During the previous year I had organized a real estate seminar business, had written a book on real estate investing, and had just completed a national media tour to promote it.

My life was ruled by a black leather time management system that weighed five pounds and took up half my desk space. My day was driven by the classic prioritizing question, "What is the best use of my time right now?"

Sometime after college I began, as many of us did, to work at two speeds: faster and fastest. I moved at this pace from six in the morning until seven or eight o'clock at night for more years than I care to count.

It would probably be accurate to say that I had become a fairly typical urban professional on my own fast track.

Though my husband, Gibbs, who is older and wiser than I am, was never technically a yuppie, his life was complicated by the fact that he was married to one. And he, too, maintained a full career schedule as a magazine editor, while at the same time writing a series of adventure novels. He was also an active volunteer with various community organizations.

In addition to our time-consuming careers, we had all the other duties and responsibilities associated with maintaining our lives. Though my two stepsons—who had been with us on weekends for the previous eight years—were now out on their own, we still had four cats and a busy social life.

The gods must have been smiling on me in the summer of 1990. I stopped for five minutes in the middle of July that year, and in a quiet moment I looked at my time management system as though I were seeing it for the first time. As I went over the list of phone calls I had to make, the people I had to see, the places I had to go, and the things I had to do, all of a sudden a light bulb went on. I realized my life had become too complicated, and I made the decision then and there to start simplifying it.

I had finally reached a point where keeping up such a hectic pace no longer seemed worth it. It occurred to me that we had, through long hours and a lot of hard work, achieved a modicum of success. We had many of the trappings of the modern lifestyle, but we didn't have the time, and sometimes not even the energy, to enjoy them. And even worse, we had little time for each other, and practically no time for ourselves.

A large part of the dissatisfaction for me was that I had never particularly enjoyed my work. I had continued to do it because I hadn't a clue what else I might be able to do. At that moment it was unthinkable that I could change my career or cut back on my work schedule.

But I decided there were many other areas where we could begin to cut back. My first objective was to create some breathing space so we could start to figure out how we could do things differently.

• • •

And so we began the process of simplifying. In the first couple of months we eliminated a lot of the clutter that was taking up our time and energy, and we moved to a smaller home. Over the next couple of years we made significant changes in our household routines, our social lives, our entertainment patterns, our civic and volunteer schedules, our financial picture, our personal lives, and eventually even our work lives.

I then got the idea to write a book on the things we had done to scale back. That book, *Simplify Your Life: 100 Ways to Slow Down and Enjoy the Things That Really Matter*, was published in May 1994. It outlines many of the steps Gibbs and I took to simplify.

In the process of simplifying the outer areas of our lives, we freed up close to thirty hours a week. This gave me the opportunity to begin the daunting prospect of thinking about making some career changes, and also the chance to address some of the emotional, psychological, and spiritual issues that had been bubbling beneath the surface of my fast-paced life, but that I'd seldom taken the time to explore.

I then decided to write a book that would discuss some of those issues. And so I wrote *Inner Simplicity: 100 Ways to Regain*

*Peace and Nourish Your Soul*, which was published in May 1995.

When we first made the decision to simplify, we had no idea that we were in the beginning phase of a major national trend. We simply wanted to get out from under the complications that twelve fast-paced years had generated.

If you, too, are thinking about making some changes and simplifying, or have already started the process, you're not alone.

According to the Trends Research Institute of Rhinebeck, New York, a privately funded organization that forecasts and tracks changes in our culture, simplifying is one of the leading movements of the decade.

A 1995 nationwide survey of a cross section of Americans revealed that close to 30 percent of the respondents had *voluntarily* downshifted, and were working fewer hours for less pay so they could spend more time with their families.

Numerous other surveys have shown that anywhere from 60 to 80 percent of those questioned would be willing to accept a reduction in pay if they could work fewer hours.

This represents a major nationwide change in personal priorities. It says that many of us have had enough of the fast-paced, hard-working lifestyle that has become "the norm" over the last decade. It says millions of Americans want to live their lives differently.

The Trends Institute estimates that by the end of the decade, a total of 15 percent of the 77 million baby boomers will have made significant moves toward creating simpler lives, some voluntarily, others involuntarily.

When I wrote Simplify Your Life, I thought I was writing it for maturing yuppies, who, like Gibbs and me, had been seduced by both the work and the consumer culture in recent years, and who in the process of overdoing it, had begun to lose sight of the important things.

But based on the letters I receive from readers around the country, it would appear that the desire to simplify crosses most generational, economic, educational, and professional lines.

I hear from teenagers, single men and women, married couples, retirees, the affluent, the not so affluent, and people from every walk of life—teachers, nurses, computer specialists, actors, journalists, artists, psychotherapists, legislators, lawyers, corporate executives, police officers, students, and media personalities. They are among the millions of Americans who are reducing, voluntarily or otherwise, the hours they spend earning a salary, their housing requirements, and the money they spend on goods and services.

They, like Gibbs and me, are realizing that they've given up too much in the effort to have it all. The primary objective for most of them is to have more time for their own life dreams or for the people they love, and for doing the things they really want to do.

When you stop to think about it, it's not surprising that so many of us want to simplify. Never before in the history of mankind have so many people been able to have so much, go so many places, and do so many things. We've worn ourselves out trying to have it all.

And now we're ready to look at other options.

In Living the Simple Life, we'll explore what simple living means to different people and look at what complicates our lives, what we can eliminate, and ways we can play the game differently (Chapter One). I'll outline some ways to get started, especially for those who feel their lives are too complicated to even think about simplifying (Chapter Two), and for those who may not have stopped long enough recently to get in touch with what really matters to them (Chapter Three).

I'll point out some of the things Gibbs and I have learned over the past few years about having more time to call our own, and suggest how to deal with people who don't understand the desire to simplify (Chapter Four).

In my experience two major issues complicate our lives above all else. The first is our ongoing battle with consumerism and the stuff we've accumulated. As with any problem, awareness is the first step toward resolution. And so I'll share what we've learned about letting go of a lot of that stuff, and some of the ways we've dealt with the media-generated imperative to consume (Chapters Five and Six).

The second challenge is the tendency for many of us to say yes when we'd like to say no, a habit that affects all areas of our lives. In Chapter Seven, I'll discuss ways we've used to approach this.

One of the great dichotomies we face is that because our lives are so complicated we don't have time for ourselves and at the same time we often keep our lives complicated so we won't have to address some of our inner issues. I'll talk about this and some ways we can bring our outer and inner lives together in Chapter Eight.

Each passing year leaves us with personal, household, and lifestyle choices that can either simplify our lives or complicate them even further. In Chapters Nine and Ten, I'll share my experiences—as well as some readers' ideas—about these choices.

There is perhaps no one for whom the problems of consumerism and learning to say no are more important or more challenging than for parents. In Chapter Eleven, I'll combine my own observations with the wisdom of several readers and an expert or two to outline some ideas for simplifying with children.

Having no options complicates our lives. Having too many options complicates our lives as well. In Chapter Twelve, I'll discuss some ways I've learned to deal with the clothing options for women. In Chapter Thirteen, Gibbs discusses some things he's always known about clothing options for men.

I've also included a Reading List, a selection of books that explores some more of the organizational, financial, lifestyle, and work-related questions of living a simpler life.

An interviewer asked me recently if I was glad I made all these changes and had simplified my life. I said I was, absolutely.

Then she asked if I'd do it again. I said yes, absolutely. There's no way I'd ever want my life to be so complicated again.

Then she asked if I would have simplified if someone else had suggested it to me—before I came to the decision on my own. My initial reply was, probably not!

But as I thought about it some more, I realized that if someone had outlined easy changes I could make which would free up some time without derailing the rest of my schedule, I believe I would have paused long enough to consider them.

If someone had been able to show me that just by tweaking my daily routine I would have more time each week—not to work more but to play more and relax more—I like to think I'd have been open to that possibility.

If someone had pointed out that reducing the hours I spend in the office each day could actually make me more productive, I would have been open to experimenting with that.

If I could have seen that freeing up more time for leisure would help open me up to my creativity, which in turn would make it possible for me to move away from a career I'd never been happy in and into one that now is a constant source of joy...Well, I might have been skeptical, but because hope springs eternal, I'd have sought out that leisure time.

And if someone had convinced me that eventually I could use some of my newfound time to face the more difficult challenges I'd spent years avoiding—such as conquering my fears and learning to forgive—and that doing those things in turn would free me for unprecedented personal and inner growth, I like to think I'd have gone for it.

So that's what I'd like to do for you in Living the Simple Life. If you're just starting to consider the possibility of simplifying, I want to give you a glimpse of the tremendous freedom you'll experience when you start to eliminate some of the day-to-day complexities.

You'll see that simplifying is not necessarily about getting rid of everything we've worked so hard for. It's about making wise choices among the things we now have to choose from. It's about recognizing that trying to have it all has gotten in the way of enjoying the things which do add to our happiness and well-being. So it's about deciding what's important to us, and gracefully letting go of the things that aren't.

You'll see that simplifying is not necessarily about moving to Walden Pond and sending the laundry home to Mother. It's about simplifying our lives right where we are. It's about learning to reduce the laundering chore, along with all the other chores and frequently self-imposed obligations, so we can begin to make the contributions we all, in our heart of hearts, want to make to our family, to our community, to our environment, and to the world.

If you've already begun taking steps to simplify, *Living the Simple Life* will help you continue on your way, perhaps with some ideas you may not have thought of, and possibly with some different ways of thinking about the process.

If you've long been living the simple life, I hope you'll find here some reinforcement and even validation for the sometimes easy, sometimes difficult, but almost always rewarding choices you've made.

When you start slowing down, cutting back, creating time— real time for yourself—the important things become obvious. Once you simplify your life you begin, perhaps again, to do your best work. You can start, perhaps all over again, to live your best life, whatever that is for you.

Simplifying is not a panacea. It won't solve all the problems of our lives or of the world. But it's a good beginning.

# ONE

# The Simple Life

# 1. What Living the Simple Life Means for Me and Gibbs

When my husband, Gibbs, and I first made the decision to simplify our lives in the summer of 1990, we weren't sure what living the simple life would mean for us. In many respects we had a good life; we just didn't have the time or the energy to enjoy it.

We knew we didn't want to drop out. We weren't ready to move to the woods. We didn't want to give *everything* away. We're too young to retire, and were not in a financial position to do so, anyway. Our challenge was to create a simpler life right where we were, in a town we love, with people we care about.

For us, simplifying meant, among other things, getting rid of an accumulation of possessions that were no longer adding anything to our lives and were taking up a lot of space in our closets and storage spaces. It was about moving to a smaller, easier-to-maintain home.

It was about cutting back on the daily and weekly household routines—cooking, grocery shopping, housecleaning, yard maintenance, errand running—and using the time we'd freed up to watch the sunset, or to putter in the rose garden, or to spend time with family and friends.

It was about changing our buying patterns, not only to reduce our consumption of the earth's resources, but also to minimize the stuff we have to take care of, insure, and provide space for.

It was about learning to say no to many of the social and civic activities we'd often felt obligated to do, so we'd have time to enjoy the silence, or start one of our creative projects, or learn to do nothing for a change.

For Gibbs, who loves his work, it was about eliminating a stressful three- to four-hour daily commute so his workday wasn't so exhausting and so we had more time together. He also wanted to have more time for his writing and to pursue his community and volunteer interests.

For me, it was about going from exhausting ten- and twelve-hour workdays in a career that never fed my soul to a six- to eight-hour day of writing that thrills me to the core.

It was about gradually, over the course of a couple of years, changing our daily routine so that, rather than having to rush mindlessly to begin our respective work schedules, we now have four uninterrupted hours to read, to contemplate, to take walks along the beach together, to chat on the phone with a friend, and possibly to romp with the dogs before we start our workday.

We're still in the early stages of simplifying, so we don't yet know all the benefits that will come from continuing to live the simple life. But we see this as a good start and a big improvement over the hectic lives we'd been living for too many years.

## 2. Some Other Views of the Simple Life

Keep in mind that simplification is all relative. For example, Oprah Winfrey simplified her life by unloading, via a charity auction, several thousand of the exquisite outfits she has worn on her daily television show for the past ten years, and by figuring out that she can turn off the ringer on her home phone so she doesn't have to take calls if she chooses not to.

Barbra Streisand simplified her life by getting rid of five of her seven houses and her Tiffany lamp collection.

For David, a 42-year-old teacher who told his story at a presentation I gave in San Diego, simplifying means keeping his possessions down to eight boxes of personal items and one lamp to read by.

David uses his master's degree in education to tutor the children of affluent families. He decided twenty years ago to limit his work schedule to two hours a day, four days a week, which provides him all the income he needs to maintain his simple life. A good deal of the rest of his time is spent doing volunteer work with underpriviledged kids.

For Ellen, a 41-year-old single attorney who wrote to me from the Northwest, simplifying is about selling her home and unloading her private practice so she can take time off to figure out what she wants to do next (which definitely won't involve law and most assuredly won't involve maintaining a huge house).

Based on the letters I get from readers of *Simplify Your Life* and *Inner Simplicity* and the stories I hear from people I talk with around the country—as well as on reports circulating in the media—simplifying means taking one or two or a combination of steps to reduce the stress that has become a permanent fixture in our lives.

Sometimes it means exploring new career options, sometimes it means quitting our jobs altogether, but almost always it means cutting back on our heavy work schedules.

Sometimes it means moving to a smaller home or moving across country, and sometimes it means simply living differently in the space we have.

Sometimes it means getting rid of everything, but more often it means merely cutting back on the amount of stuff we've accumulated, and changing our spending habits because we're finally learning that too much is too much.

And sometimes simplifying means searching for balance between our need for a satisfying career, our desire to spend time with our families, and the need to nourish our inner selves.

For most of us, simplifying is any one or a combination of steps we can take to get back in control of our lives.

## 3. A "Corporate Yuppie" Approach to Simplifying

Dear Elaine,

I enjoyed Simplify Your Life and wanted to respond. We, too, have made a drastic lifestyle change for the better. We were yuppies at major corporations and enjoyed the material things and the fast-paced life in Dallas, Texas.

Then the kids came. They are now 2 years old and 7 months old, and they keep me busy. I have no time for fussiness or complications. People ask me how I do it, and I reply, "Simplicity and organization." We moved to a rural area up north and look forward to raising our kids with values and a wholesome environment.

The first thing I did when we decided to simplify was to quit my job. That step in itself eliminated day-care and transportation hassles. I'm trying to get another career going from my home.

I've always been a minimalist, but I really kicked into high gear after the kids came along.

I do a lot of the things your book mentions. I feel so free from our past stresses. The thing that makes me happiest is that I'm only 31 years old and learned this early in the game.

The hardest thing is trying to explain our lifestyle to people my age because they think our downscaling was motivated by a negative, such as my quitting my job, or because we can't afford things. It's the opposite, but people don't get it. We don't want an answering machine or call waiting. It's not that we can't afford it. Like you, I was constantly on the phone on my last job, and am not fond of the phone.

I've stopped trying to explain to people. Now I let them wonder why I'm so happy and secure in myself these days.

Sincerely,
Cynthia Ferguson
Byron Center, MI

# 4. A "Cabin in the Woods" Approach to Simple Living

Dear Elaine,

I live in Skagway, Alaska, ninety miles north of Juneau. Your book Simplify Your Life made it to my morning "wake up slowly time" (by reading a book and sipping warm apple cider) just this morning. It was a gift from relatives in Vail, Colorado. I had been feeling complicated and rushed lately, and decided to see what you had for me!

Soon, with a big smile, I realized that I had actually graduated from most of the one hundred simplifiers. Thank you for reminding me how most Americans live a crazy busy life compared to mine.

As I looked around my one-room cabin, taking in all 400 square feet of it, I laughed at myself for thinking my life was too complex. I live eight miles out of Skagway (population 720) in my cabin that has no electricity or running water other than the mountain creek that "runs" by my cabin that I've been drinking from for over five years. I have wood heat, a propane stove, and a neat and clean outhouse. I use the creek for refrigeration in summer, and a window box for a fridge in the winter. I can look out my window and see the harbor seals playing and hear the dolphins exhaling out of their blowholes.

For exercise, I chop all my own wood to burn and bike the eight miles to work most days of the week. In winter there are no open businesses in town to use me as their bookkeeper, so I have about five or six months off a year.

My quality of life is fantastic. Yesterday I saw both a bear and a coyote in my neighborhood. The eagle on the front of this card follows me to work in the mornings! I have clean air, clean water, and many loving friends who all live as simply as I do. I actually forget that most people don't live like me and my neighbors.

We aren't hippies or revolutionists. We simply simplified. You'd be amazed how much you can really pare down. I have hauled up a car battery that I run my radio/CD player on, but imagine how much space you'd have without all of your plug-in gadgets! Sometimes we rent movies and watch them at the public library. But the TV was the first thing I was delighted to part with.

Thank you for making your great ideas feasible for people who would not be able to make such a big step over to my lifestyle—but perhaps they'd be able to fire their personal trainer, or simplify their diet, or just smile at their neighbor.

Have a great day.
Carlie Gnatzig
Skagway, AK

## 5. What Does Simple Living Mean to You?

The levels of stress many of us have experienced in our fast-paced lifestyles have made us long for respite from the pressures of the modern world. The temptation is strong to think that respite would come from packing up and leaving it all behind.

But as Carlie Gnatzig points out, moving to a cabin in the woods is a big leap. Many people have left everything behind to move to the country, and then found that it's not necessarily simple or suitable.

Tempting as it might be to some, escaping to the woods is not the only way one can live a simple life. And it's probably not a realistic option for most of us.

And it's not necessary to make such sweeping changes in order to simplify, at least not to begin with. For many, even minor alterations to the lifestyle we're now living can bring significant relief.

So before you order up the proper attire from L. L. Bean, you may find it helpful, if you haven't done so already, to take some time to figure out what simple living really means to you.

What do you hope to achieve by making some changes that would simplify your life? What would have to happen for you to live more simply? And how will you know when you've gotten there? Can you make some easy changes right where you are? Or would you have to move across town, or possibly across country to get to simple?

It's possible your ideas about simplifying will change as you go along. Keep in mind that what may be simple for someone else may not be simple for you. You may end up with an entirely different understanding of simple living than the one you start out with.

But it's so much easier to reach our destination when we at least have an idea of where it is we want to go.

## 6. The Things That Complicate Our Lives

Many things make life complicated for us. Here is a list of one hundred of them:

Big houses. Big mortgages. High-maintenance automobiles. Property taxes. Home remodeling. Inflation. Revolving charge accounts. Easy credit. Multiple credit cards. Credit card debt. Consumer debt. The national debt.

Not having time to spend with our spouses. Not having time to spend with our children. Difficult spouses. Children who are difficult because we don't have enough time to spend with them. Ex-spouses. Family obligations. Ailing parents. Step-parents. Uncooperative siblings. Stepchildren. Difficult in-laws. Family expectations. Our own expectations.

Fifty-hour work weeks. Sixty-hour work weeks. Having to hold down two jobs to meet the big mortgage payments and the multiple car payments. Long commutes. Heavy traffic. Traffic jams. Traffic accidents. Difficult bosses. Obstinate employees. Grudging co-workers. Demanding clients. Irksome partners. Silent partners who won't remain silent. Staff meetings. Breakdowns in communication. Work we don't particularly enjoy. Work we actively dislike. Working too many long hours, even if it's work we love. Unemployment.

Not having time to spend with friends. Not having time to spend alone. Pressing civic obligations. Committee meetings. Social commitments. Noisy neighbors. Incompetent physicians. Politics. Equivocating politicians. Congress. Attorneys. Lawsuits. Delivery people who show up a day late. Repairpeople who never show up. Contractors we wish had never shown up.

Publisher's Clearing House mailings. Unrelenting charity requests. Television. Advertising. Televised court proceedings. Telephone solicitors. Call waiting. The Net. E-mail. Registered mail. Junk mail.

Having too much stuff. Having no options. Having unlimited options. Planned obsolescence.

Alcohol. Drugs. Cigarettes. Pollution. Taxes. Unsafe sex. Dieting. Health fads. Exercise equipment we don't use. Over-the-counter medications that don't work. Cheap gadgets that don't work. Expensive gadgets that don't work. Relationships that don't work. Prescription medications that may solve one problem while creating another. Illness. Choosing an HMO.

Anger. Worry. Fear. Negative cash flow. Bad weather. Natural disasters. Inadequate day-care arrangements. Plastic grocery store baggies that don't open. Tax returns. Blown-in subscription cards.

Not necessarily in this order.

# 7. What We Can Eliminate

Not all of the previously mentioned things complicate life for all of us all of the time. But a lot of them make life difficult, sometimes more often than we're aware of.

In this culture, at this point in time, most of us won't be able to avoid all complications completely. But we can eliminate more than we think we can. We just have to learn to be selective.

And that's a big part of what simplifying is all about.

Reread the list of things that complicates our lives and mark any that apply to your life at the moment. If you think of any other things, add them to the list.

In this list there are less than a dozen that we probably won't be able to do anything about—not in this lifetime and not legally. They include inflation, the national debt, politics, attorneys, Publisher's Clearing House mailings, planned obsoles-

cence, taxes, bad weather, natural disasters, and blown-in subscription cards.

Everything else on the list, and probably most of the items
you may have added, we can either do something about or se-
lectively avoid in one way or another.

Recognizing this will simplify your life. The rest is just details.

## 8. Remember a Time When You Were Truly Happy

Ask anyone who is past the age of 35 to recall a time when they were truly happy. Most people will say they're pretty happy now, though they may admit they sometimes feel overwhelmed by the demands of life these days.

If you press them further, a lot of people will remember a time in their youth, perhaps a particularly wonderful summer when they had few cares or responsibilities and spent seemingly endless weeks fishing on a quiet stream or lazing by the neighborhood pool.

Or perhaps they'll remember the joy of being young and single, or of being newly married and madly in love. They had few possessions to weigh them down, no house payment, maybe only a small car payment. They worked hard, but work didn't consume all their time and energy. Mostly they didn't worry about health insurance, life insurance, home insurance, interest rates, the Dow, or taxes. Life was simple.

Most of us wouldn't go back to being young and totally independent and having nothing at all to call our own. But many of us would like to recapture the *feeling* of those carefree days.

And sometimes, in the midst of simplifying, things can get overwhelming. If you're changing jobs, reducing your income, letting go of the clutter, cleaning up relationships, dealing with some of the inner issues, or changing your long-established habit patterns, life can, in the short term, seem pretty complicated.

So reconstruct your fond memories of happy, simpler times. Let them help create a clear picture of what simple living means for you. It will stand as a beacon for you in the process of getting back to the simple life.

# 9. Be Willing to Change the Way You Play the Game

Often one of the stumbling blocks to living a simpler life is our inability or unwillingness to change how we play some of the games that got us into these complicated lives in the first place.

For example, for many years I was driven by the "need" to maintain our home to certain standards of cleanliness, organization, efficiency, and so-called style. After we'd taken some of our first steps toward simplifying, such as moving to the smaller place and changing a lot of our buying patterns, I realized this was one area in which I wanted to make some significant changes.

When the town we live in was considering rationing water because of severe drought conditions, we made the decision to cut back on the amount of laundry we wash. This meant wearing our clothes a bit longer than we'd been used to, and not changing the sheets and towels every week as I'd always done.

To my surprise, I didn't have a problem with wearing our clothes longer between washings. Gibbs was once editor of *Yachting* magazine, so we've spent a lot of time on boats over the years and learned how to stand downwind from people!

But I grew up, as many of us did, in a household where we changed the sheets and towels every single week no matter what, so I had some difficulty reducing the frequency with which we laundered the linens.

Fortunately, my younger stepson, Eric, who had recently graduated from college, gave me some sage advice. He said, "Elaine, relax. I went for four years without changing the sheets."

The drought forced us to change the way we had always done the laundering chore. But Eric's comment helped me put things in perspective, and I began to see how approaching that weekly task differently had simplified our lives.

Gradually, I started to change some of my other expectations, such as how spotless my glasswear was or how clean my floors had to be. I began to look carefully at some of the routine household chores I'd always considered sacrosanct, such as the idea that our clothes have to be whiter than white, that our blues have to be bluer than blue, that our mirrors have to shine with a brilliant luster, or that our hardwood tabletops have to be polished to a blinding brightness.

When you examine these precepts closely you begin to see how absurd they are. Has anyone ever been fired for having a ring around the inside of a shirt collar? Is our spaghetti bolognese less delectable because we can't see our reflection off the side of the pan? Would houseguests actually leave, never to return again, if we didn't use fabric softener on our bath towels?

This is not to suggest that we eliminate housecleaning or laundry routines altogether, but simply that it's possible to think of doing them differently, or that we can set our own standards rather than dutifully accepting those advertised by cleaning product manufacturers.

Few of these dictates were determined by actual need, or even by our desires. They were set in the boardrooms of UniLever,

Bristol Myers/Squibb, and Johnson Wax, among others. Many dollars are spent each year to get us to accept these and countless other ideals as our own. We've been made to feel inadequate, incompetent, insecure, dissatisfied, and socially unacceptable if we don't meet them at every level.

In the last thirty years we've given up time with our families, our leisure time, our sleep time, our money, our rapidly depleting energy, and our own free choice in varying attempts to maintain many of these conventions. In doing so we have generously lined the pockets of a couple hundred corporate executives while vastly complicating our own lives.

Household cleaning routines are only one area in which we've abandoned our freedom of choice to the strategies of marketing gurus. Few areas of our lives are untouched by products that are designed for the sole purpose of getting us to feel insecure enough to part with our money. Our tastes in clothing, personal hygiene, health care, food, travel, automobiles, children's toys, and practically everything else is manipulated by the pronouncements of those cunning advertising demons.

I don't claim to have been able to free myself completely from all of these mostly preposterous decrees. Far from it. I'm still emotionally attached to my BMW, and it's unlikely I'll ever be able to let go of my Revlon-generated need for lipstick. But becoming aware of the origin of a lot of these attachments has made it possible for me to simplify in many other areas.

It's sometimes difficult to know where to draw the line. But as you start to think about ways you could simplify, become mindful of the number of things you do each day because of standards that were set in a marketing session at Procter & Gamble.

# 10. You Can Have a Simpler Job

For many of us, our jobs and our work schedules have been one of the major complications of our lives. Our material well-being depends on our paycheck. Without our monthly income how could we eat or make the mortgage or the car payments? Without our jobs, the whole house of cards would come tumbling down. Often our very identity depends on our being employed.

And so I often hear people say, "I can't simplify my life as long as I've got to make a living."

But if you've got a demanding, time-consuming job, that alone might be sufficient reason to simplify your life.

As we've seen, many people have already made changes in their lifestyle or are thinking about the possibility of downshifting, or possibly changing their career path altogether so they can free up time to spend with their families, or to create more leisure time.

According to a survey conducted by the Merck Family Fund, 28 percent of working adults said they had voluntarily reduced their income in the last five years because of changes in their priorities. Others are being forced to make such changes due to corporate downsizing and changes in the economy.

But if you're like I was a few years back, you may not be open to the possibility of making career changes right now. You could well be thinking, as I did, "You gotta be kidding. There's no way I could quit my job. And I could certainly never work part time. How could I support or help support my lifestyle if I did? I've got to make a living."

And, most likely, at this moment it's true: You can't quit your job. Not today. Not tomorrow. Maybe not next month. Maybe not even next year.

Once I could see my way clear to simplifying my life, it was not that big a step to begin cutting my workday back to eight or nine hours. But it was several years before I could seriously think about unloading the real estate and doing something else. In the midst of a complicated life, it often is impossible to change jobs, or even to think about it.

So if the thought of making changes in your job picture presses all your buttons, don't even think about it now. Instead, look at all the other areas of your life you can simplify.

Simplifying in other areas will give you some breathing room. It'll give you more time. It'll give you more energy. It will reduce many of the financial pressures—if you're living more simply, you'll simply be spending less money.

Having more time and less stress will open your mind to possibilities you may not even be able to think about now. And eventually, as you pare away all the extraneous stuff, a new way of approaching your present job or an entirely different career option may be staring you in the face.

Yes, most of us have to make a living. And we have to look at ways we can support ourselves not only now, but throughout our retirement years. But if Vicki Robin and Joe Dominguez, authors of Your Money or Your Life, have been able to live on $500 a month for the past twenty years, then many things are possible in terms of career and employment changes for all of us.

This doesn't mean we all can live on $500 a month, but it

shows us that it is possible to live, and live well and happily, on a lot less than we've led ourselves to believe.

By slowing down, by simplifying, by breaking some of our consuming and spending habits, by teaching our kids simple pleasures, and by adopting simple pleasures ourselves, we can create a beautiful, happy, fulfilling life. And we won't have to work as hard as we have been to maintain it.

## 11. You Can Live a Simpler Life

I spoke to a bookstore owner recently who described people's reactions when they came up to the cash register with their books and saw a copy of Simplify Your Life sitting in a stack on the counter. Time and again he saw people pick up the book and read the title. And then they'd laugh. He said they laughed right out loud because the idea that anyone could actually simplify his or her life in this day and age seemed so preposterous.

But, while waiting for their purchases to be totaled up, they'd flip through the book, just out of curiosity.

Then they'd say, "Ah, yes, if I dropped call waiting, that would simplify my life."

Or, "Yes, if I didn't have to answer the phone every time it rings, that would simplify my life."

Or, "Yes, if I started doing just one thing at a time, that would simplify my life. And if I cleaned up my relationships, that would *really* simplify my life."

And they began to get the idea that there *are* things we can do to simplify. Easy things—like leaving our shoes at the front door or changing the way we do the holidays—that would make a difference.

They also see there are other steps—like changing our expectations, or learning to forgive, or getting out of debt—that are more difficult perhaps, but are possible, and that would significantly reduce the complexity of our lives.

But I understand the initial skepticism. At first glance, the idea of creating a simple life often seems out of the question.

When we're in the midst of a complicated life, we think it would be impossible to slow down. When we're constantly racing against the clock, it feels like there's no way to create some extra time. When we're so exhausted from moving ninety miles an hour, we're certain we don't have the energy to figure out how to do things differently.

When we're torn between the pressures of work, the demands of our children, and the needs of our inner selves, it feels as though there's no way we could add one more thing, like simplifying, to our list of things to do.

But it is possible. And there's a magical, almost exponential quality about time. Once you free up even a little bit of it, other ways will start occurring to you to help free up even more.

If you don't know where to begin, start with one of the easy steps outlined in the next chapter.

# TWO

# Getting Started

## 12. A First Step

People frequently ask me, "How can I possibly simplify my life? I'm working too hard. I'm moving too fast. I've got my career, my marriage, the kids, the mortgage payment, and the car payments to think about. My life is too complicated for me to take the time to stop and simplify."

I know exactly what they mean. My life was that complicated a few years back. Even if I could stop for a bit, I felt I wouldn't know where to begin. But finally, as many of us have, I reached the point of desperation. I had to start making some changes, and begin to simplify my life.

But it didn't happen overnight. It took us several years of concerted effort to create a simpler life.

This is not to say that everything we did to simplify was difficult. Far from it. There were many things—like changing our exercise regimen, spending more time in nature, and creating time for solitude—that were relatively easy and gave us immediate relief.

But if you've been living what we have come to think of as a normal life in this culture, it's unreasonable to expect that you can simplify your entire life this Saturday between noon and 3 p.m. Realistically, it's just not going to happen.

Simplifying is a process. It no doubt took you years to build your complicated, high-pressure life. It will take some time to simplify it. You can't undo it all today. But you can get started today.

To start simplifying the only thing you have to do right now is decide that you really want to simplify, and then schedule some time to think about it. That's it. Making that decision and setting aside the time is enough for one day.

How much time do you need to schedule? It depends to some extent on how complicated your life is and how adept you are at changing gears. When I decided to simplify, I scheduled a four-day weekend at a local retreat house. It took a day and a half for me to unwind enough just to get to the point where I could begin to think clearly about my life. If you mull it over for a few minutes, you'll know whether you can get started in an afternoon, or whether you need a couple of days or more.

A weekend provides a reasonable amount of time for most people. If you have a very complicated life, you may need that much time just to get into the process.

If you feel you can't take the whole weekend right now, take half of it. If you can't spend a whole day, then take half a day.

In the next week, just schedule whatever time you think it'll take. That's the first step.

Don't underestimate the tremendous power of taking a simple step like this. An amazing thing starts to happen when you begin to simplify your life: Each step you take will make it easier for you to take the next step. I promise you, if you make the decision to simplify, and commit to it, incredible things will happen.

## 13. Ten Ways to Free Up an Hour or More Each Day for the Next Thirty Days, So You Can Start Thinking about How to Simplify Your Life

If you feel your schedule is so jammed that you don't see how you could slow down enough to even begin thinking about simplifying, take a few moments to consider some of the suggestions here.

This is a list of reasonably painless ways to free up an hour or more each day—that's ten to twenty hours each week—for the next month.

For right now, you don't have to think of these as long-term changes—or as something you'll have to do forever in order to create more time for yourself—although you may ultimately want to incorporate many of them into your simple life.

There may only be a couple of ideas that apply to your life at the moment. Pick one (or two or more) that will work for you, and stick with it for thirty days:

1. If your job allows, quit work an hour earlier than you usually do and use that time to think about your life.

2. If your job allows, start work an hour later than you usually do and use the quiet time at home—after everyone else has gone—to think about your life.

3. If possible, stay at your office an hour later than you usually do, and use the time to think about your life. Do this only if you can be certain you will have uninterrupted time there.

4. Get up an hour earlier. This may also mean you go to bed an hour earlier; but an hour in the morning when you're rested and refreshed is worth two hours at the end of the day when you're exhausted.

5. Stop watching TV news.

6. Stop watching TV (period). Unplug it and move it to an out-of-the-way spot if necessary. Do this even if

you believe watching television relaxes you. It may, but it also programs you—in ways we're often not even conscious of—to continue to complicate your life. And it clutters up your mind with distractions that keep you feeling overwhelmed.

7. Don't schedule any lunch dates.

8. Don't schedule any after-work social hours. No coffees. No pre-dinner drinks. No dinners. No after-dinner drinks.

9. Stop reading the daily newspaper. (It's only for a month!)

10. Change your exercise regimen. For example, cut your daily program in half. Or, if you commute to a gym or an aerobics class, exercise at home and save the commute time. Or exercise just two or three days a week. Be creative here; it's only for thirty days.

# 14. Ten Ways to Free Up Miscellaneous Amounts of Time over the Next Thirty Days, So You Can Start Thinking about How to Simplify Your Life

Many of these ideas are not only about freeing up time, they're also about reducing the physical, mental, and emotional static that constantly occupies our minds, drains our energy, and keeps us from being in touch with how we would live our lives if we didn't have so many distractions.

1. Plan to stay off the phone, except for business or for emergencies. Announce to family and friends that you won't be chatting on the phone for the next month. (You might be astounded at how much time you save and how much internal noise you eliminate each day by cutting back on your social phone calls.)

2. Stop listening to the radio, the CD player, and your Walkman—at home, in the car, at the office, when you exercise.

3. Stop reading magazines. Recycle or pass on to a friend the stack of magazines sitting on your reading table waiting for you to find the time to read them.

   Do the same with any magazines that arrive in the mail during the next month. Don't set them aside and think you'll read them when the month is up. If you do that, you'll be just as behind then as you are now. You have to start someplace.

4. Stop all escape-type reading—detective stories, murder mysteries, fantasies.

5. Simplify your family meals as much as possible. Plan to prepare batches of soups or casseroles ahead of time and freeze them in serving portions. Or buy a month's supply of frozen dinners. (It's only for a month.) Make sure there is plenty of fresh fruit available. Dr. Spock always said if kids have fruit, they don't have to eat their vegetables. Use paper plates to minimize cleanup.

Enlist the help of your mate and children in the preparation, provisioning, and cleanup of meals, including breakfasts and lunches. Make a game out of this for your kids. Make a challenge out of this for your spouse.

6. Do only the minimal housekeeping chores. Keep the house picked up and orderly, but don't worry about dusting, vacuuming, window washing, mowing the lawn, waxing the car, or polishing the candelabrum.

   You may have to change your expectations about how clean your house has to be to do this. Or you may have to change the expectations your mate or your mother or Madison Avenue has laid on you (#9).

7. Do minimal laundry. Our mothers did the week's laundry for the entire family in one day or less, without the high-tech machinery we have today. I know women who now wash a load or two every night of the week.

   If we learn to be careful about how we wear our clothes—and train our kids to be careful, too—we can greatly reduce the laundering chore, at least for a month.

We can let the sheets and towels go for a week or more.

Make a quick calculation right now as to how much time you'd save you if you allowed yourself to do the laundry differently. How many evenings would it free up? How much of the weekend?

8. With the exception of groceries, eliminate all shopping. Stock up on things you might need ahead of time. Or simply do without. No one has ever died from running out of eye shadow. Or shaving cream.

Think of this as a personal challenge, and be prepared to use some of your self-discipline. The urge to rush out and buy something we think we need has become overwhelming in this culture. Multibillion-dollar media campaigns ensure that this urge continues. You'll be amazed at how much time you'll save when you learn to break this habit.

9. Don't accept or arrange any social or family engagements.

10. Cancel all civic or volunteer obligations. Simply say, "Sorry, but I'm starting a new project and won't have time for anything for thirty days."

Take five minutes right now to see if there are any other things particular to your schedule and lifestyle that you could change or eliminate to free up some time over the next thirty days.

Obviously you can extend any of these ideas into a 60- or a 90- or a 365-day plan. The idea is to free up as much of your time as possible so you can start thinking about some long-term changes you can make in your life.

## 15. Five Ways to Free Up an Entire Day or More over the Next Thirty Days, So You Can Start Thinking about How to Simplify Your Life

1. Take vacation days on Mondays or Fridays to give yourself a couple of three-day weekends. Or take some stand-alone vacation days in the middle of the week.

2. Take a week or more of vacation time, and use it to get started simplifying your life.

3. Take a couple of sick days or personal days.

4. Make an arrangement with your boss to work four ten-hour days for the next month (or permanently), and use the fifth day each week to start simplifying.

5. Plan to spend a Saturday or a Sunday or an entire weekend at home with no social or family commitments (except for your immediate family). Remember to eliminate the standard distractions, such as the radio and television, during this time.

## 16. Escape to a Quiet Spot

No doubt some people can arrange quiet time at home and actually make progress there in these first few steps.

But if your life is anything like mine was, you've got so much going on at home that you wouldn't be able to have an extended period of time without interruptions. Therefore, it might be easier if you can get away from your home or work environment.

This includes being away from phones, faxes, radios, television, the fridge, laundry, friends, neighbors, bosses, co-workers, and all other potential preoccupations.

One of your best options for an extended period of undisturbed time would be a nearby monastery or retreat house where you'll have a simple but comfortable room without a phone—where meals are included, and the entire atmosphere is arranged for a contemplative withdrawal from the world. (Check out *Sanctuaries,* by Jack and Marcia Kelley.)

As an alternative, consider renting a convenient motel room for a couple of days, and give out the phone number only for use in emergencies.

Spend some time right now thinking about the ideal place that would suit your circumstances.

Maybe you have friends who will be away on vacation and would be open to having you use their space for a couple of days.

Or perhaps you know someone who has a summer home or a cabin in the woods that you could rent or borrow for the time you need.

Or if you're comfortable with roughing it, get out your camping gear and head for the hills.

If you can't get away from home for a couple of days right now, but can see your way clear to freeing up an hour or so every morning, consider finding a quiet table at your local library, or an empty pew in a church, as a place in which to get started thinking about your life.

Another alternative is the great outdoors, perhaps on a park bench.

If you simply can't get away from your home, then do what you can to create the time and space there for quiet contemplation without the usual interruptions. Unplug the phone, turn off the radio and the TV, cancel your coffee break with your next-door neighbor.

If you're a mother with young children, hire a babysitter for a couple of afternoons. Or find a friend who wants to simplify, too—or who at least is sympathetic to your desire to simplify— and trade babysitting for a couple of afternoons or evenings.

Do whatever you need to do to find a space that will work for you. And do what you can to make it special. It's possible that this time will be for you, as it was for me, a major turning point in the way you live your life. It will be fun for you to be able to look back on this time and space fondly, and with sweet memories.

# 17. What to Take with You

This might seem like a minor point, but for those of us who are addicted to our stuff, it will serve as a helpful reminder.

To some people it's probably obvious that if you're going to hole up for a couple of days away from home with the purpose of thinking about simplifying your life, you'll want to take only a minimum amount of paraphernalia. However, it wasn't apparent to me when I left for my retreat, so I'll mention it here.

When I headed off to the hermitage for a mere four days, I had two satchels packed with personal belongings. One was full of clothes, shoes, and other personal items I didn't need and, in fact, most of which I never used. The other was loaded with books, magazines, notebooks, paper, pens, tapes and a tape player, and other miscellaneous stuff—most of which I also never used but had included on the "you never know when you might need it" theory.

I lugged all this baggage up a couple of flights of stairs and into my simple room, which was suddenly no longer quite so simple. After sorting through it all, I realized there was more than I'd actually use. Since it was getting in my way, I packed some of it up and took it back down to the car.

When I set out on similar missions these days—which I do on a regular basis—I leave the books and the tapes behind. I take a change of clothes, a toothbrush, a pen, and a notebook. When I thought about it later, I realized that's all I actually used, though I spent a fair amount of time and energy being preoccupied with all the other things.

This is a microcosm of the macrocosm for a lot of us in this culture: We're continually overwhelmed with and distracted by our stuff.

You might want to keep this in mind if you're packing for a brief retreat from the world.

## 18. Ask Yourself Some Simple Questions

Once you've created the time and have found a quiet place in which to think, a powerful next step is to ask yourself some simple questions.

One of the most obvious things to ask is "What is complicating my life right now?" Is it career pressures? Your relationship with your boss? With your co-workers? Are you spending too much time working? Too much time commuting? How could you cut back in these areas?

Sometimes simply taking the time to pinpoint the hot spots can go a long way toward alleviating the pressure.

The next obvious question to ask yourself would be "What do I need to do to simplify these areas?"

No one knows the minute details of your day or the secret wishes of your psyche better than you do. No one knows the answers to these questions better than you do, either.

Of course, your life may have become so complicated that even you are momentarily out of touch with the innermost workings of your being.

So getting to the point where you can ask the questions could be the easy part. Waiting for the answers can be the hard part. You may have to be patient. You'll definitely have to cut back on the distractions to listen carefully.

One of your toughest tasks may be forcing yourself to pay attention to the answer. You may be hearing things you don't want to hear. Your inner voice may be telling you that what you need to do is to quit your job or to find a new career or to move on from a relationship that isn't working. Remember, one of the reasons we keep our lives complicated is so we won't have to listen to our inner voice telling us what we need to do to make our lives work better.

But asking these questions can start the ball rolling. Keep a journal or notebook handy and write down any thoughts, insights, or solutions that come to you.

Even now, several years later, I've found it helpful to keep these questions in mind if I notice my life starting to get complicated again.

## 19. Set Your Own Pace

I've heard from many people who quit their jobs, left their mates, moved across country, and virtually started their lives over, all in one fell swoop.

But there are many for whom that drastic approach would be neither comfortable nor appropriate.

Where you start and how quickly you move along will depend to some extent on where you're at in your life right now, as well as on the type of person you are.

Obviously, there is no right or wrong way to begin the process of simplifying. If giant steps work for you, take them.

If you're not sure where to begin, creating the time to think about your life would probably be essential. Where you go from there and how quickly you do it will be up to you.

# THREE

# The Things That Really Matter

# 20. You May Not Know What Really Matters

According to a recent TIME/CNN poll, close to 65 percent of us spend much of our so-called leisure time doing things we'd rather not do. That is a staggering statistic, especially when you consider the incredible number of options that are available to us today.

I think there are two reasons a lot of us aren't doing the things we really want to do. First of all, many us don't know what those things are.

When I think back to my hectic lifestyle, I have to admit that one of the reasons I allowed my life to continue to be so complicated is that I hadn't slowed down enough in recent years to figure out what I wanted to do, not only in terms of my work life, but in terms of a lot of my personal choices.

I knew the basic things: I knew that Gibbs, and family, and special friends were important. I knew that for me, spending time in nature was important. I knew maintaining my health with exercise and an appropriate diet were important.

But there were other areas, such as my life's work and many social and leisure activities, I just sort of drifted along with because it was easier than taking the time to come up with alternatives.

For any number of reasons we lose sight of what we want to do. Perhaps we weren't encouraged as children to make our own decisions.

Or maybe we have easygoing, compliant personalities and have gone along with what other people have wanted to do, or wanted us to do, for so long that we've forgotten what's important to us.

Or perhaps we never allowed ourselves to believe that doing the things we enjoy is even a possibility for us.

If you've spent a lot of years not knowing what you really want to do, either in terms of your career or in terms of your personal, social, civic, or family life, it can seem like an impossible task to stop what you've been doing—or at least slow down for a bit—and figure it out. It often seems easier to keep on do-ing things we don't want to do.

Secondly, what we want to do can often be difficult to do.

For example, if your deep, dark, hidden desire is to write the great American novel, it would seemingly require a major dis-ruption in your life to arrange things so you could even get started on it. Often it's easier to continue doing things you al-most want to do, or don't mind doing.

So our lives get frittered away by a social engagement here, a luncheon there, an evening of television here, or the habit of working evenings or weekends or both on projects that we don't have all that much interest in. And the things we really want to do, in our heart of hearts, get put on the back burner.

One of the things simplifying your life will do is free up time for you to figure out what really matters to you, and then enable you to arrange your time so you can do it.

## 21. Reexamine Your List of Goals

Not being clear on what I wanted to do didn't keep me from having lots of lists of things I thought I wanted to do. Paradoxically, it may have contributed to the length of my lists.

When I made the decision to simplify my life, I had a full-sized three-ring binder time management system in which I had a goals page for each of the major areas of my life, including personal, career, social, financial, spiritual, and civic. In each of these categories I had a to-do list that included projects I thought I wanted to start.

For example, my personal list included the following projects, among others:

Start painting

Start drawing

Study landscape gardening

Learn to write

Join a choral group/study voice

Learn Spanish. Brush up on French and German.

Learn speed reading.

Learn flower arranging, especially Ikebana

Study art history

Start bird watching

Study the Middle East situation in depth

Get into hang gliding

Start writing letters

Study screenwriting

Study filmmaking

Learn Beethoven's *Moonlight Sonata* for Christmas recital

Become a gourmet cook (!)

Learn the basics of interior design

Learn about growing roses

Start mountain hiking

This time management system also included the following: time lines with starting and completion dates and to-do sheets for each of the items within the above mentioned categories; a mission statement; a purpose statement; and a three-page constantly expanding reading list. It also, of course, had a two-page spread for every day of the year on which were outlined the activities connected with my daily schedule.

Obviously, if I was going to simplify my life, one of the first things I was going to have to do was to reconsider my goals.

Though it's difficult for me to believe this now, before I simplified my life I was committed to the idea that I'd eventually—and sooner rather than later—be able to do all the things I had on these lists.

If you'd asked me at that time what really matters, I'd have insisted that it all mattered. It never occurred to me to give up any of it.

I look at this list now and I can laugh. The only reason I have the courage to reveal the absurdity of these lists is that now I know I was not alone. There are millions of other people out there who believe, as I did, that we can do it all, have it all, be it all. Or at least do most of it; and who perhaps even yet are carrying around similar lists—comparable in scope if not in content—in their leather-bound time management systems.

I know that keeping lists can be beneficial in terms of helping us figure out what's important. But if, as many of us did, you got carried away with your lists, you may have to reconsider and cut your lists back to more realistic proportions.

I found this to be an ongoing process that unfolded over several years. I made continuous changes and adjustments to my lists as I learned how to be more realistic about the time we have available and to make wise choices among all the options we have to choose from, and as I got better about figuring out what it was I really wanted to do.

If you never got into extensive list making, or were able to keep it under control, your job of simplifying may be easier than you thought.

## 22. Zero In on Your Top Four or Five Priorities

There were many intermediate steps along the way, but I have only one list now. It looks something like this:

Spend time with Gibbs

Pursue my writing career

Have quiet time alone for my inner work

Spend time with family and friends

Have quiet time for reading and drawing

This is a far cry from my previous lists, but when I factor in all the activities of daily living—the things we have to do to survive, like food shopping, cooking, eating, sleeping—realistically, this is what I have time for.

It was a tremendous relief for me to look at all the other things I'd been carrying around on those lists, and to finally get the picture that there were simply not enough hours in the day or in the week or in the year to accomplish them all, and that I was going to have to let most of them go, at least for now.

In my experience, as people start to simplify their lives, the things that really matter naturally come to the forefront. Ideally, you reach the point where all the distractions have been minimized or eliminated from your life. The things that are important to you are so few and so obvious that you don't even need to write them down. Instead, by simplifying you've been able to arrange your life so that each day automatically revolves around those things.

If you're an incurable list maker, be open to the possibility that you may have to cut your lists back to more realistic proportions.

If you're not a list maker by nature or by habit, you might find it helpful to come up with a brief list of four or five things you'll want to concentrate on as you begin to simplify your life.

Just don't get carried away.

# 23. Remember, There Are Only Twenty-Four Hours in the Day

I have long been aware of the notion that there are only twenty-four hours in a day. But until I simplified, I hadn't stopped long enough to figure out how that frequently overlooked detail affected my life.

It's very deceptive. Twenty-four hours sounds like a lot of time, and so it feels as though we should be able to fit into the day all the things we think we have to do as well as all the things we want to do.

But the fact is if you work eight hours a day and sleep eight hours a night, that leaves only eight hours for everything else.

Most of us spend roughly half of those eight hours provisioning for, preparing, eating, and cleaning up after our meals; bathing, brushing, and flossing; finding the right necktie or looking for a pair of stockings without a run in them;

and if we're lucky, cycling, jogging, or walking around the block.

If you factor in commute time, housekeeping chores, mail sorting, bill paying, sex, social phone calls, duty phone calls, feeding the dog, cleaning out the cat's litter box, and scheduling the next day's activities, you can use up more than half of those four hours before you even turn on the TV or pick up a newspaper.

If you have child-related duties or volunteer commitments, or if you spend extra time at the office or excessive time commuting, that leaves approximately no quality time with your spouse, your kids, your friends, no quiet time alone, and no time for your creative interests, which are the things the majority of us agree are the most important.

We may believe, for example, that we can get ready to leave for the office in forty-five minutes. But the reality is that, in addition to all the things we have to do in that time to get dressed—shower, shave, blow dry, and stand in front of the closet for ten minutes trying to figure out what to wear—we also have to squeeze the orange juice, pack the kids' lunches, walk the dog, bring in the paper, and feed the cat. And we wonder why we're dashing out the door fifteen minutes late for the office.

We think we can do it all. But in the reality of the twenty-four-hour day, it seems unlikely. It takes a tremendous amount of time just to keep up with spouses who want our attention, kids who need our love, employers who demand our souls, homes that take a lot of our energy, friendships that require nurturing, and our own inner cravings that need to be met. That's enough for one twenty-four-hour day.

For many of us, all the other things we think we want to attend to will have to wait until they start making thirty-six-hour days.

## 24. Remember that Relationships Take Time

When you're zeroing in on what's important to you, keep in mind that our close relationships frequently need more time than we've devoted to them in recent years.

This seems so obvious, but given the fact that one out of three marriages ends in divorce and our children feel disenfranchised, it's apparently easy to overlook. Not that inattention is the only cause of divorce, but it's certainly a contributing factor.

Gibbs and I have always felt that our marriage was one of our very top priorities, but we'd gradually begun to devote more and more energy to our goals without realizing that the time we had for each other was getting lost in the shuffle.

Considering all the other pressures and the time demands that we allow to impinge on our day-to-day activities, it's easy to get into the habit of taking our closest relationships for granted.

I believe there's also a subtle tendency to think that once

we've landed the person of our dreams, we can check "get married" off our list. Then we move ahead, have our 2.3 children, and check "have children" off the list.

Then we get so caught up in the work we do to support these relationships—and the home, the cars, the clothes, and the never-ending cultural and social and educational activities that seem necessary—that we lose sight of the relationships themselves.

We can so easily end up with a variation of the famous Roy Lichtenstein cartoon of the 1980s. One that says, "Oh my God! I forgot to make time for my family."

If you're in a relationship or have children, these are no doubt going to be a top priority. Devote some of your newfound free time to your nearest and dearest.

## 25. Stop Feeding Your Ego

A few years ago I was asked to write book reviews for one of the major book clubs. At the time, I was delighted to accept this offer. It gave me the chance to keep up with the latest books in my field of investing, and it also gave me the opportunity to say that I was doing reviews for this prestigious book club.

While that sounded impressive, at least to my ear, the reality was that the work was intermittent, the manuscripts were often tedious, the deadlines were urgent, and the pay was lousy. As time went on, it became a major complication in my life.

As my field of interest changed, it would have been logical to discontinue this work. But I kept doing it far longer than I should have, somewhat out of habit, partly out of feeling fortunate to have been asked to do this thing (that I didn't really want to do), but mostly so I could continue to say, if only to myself, that I was doing reviews for this book club.

Eventually, I figured out that if I stopped doing the reviews, I could still say I *used* to do book reviews for this prestigious book club, and it would carry almost the same weight in terms of ego gratification. So I finally got wise, and retired from this activity.

Even though it's embarrassing for me to admit this, I know from talking to people that this kind of behavior is not unusual.

We often get into work situations, social commitments, volunteer obligations, sports routines, and other types of activities that complicate our lives. We stay in them far longer than we need to because it looks good on paper, or because it sounds good when we have the opportunity to drop it into conversations, or because in some way it meets our own or someone else's expectations of the kinds of things we think we should be doing.

We each have to decide for ourselves when it's appropriate to bow out of these kinds of endeavors. This might be a good time to take a look at your life and see if there are any activities you're involved in that are no longer serving a purpose for your simple life. Then drop them.

## 26. Learn to Make Good Choices

In order to simplify, we have to start making choices, sometimes difficult choices. And often it means saying no, even to the
things we want to do.

Shortly after Gibbs and I began to take steps to simplify, we
found ourselves having dinner with some friends who were into
hang gliding.

We spent the entire evening listening to them rave about the
thrill of this fascinating sport. As we sat there being seduced by
yet another activity, we imagined ourselves leaping off the cliff
and soaring silently over the beautiful hills behind our home.

By the time the evening was over we'd promised our friends
we'd meet them at six o'clock the next morning on a nearby
peak to try out their gear and have our first lesson.

All the way home we talked about how wonderful it would be
to start hang gliding.

Then we walked through the front door, looked at each other, and reality began to set in. We reminded ourselves of how little time we actually have available. We realized there was no way we'd be able to fit a new sport into our schedule, especially one as time and energy consuming as hang gliding. We knew that our short list would suffer if we did. And our short list had been suffering long enough.

When we analyzed it carefully, we realized hang gliding was not as high on our list as we'd originally thought.

Reluctantly, we called our friends and explained why we wouldn't be able to join them.

"Sorry, we got carried away. We'd truly love to meet you tomorrow morning, but we're making some changes in our lives, and we simply won't have time to get involved in hang gliding for the time being."

When we thought about it later, we realized this was progress for us. In the past, we'd have purchased all the equipment and had six weeks of lessons before it dawned on us that we couldn't fit this new activity into our schedule.

And all the time, we'd have been wondering why, when we

were at last engaged in this wonderful activity that we both had thought we wanted, our lives had become even more complicated and stressed out. The choices then would have been to stop hang gliding and feel guilty about all the time and money we'd wasted, or to keep trying to justify the expenditure by continuing with an endeavor that we didn't have time for.

The need to make wise choices encompasses every area of our lives. Since we have time for only a limited amount of stuff, we need to choose wisely what stuff we're going to allow to take up that time. Since we have only a limited amount of time to spend with friends or to engage in leisure activities, we need to choose our friends and our activities wisely.

Take a look at your own life to see if there are any choices you might be able to make that would free up more time and energy for the things that are higher up on your list.

## 27. Set Your Time Management System Aside

If you've got an extensive list of all the things you want to do or feel you have to do, how do you get to a simple list?

One possibility is to try a fresh approach.

One of the best things I did when I went on my four-day retreat was to leave behind that time management system with the interminable lists.

No doubt there are people who wouldn't agree with this tactic. After all, frequently our whole lives—our goals, our aspirations, our life purpose, our priorities, our to-do lists—are laid out in those systems. And we've become addicted to them. We've spent untold dollars learning to use them, and countless hours keeping up with the process.

But many of us have found that those systems don't manage as well as we'd thought they would. I finally began to suspect that my lists were part of the problem.

In addition to including all the things we think we want to do, often our goal lists reflect what we feel we ought to do. In many cases these lists are determined, sometimes without our even recognizing it, by outside influences such as career demands, peer pressures, parental expectations, family obligations, or media enticements. Frequently we've lost touch with what we truly want to do.

I looked at one of the bestselling books on time management recently. The charts, lists, goal planners, and other strategies required to manage our hectic days made my head spin. It's my belief that those systems don't simplify our lives; often they assist us in keeping them complicated.

Even more insidious is the subtle underlying message in many of these systems that somehow we're missing out on life, or in some way are not doing our part if each day isn't scheduled down to the last minute.

I'm not suggesting that you shelve your time management system permanently, but merely that you set it aside as you figure out what matters.

It may well be that some of those things that matter are already on one of your existing lists. That's okay. The idea here is to let the list you'll be forming now come from your heart rather than from your own or someone else's expectations.

As you reduce the stress and time demands of your hectic life, your new list may turn out, as mine did, to be not only shorter, but quite different than you expected.

# FOUR

# Some Things to Think About

## 28. Simplifying Is Often Two Steps Forward, One Step Back

One of the things Gibbs and I did to simplify was to get rid of a lot of the clutter in our lives. That was two big steps forward for us.

It took us several weeks to complete this process and it was several more weeks before we could hold a garage sale to unload the stuff, so in the interim our living space was in a state of chaos. That was a temporary step back.

Then, after the thrift store truck pulled out of the driveway with everything we couldn't unload in the garage sale, we decided to move to a smaller house. Two steps forward.

We went through another month of disruption until we could get into our new place. One step back.

It was another week or so before we were completely settled into our small but cozy condo. Two steps forward.

It was only a couple of months later that we noticed we were going out and acquiring things to fill it up again. Ten steps back.

One of Gibbs's objectives in simplifying was to have time to devote to some of his volunteer projects, and so he started reading for Recording for the Blind. Two steps forward.

A year later he stopped one day and realized that in addition to his weekly reading, he was also now participating in the local adult literacy program and had become an active member of the Coast Guard Auxiliary. He was beginning to feel overwhelmed again. One step back.

When I made the decision to write *Inner Simplicity*, I realized I had found a new career possibility. A major step forward in terms of finding my life's work.

But I committed to a tight deadline, which meant I wrote practically around the clock during that time. Even though I loved what I was doing, it was definitely two steps back in terms of scheduling balance into my routine.

It might be helpful to know that the two step one step phenomenon can occur on the way to living the simple life. The habits of a fast-paced life die slowly. And change by its very nature is disruptive. Even with the best planning, it may not be possible to avoid periods of upheaval and disorder—and possibly even confusion—on the way to a simple life.

## 29. Be Aware of the Pitfalls of Having Extra Time on Your Hands

Making changes in your schedule so you can free up an hour or two every morning for the next month will make it possible for you to start making some dramatic changes in your life.

It can also be terrifying. Or tremendously challenging. You might feel guilty. Or you might want to run screaming back to some time-consuming drama so you don't have to deal with the real issues. Or it can be all of the above.

Keep in mind that the complications in our lives can take on a momentum of their own. They can rapidly expand to fill the time allotted for them. They can also expand to fill time that is not allotted for them. Stay focused, and no matter how strong the temptation, don't let the latest crisis—yours or anyone else's—eat into your newfound time.

This is one reason to schedule some of your quiet time away from your usual setting where most of the distractions occur with predictable regularity.

If you're in the habit of feeling rushed and overpowered by your schedule, don't allow that habit to carry over into your new free time. Make a concerted effort, especially in the early stages of simplifying, to stay loose and relaxed.

You may reach a point where it feels as though it would just be simpler to continue with your hectic life. It's clear to me now that one of the reasons I maintained a complicated life was because I was afraid of what I'd have to unravel in order to simplify it. Having taken major steps to eliminate the complexities of my life, I can assure you that, even in the short run, simplifying is easier once you've taken the plunge.

Also, remember we know how to move at breakneck speed, so at one level that feels comfortable. Most of us haven't had as much practice moving slowly, so doing so with ease can be a real challenge.

Be prepared for change. When I simplified, my whole life was transformed dramatically: I reduced my living space by more than half, I moved away from relationships that weren't working, I let go of a lot of my limiting beliefs, I found a new career, and was compelled, ultimately, to confront a lot of my inner demons. All this can make you feel like you're standing at the edge of a cliff.

If you find yourself feeling uncomfortable with a lot of extra time on your hands, try to figure out exactly what it is you're experiencing. Identifying your reactions is the first step toward moving beyond them.

Don't let an initial feeling of discomfort keep you from making the changes you want to make in your life. Realize that once you get into the process and actually begin taking steps to simplify, you'll leave those feelings behind pretty quickly.

# 30. Get Off Automatic Pilot

O ne of the things that made it possible for me to keep going at high speed until I simplified my life was an innate ability to race through my day on automatic pilot. I think this is true for a lot of us.

We're used to rolling out of bed in the morning, moving quickly through our ablutions, grabbing a bite to eat while we read the paper or watch the morning news, packing the kids off to school or day care, putting the finishing touches on a report for the boss, having a final swig of coffee, then flying out the door to start our workday, without reflecting on what we're doing.

We take the same route to work, so we don't have to think about it, and our minds easily fill with a million other things—worries, responsibilities, obligations—on the way to the office.

While some of our daily work procedures are less automatic than others, there's still a certain predictability about a lot of the tasks we take on. Mostly we don't have to analyze it much. We just get through the day so we can hop in the car, and go back home, on automatic.

Then we fall immediately into our evening schedule, what ever that might be for us: exercise, on automatic; dinner, on automatic; cleanup, on automatic; meetings, on automatic; watching television, on automatic.

The weekends are frequently the same, though they usually allow for a little more latitude in terms of the routine. But most of us tend to do the same things over and over again, week in and week out.

Yes, we may vary the specifics somewhat. We may have social or cultural or recreational outings on a regular basis. But those can easily become automatic as well. We tend to go to the same places, see the same people, discuss the same issues.

There's a certain comfort in moving through our lives this way. The world sometimes seems unpredictable, and the grooves we establish give us a feeling of order and of being in control. That's fine as long as the things we're doing on automatic are the things we really want to be doing. Often they're not—or maybe they were once but aren't now—and we haven't stopped long enough to realize it.

And paradoxically, living on automatic complicates our lives. Living on automatic is often what makes it possible for us to do all the things we feel we have to do. We squeeze into our days new chores or commitments, adding another errand here, another lunch date there, without considering whether we really have the time to do them, let alone the desire. We just take a deep breath, put our nose back to the grindstone, and add one more item to our list of things to do.

This is where building some air into our schedule pays off. We can create the time to have a leisurely breakfast with our family, or take the scenic route to the office and enjoy the ride. We can create daily and weekly variations that will make it possible for us to savor special moments throughout our days, throughout our weeks, and throughout our lives.

Changing gears from time to time makes it possible for us to get into the habit of being aware and alive each moment, or at least for a lot more of our moments. And the more aware we are, the easier it is to get back in control of our lives.

The process then builds on itself. Each time we become conscious of the fact that we're doing something we'd rather not be doing, we can make adjustments in our schedule. Gradually we can learn to eliminate those activities and substitute more appealing pursuits.

# 31. Some Ways to Change Gears

Here are some things you might think about doing to get off automatic for a bit:

Get up earlier and go out to eat with the family at a local breakfast dive. Or pack some muffins, juice, and coffee for a picnic breakfast to watch the sunrise.

Walk to work. Cycle to work. Take a bus to work. Take a different route to work.

Walk the kids to school instead of driving them.

Do your grocery shopping early in the morning before the store gets crowded. Shop at a different store altogether to get a fresh perspective on the items you purchase.

Meet your spouse and/or kids for lunch in the park. Or leave the office early, pick up a deli basket, and have dinner in the park at sunset.

Let the housekeeping go this week. Spend the time with your kids instead.

Let the laundry go this week. Or assign the routine chores to someone else if you can.

You might come up with a slightly different way of approaching these tasks that would make them simpler for the time being. Recently a friend of mine asked her 10-year-old to make her bed before guests arrived. "Can't we just close the bedroom door?" her daughter asked.

There are many circumstances in which just closing the door for the moment would make life simpler.

Take a vacation day in the middle of the week with your spouse and kids, and go play together. If you can't take the whole day, take the afternoon off together.

Exercise at a different time; or do it at a different place; or do it with someone else; or do it alone.

Unplug your phone for a week. Or change your outgoing message to say you'll return all calls next week. When I started simplifying some of my office protocol, I was amazed to learn how few phone calls need immediate attention.

Or sit in a different chair or at a different desk. If possible, work in a different office, or take your work to an empty table in the local library or your favorite café.

Take some time right now to come up with two or three things you could do this week that would help you break, even for a short while, the patterns that keep you moving through life on automatic, the patterns that keep you trying to do it all.

## 32. Involve Your Children in the Process of Simplifying

If you've got kids, your simplification program will obviously be easier to put into place if you include them in the process and enlist their help in making your lives simpler.

I hear wonderful stories from families who've worked together to simplify their lives. I also hear from teenagers who long for simplicity in their world. They've seen how all the complications, commitments, and stress have kept their parents from being happy, and they're determined not to let their lives be that hectic now, or get that overwhelming as they grow older.

It might be helpful to schedule a family powwow with the stated intention of setting up a program to simplify all your lives. You could start with a discussion designed to help everyone figure out what their own priorities are as well as what the family priorities are. Then take a close look at your schedules to see what kinds of changes you can make to free up time together as a family.

Assign each child chores in the preparation and cleanup of daily meals, and with the laundry, housekeeping, and yard maintenance. This will give the kids a feeling of responsibility for the family well-being and relieve some of the time pressures of the primary caretaker.

Not every family member is going to respond favorably to a plan to simplify. The ages of the children and the dynamics within the family will determine, to some extent, how receptive your kids may be to the idea of making some changes and simplifying. But don't automatically assume that your children will not be interested. With the pressures on kids today, they may be as ready to simplify as you are.

## 33. When Your Significant Other Doesn't Want to Simplify

It's one thing to get your children involved in your plans for simplifying or, if they're not interested, to work around them. But it can be another issue entirely if your spouse is not open to the idea.

If this is your predicament, don't give up on the idea of simplifying. There are a number of things you can do.

First, you can look at all the areas of your own life that you can simplify, such as your work life, your social life, your volunteer projects, your exercise routine, your wardrobe, your car, your desk, your side of the medicine cabinet, and so forth.

It's entirely possible that as you begin to simplify your life so you can do the things you really enjoy doing, your partner may be inspired and decide to join you. If nothing else, at least you'll have created energy to put up with someone who wants a complicated life.

Whatever you do, don't spend a whole lot of time trying to change the other person. If he or she is not interested in simplifying, the chances are good that no amount of nagging is going to transform them, and it will only complicate *your* life.

Another thing you can do is change your expectations about how simple their life has to be. It's possible that two people with disparate lifestyles can each make a valuable contribution to the other's life. If you love one another, and are close in many other areas, you may each have to allow the other to pursue his or her own level of complexity.

If, as often happens, the main issue is the other person's clutter, the situation can be tricky. Many people have a lot of stuff because they've never learned how to throw things out, but under the right circumstances, they would be open to learning.

Also, some people thrive on clutter and complexity, or think they do. It's possible they've never stopped to think about how clutter can get in the way of living their lives, or how it's getting in the way of your life. Often, these situations offer the potential for change, or at the very least, compromise.

But when you're dealing with someone whose clutter is a substitute for the love they never got as a child—or is a refuge from earlier abuse or deprivation—then you both might need to find professional help to deal with this issue.

If the situation is or becomes untenable for you, it may be necessary to consider a permanent change. Although this is obviously a drastic measure, I've heard from many people who've said that one of the most important steps they took was to move on from a spouse whose life was incompatible with their own desire to live simply.

Of course the other thing that can happen when one person starts devoting more time to the relationship is that the other person's priorities change. They, too, become more attentive, and so the whole relationship improves.

The other option is to try to find a friend (#34) who supports you in your desire to create a simple life and accept that, possibly for the time being, your spouse won't be joining you.

# 34. Find a Buddy

If you feel you need help creating a simpler life, and your partner is not enrolled for the moment in your simplicity program, then find a sympathetic friend, or two or three, and connect with them on a regular basis so you can share ideas and provide encouragement as needed.

Having even one other person who understands and approves of your need to simplify will make your task a lot easier. Our desire to simplify our lives goes against the mainstream in this culture, so going it alone can be a real challenge.

If you have just one person supporting you in this, plan to connect by phone at least once or twice a week. Limit your phone calls to ten to fifteen minutes, or less if possible. It's so easy to launch into a lengthy discussion that can derail your intention to have time for yourself.

If there are three or four of you committed to simplifying, it might make more sense to arrange for a weekly meeting where you can all get together and share in round-robin fashion.

For five people, for example, you could plan to meet for an hour and a half, allowing fifteen minutes for each person to share their own experiences from the week, followed by a wrap-up for fifteen minutes or so.

Agree on the meeting arrangement in advance so you can launch right in without wasted time or effort. Use the wrap-up to evaluate the effectiveness of your session and determine whether or not you need to make any changes in the process.

Make this gathering a model of simplification. Eliminate the extraneous stuff, such as refreshments, that quickly become one more complication in your life. For now, the goal is to use the group meeting as an aid to get to the simple life as efficiently as possible.

## 35. How to Deal with People Who Don't Understand

In making the decision to simplify your life, you run the risk of going against the generally accepted American standard of success. Friends and associates who are still looking to Madison Avenue or to corporate America or the media to define what success is for them may well find your desire for a simpler life tantamount to heresy. They'll think you've gone soft. Or that maybe you just don't have what it takes to succeed in the "real" world.

Sometimes—though they wouldn't admit it—they see your new lifestyle as a threat to their own.

To many, the idea of paring down and living a simple life seems not only impractical, it's unthinkable. The question often is, "Why would you want to have only a little when you can have a lot? Or even have it all?"

The reactions you receive can range anywhere from friendly teasing, to well-intentioned advice about hanging in there, to outright ostracism.

And you may go through your own period of confusion. If you've spent a good deal of your life in recent years allowing your professional persona to define who you are, not only to yourself, but to your family, your friends, your colleagues, and your community, you may sometimes find yourself in situations where it's a real challenge to let go of that identity.

As you move along in your plan to simplify, take whatever time you feel is necessary to explain to friends your plan to create a life outside the narrow confines of what passes for success in the world. But don't be surprised if they don't immediately join you in your quest.

It takes courage to buck the tide, but once you start to experience the freedom that comes from actively creating your own interpretation of success, you'll find it easy to move on from people who haven't yet figured out that having it all or spending long hours at an unsatisfying job will never define who they truly are, no matter how high the pay.

You'll no doubt soon reach the point, where you can say, as Cynthia Ferguson did (#3), "I've stopped trying to explain to people. Now I just let them wonder why I seem so happy and secure in myself these days."

# 36. Find a Happy Medium That Works for You

One of the things I did in the early stages of our simplification program was to get rid of our houseplants. Our cat, Speed—named after a strong female character from one of Gibbs's novels—was a strong female cat who got into the habit of eating the leaves of the plants; then she'd throw up on the carpet. It got to be such a hassle that it came down to deciding whether to get rid of the plants or to get rid of the cat.

Because Speed is such a wonderful cat in every other respect, we decided the houseplants would have to go.

It was only after I'd passed my plants on to friends and neighbors that I saw how much effort they'd been. As one reader wrote, "I had never realized how time consuming my houseplants were. They're like kids—you've got to feed them, water them, and pick up after them. Like you, I got rid of all my plants and simplified my life!"

But after several years without plants, I reached a point where I missed having them. I also realized that one of the reasons they'd been such a complication earlier was that my plant population had gotten out of control—I'd had far too many of them.

A while back a friend gave me a beautiful Phalenopsis orchid and I've found, to my delight, that this is one plant Speed won't touch. Orchids are low-maintenance plants that require minimal care, never drop their leaves, and have an exquisite bloom that lasts for months. So now I have a couple of gorgeous orchids around the house that I enjoy immensely. Not only are they beautiful, but they're so simple.

So, in getting rid of *all* the plants, I'd gotten carried away. Even though it simplified my life in the beginning stages to be free of them, I eventually found that having one or two beautiful plants added a lot to my life. I'd come back to a happy medium for me.

Just be aware that you may have to take some drastic steps in the early stages of simplifying your life that will make things easier for you during the process of getting to simple—such as cutting out the newspapers, eliminating some of the routine household chores, or temporarily dropping a lot of your social activities.

Then, as you achieve a certain level of comfort and ease by simplifying other areas of your life, you may decide to go back to some of your previous practices. Or you may find that by doing them differently from the way you did when your life was hectic, they can contribute something to your life in their new incarnation.

## 37. Keep Asking, "Is This Going to Simplify My Life?"

$A$s Gibbs and I went through the process of simplifying, we got into the habit of asking ourselves, "Is this going to simplify our lives?" every time we considered a potential purchase, or a new service, or a change to our routine.

For example, one of the things we thought we wanted to do, as we were offloading many of the possessions we'd accumulated during our hard-charging years, was cut back to one car. Since I work at home and Gibbs now had an easy ten-minute commute to his office, we thought that with a bit of judicious planning, we could easily get by with only one set of wheels.

So when we moved to the condo and found ourselves on a bus line that provided direct access to Gibbs's place of work, we thought, Aha! Now is the time to get rid of the old Plymouth.

But before we did, we decided to try the bus schedule. It worked well for some months, until Gibbs's office setup changed and the bus schedule was no longer convenient. And at the same time, my schedule required that I spend more time on the road and so I needed the car more than I had.

We were still philosophically disposed to getting rid of one of the cars, but the reality was that, given our new schedule and the limited public transportation in a part of the country that relies heavily on the automobile, it wouldn't actually simplify our lives to do so.

At another point we were doing some minor renovations to our home and had drawn up a list of the changes we wanted to make. By this time we'd gotten into the habit of asking ourselves, "Is this going to simplify our lives?" So we went down the list and were able to eliminate over half the things we'd originally thought we'd need to have done.

Yes, it would simplify our lives to replace the aging, small-capacity washer that tended to mangle the clothes and the decrepit dryer that had only one setting (fry). And, yes, adding a kitty door to the cat box would simplify not only the cleanup and maintenance, but would provide more space in the already limited closet where the cat box was housed.

But the kitchen countertops were fine, and replacing them would add nothing to their serviceability, but a good deal to the expense and a lot of disruption to our lives in the interim. It was simpler to leave them as they were.

Our culture is replete with so-called convenience items—call waiting, E-mail, the food processor—or alternative approaches to situations that at first glance appear to be simplifiers, or which might simplify someone else's life, but which on closer inspection would only complicate our own.

We've found the habit of asking "Will this really simplify our lives?" a powerful weapon in the ongoing battle against the complications of modern life.

# FIVE

# Getting Rid of
# Our Stuff

## 38. Where to Start

If you're ready to begin unloading the stuff that's been cluttering up your life, and you don't know where to start, start with the easy stuff.

I heard from a woman recently who had an office full of files, family papers, legal documents, reports, journal articles and other paraphernalia for projects she had worked on.

She knew she needed to bite the bullet, go through all that stuff, make some difficult decisions about what to keep, and eventually throw out a lot of it. But because it seemed like such a monumental task, she couldn't seem to get going on it.

So I suggested she leave the office alone for the time being, and start somewhere else. Like with the linens.

Has there ever been a linen closet that wasn't chock full of well-worn, mismatched sheets that will never be used again? Or sheets that may be in perfectly good shape, but that fit the bed you gave away three years ago? Or stacks of bath towels and washcloths that don't match your current color scheme and you'll never again hang on a towel rack?

What about the tablecloths and napkin sets that you haven't used in years because you can't bear the thought of ironing them? You know you'll never use that stuff again. Pass it on to someone who can.

The kitchen is often another safe place. Start with the very top shelves in the kitchen cabinets. Get rid of anything that is covered with a thin coating of grime—it's a safe bet you haven't used it in a while, and probably never will again.

Pull out all the so-called convenience items such as the bread makers, plate warmers, and the pasta machines you've only used once in five years, and pass them along to someone who might like to have them. (They won't use those things more than once or twice either, but at least they won't be sitting on your shelves collecting dust.)

Look at any other areas in your home where it would be easy for you to go in and clear out—under the sinks, or the shelves in the laundry room, or the inner depths of the basement, perhaps the front hall closet, and start tossing.

This sounds so obvious, but often people feel trapped by the things they're afraid to let go of or that they know will be difficult for them to deal with, so they never get started at all. But if you get going with the easy stuff, and you see how good it feels to be free of it, it's so much easier to go on to the harder stuff.

Once you're in the decluttering mode, get to the hard stuff as quickly as you can. One of the objectives here is to use the momentum you've generated on the easy things to propel you into the discarding mode for the harder stuff.

As reader Nancy Hawkins wrote, "After buying and trying to follow books about how to be organized I was thrilled to realize I needed to simplify and *get rid of the clutter*, not just rearrange piles of stuff in a new way."

It's so true. If you just get rid of the clutter you never have to *organize* it.

## 39. Getting Rid of the Stuff Doesn't Necessarily Mean Getting Rid of *Everything*

Invariably when I talk to groups about simplifying and the issue of clutter comes up, someone will say something like, "I've gone through and cleared out a lot of stuff in my home, but I've got this stash of medals from when I was an Olympic swimmer. I know they're taking up space and I never wear them or even look at them much anymore, but I can't bear to throw them out. What do you suggest?"

Sometimes, it's a box of mementos, or a record collection, or their grandmother's fine china. My answer is simple. If you can't bear to throw them out, then *don't*.

Gibbs and I both love books. We love reading them. We love having them in our home. When we first started clearing out stuff, we had no intention of thinning out our collection of books. They meant too much to us.

Then, after we'd gotten rid of a driveway full of stuff we

weren't using anymore, and we experienced the tremendous feeling of liberation that comes from unloading, we decided to rethink our position on the books.

We went through the shelves and started pulling down tomes we knew we'd never read again. Some we sold to a local used-book shop. Others we donated to our public library. Every year or so we have gone through and pulled out more books that we now see we can do without.

But we still have a lot of books, and I can't imagine we'll ever get rid of every one of them. After all, one of the main reasons we simplified our lives was so we'd have time to do the reading we want to do.

Getting rid of the clutter is not about letting go of things that are meaningful to you. It's about letting go of the things that no longer contribute to your life so you have the time and the energy and the space for the things that do.

Also, keep in mind that our identities are often connected to our stuff. When we start unloading it, it feels like we're giving away part of ourselves. But unloading some of it can also help us move into the self we want to be.

## 40. Look at All the Things You Hold on to Because You Might Need Them Someday

As we were getting ready for the garage sale that would clear out of our lives forever all the things we had decided to let go on round one of our uncluttering process, we stopped for a brief moment and looked at all the stuff we had piled in the driveway.

Gibbs pointed out that we'd been holding on to most of this stuff on the theory that we *might need it someday.*

It's so easy to do this. You come across some seemingly fabulous thing you have no earthly use for at the moment, but you think, "I never know when I might need a whatever-this-is." And you put it on the back shelf somewhere (along with all the other things you never know when you might need).

And you think, "Well, it doesn't take much room, and it's not hurting anything. I'll keep it on hand just in case I ever need it."

But often these are things you have to keep clean, or maybe you have to wrap them carefully so they don't get broken. Sometimes these things are so valuable you have to insure them. If nothing else, you have to provide that back shelf for them. And so, at some level, they are weighing on your consciousness and impinging on your life.

As we stood in the driveway that day we realized that if there was something we ever did need from all this stuff, we could, in a pinch, go out and get it again. In fact, we could've replaced the entire driveway full of stuff for a few hundred dollars.

But the interesting thing is that now, five years later, there hasn't been even one thing we wished we'd held on to.

Well, there *was* an old pair of cowboy boots I put in the pile because they'd been sitting in the closet, unused, for some time. I was afraid they were housing a black widow spider and didn't want to put my hand in there to find out. Later, I kind of wished I'd saved them. But when I remember them accurately I know that they were so worn-out I never would have worn them again.

But other than that, nothing.

So, if you ever find yourself tempted to put something on the back shelf because you think you might need it someday, remember that *replacing* it (and all the other things on the back shelf you think you might need) is probably a lot easier than maintaining the space required to store it all.

And if you ever find yourself wistfully wishing you'd held on to something, it's seldom as wonderful or as suitable for your needs as you remember it being.

# 41. One Knife, One Fork, One Spoon

Reader Grace Samis described what I've found to be a great simplifier for many areas of the house where stuff tends to accumulate.

She wrote, "I'm working on having only two items more of 'things' than people that live in the house...meaning plates, glasses, cups, knives, forks, spoons, pillows, blankets, sheets, towels, etc. For example, if there are four people in the household, keep only six plates.

"This is a threefold treasure. First, this gives you more space in your household. Second, it forces you to keep up with the cleaning—you can't let the dishes pile up if you need them for the next meal. Third, and most importantly, you can't have unwanted guests over too often. With no extra plates, no extra pillows, no extra blankets, uninvited visitors can't just come for a casual visit for any great length of time without some hard planning!"

I love this idea for a number of reasons. First, it gives you a specific goal to work toward in the ongoing process of uncluttering. Once you set this limit—or any other limit that works for you—there's no guessing. No wondering, should I keep this or that. It's so easy: Just two more things than people, and everything beyond that goes out or to someone else who can use it.

Secondly, it not only frees up more space in the household—in the kitchen cabinets, bath cabinets, linen closet—it makes it so much easier to keep track of things. I know I've got exactly what I need for our own use, and then just two more. No more digging around in the back of closets or pulling out the stepladder to climb to the top shelf of the pantry, because I think there might be something useful back there. Now I know what's there, and it's only two more than what I use everyday.

Obviously, if you entertain a lot, this wouldn't work—unless you were open to the idea of keeping some disposable plates and utensils on hand. Or, you could go for a variation on the potluck meal and have people bring their own knives and forks and spoons.

Of course, Grace, the ultimate way to deal with unwanted houseguests is to learn to just say no(#57). But this is a workable solution until we can learn to do that.

## 42. Start Over Again, and Do It Right

I've heard from and talked to many people who described how Mother Nature simplified their lives for them. They'd lost their home and many or all of their possessions through fires, floods, earthquakes, mudslides, or some other disaster. Losing everything you own under such circumstances can be devastating, but the people I've heard from all saw their loss, ultimately, as a blessing.

"The fire saved us the agony of deciding what to keep and what to get rid of," one woman wrote. And once all those things were no longer there, she and her husband saw how they had weighed them down and complicated their lives.

"There was so much stuff we never used and that was just taking up space. We vowed when we started over, we'd replace only what we needed, and this time we'd do it right. We've kept our promise: We don't have much now, but what we have is exactly what we want. "

Though we've never had a catastrophic loss such as that, Gibbs and I did have a close call shortly before we decided to simplify. At that time we lived in a fire zone. One night a firestorm raged through and destroyed over six hundred homes in our community. That tragedy gave us the opportunity to look objectively at the goods we'd accumulated.

We saw that there was so much we could get rid of and not only never miss, but be better off without. Having almost lost it all, we found it much easier to let go of the things we knew we'd never use again.

Obviously, there's a tremendous difference between geting rid of possessions and losing them through a natural disaster without having a say in the matter. And this is not to minimize the tragedy and pain such a loss can generate.

But you might think about how you would approach the acquisition process if you had it to do all over again. Look around your home and make a list of what you would replace.

Make another list of things you wouldn't acquire again no matter what, and in fact would be happy to be rid of.

When you're ready to start unloading some of your stuff, that list will be a good place to start.

## 43. Take a Picture of It

The young woman with the collection of medals and awards from her Olympic swimming days was in a quandary. She had just moved to a smaller, simpler place and wanted to keep a sparse, clean look to her life for the moment. She couldn't bear to get rid of the medals altogether, yet she didn't want them cluttering up her space.

She brought this up at a talk I gave, and one of the other members of the audience suggested that she sort the items, set aside the ones that had the most meaning for her, lay them out in an interesting arrangement, and take a photograph of them. Or she might photograph them individually, and create a photo montage she could hang on the wall.

Or she could simply photograph them, donate them to a school or an art class where they could be used by students for various projects, and keep the photos in a file folder.

This last idea appealed to her. She had already made the decision to keep the walls of her new space free of distractions, at least for the time being.

A photo montage wouldn't work for everything, but you might consider it as a possibility.

Don't let the photos clutter up your life, however. Many people wrote to say that photos, perhaps more than any other personal item, can clutter up closets, drawers, desks, shelves, and multiple nooks and crannies. If this is true in your house, gather from all the corners of your home every photograph you've taken or that has been given to you over your lifetime. Sort through them, mercilessly tossing out any shot that's out of focus, or that is of someone you've never seen before, or that you never want to be reminded of again. Arrange the remaining photos in albums in whatever order seems appropriate. This will eliminate a lot of clutter and provide a simple and enjoyable way for you to share family memories.

## 44. Never Touch a Piece of Mail More than Once

I'd heard about this approach to the seemingly endless torrent of paper that flows across our desks and through our lives. And for years I'd thought, "It might work for others, but it would never work for me." I felt I always had too much stuff coming in at any one time to handle it all right then and there. So I'd set it aside, and then I'd have to come up with *a lot more time* to handle *a lot more of it* later.

When I simplified my life, I did cut back on the number of journals, magazines, and newspapers that come into my home and office every day. I also drastically reduced the junk mail I was subjected to (#45).

As I began to simplify even more, and started letting go of a lot of the real estate and other business associations that generated a heavy load of mail, not only were there far fewer bills coming in each day, but eventually I arranged for the bills that did show up to be handled by automatic payment through my bank (#80).

But after hearing over and over again from readers of Simplify Your Life that handling it once was a major simplifier, I decided to try it.

Now I set aside an hour at the end of my workday to read the mail and to deal with the stream of paper that comes through the door. Most days it takes only a few moments to sort through the mail, send off a postcard response as needed, read any pertinent articles or newsletters, file anything I might need to refer to later, and toss out what I don't need to keep.

The better I get at making decisions on the spot as to what to keep, the more I can toss into the recycling bin, and the less stuff I have to file.

I also found it doesn't work to think "I can't read this article now, or make that decision at this moment," and set it aside for later. When I do that, I'm soon right back where I started, inundated with paperwork. But by keeping that hour at the end of the day to read it now, or to do whatever I need to do to make a decision now—place a phone call or do some research—I can usually deal with it immediately and be finished with it. We have to decide at some point what to do with it. I've learned it's better to decide now.

It's so liberating not to have stacks of paper weighing down the edges of my desk and the corners of my mind. Now the mail is all taken care of in just a few minutes or at the most an hour each day.

If it takes more than the allotted hour to deal with a particular item, then I'll set it aside for the next afternoon. Though now that I've gradually reduced the volume of mail and have increased my ability to decide right now how to deal with something, I seldom have to deal with it later.

If it takes less than the allotted hour to deal with the day's mail, which now it usually does, then I've got a sweet little bit of leisure time which I can use to stroll through the garden, call a friend, or just sit quietly and do nothing.

Learning to handle it only once ranks high on the list of steps I've taken to keep the clutter to a minimum.

This also applies to magazines and newspapers. I heard from

many people who simplified their lives by reading the morning paper as soon as it arrives, then passing it on to a friend or neighbor or taking it into the office to share with a co-worker. Not only does this practice reduce the clutter that otherwise often stays in your life, but it reduces the expense of newspaper and magazine subscriptions. As with many aspects of simplifying, it has some positive effects on the environment as well. If everyone did it we could drastically reduce the amount of paper that has to be produced for these products and, ultimately, cut back on the volume of paper that has to be recycled each day.

## 45. Junk Mail Update

Junk mail is certainly one of the major complications of modern life, and few things add more useless stuff to our clutter. In *Simplify Your Life* I describe how we cut back on the amount of junk mail that comes into our home by writing to the Mail Preference Service (P.O. Box 9008, Farmingdale, NY, 22735-9008) and requesting that our name not be sold to any mailing list companies.

As my friend Donna wrote from Chicago, that's a start, but there is much more you can do. She says, "I cut my mail down from literally two cubic feet a week to just a neat handful a day by applying the techniques in the booklet *Stop Junk Mail Forever* by Marc Eisenson (available from Good Advice Press, Elizaville, NY, 12523 (914) 758-1400 for $3). The notification of mail preferenced service alone won't do it. I found out my professional journals, professional organizations, auto insurance, charge cards, credit bureaus, and so on, were all selling my name. Also, standardizing my name and address on our self-inking stamper helped so I wouldn't get on different lists due to variant spellings, for example, without middle initial, spelling out North instead of abbreviating. I've got a little stamp made up in a red ink: DO NOT LEASE SELL TRADE MY NAME ADDRESS. My mail carrier is very appreciative too."

I took Donna's advice and ordered this booklet. In my opinion, it's worth its weight in gold. In addition to information on how to contact the Mail Preference Service, it lists roughly eighteen steps you can take to literally stop junk mail forever, and to stop unwanted phone calls, too.

It took me less than an hour to call (when 800 numbers were available) or to send a postcard to the junk mail handling organizations listed in this booklet, requesting that our names be removed from all the major lists. It has made an incredible difference in the amount of mail I have to deal with each day. And it has also greatly reduced the number of temptations we're exposed to in the form of glossy four-color catalogs filled with stuff no one really needs.

If you're burdened by junk mail or telephone solicitations, order this book.

## 46. Don't Even Think about Saving That Piece of Aluminum Foil

We've all heard the stories about the little old lady who passed on, leaving her heirs a ball of string the size of a Buick or a mountain-high stack of newspapers she'd never had time to read. Or the drawers full of stubby and broken pencils and now stretchless rubber bands that no one would ever use, even if they were the last rubber bands on the planet.

Maybe you have an accumulation of these, or similarly useless items, sequestered away somewhere. If you do, you may be ahead of the game: With an ample supply of such superfluous material, you'll never have to save another piece of string or a thumbtack with a bend on the pointy end.

I never had a problem with coupons whose expiration date had passed or last year's denomination of stamps—at least not a *serious* problem. But for years my downfall was used 8 1/2 x 11-inch envelopes.

Being married to a writer/editor who is constantly receiving manuscripts in large manila envelopes, I had a prodigious and never-ending supply of used envelopes. As a new manuscript came in, I could never throw out that envelope. I clung to it tenaciously on the theory that I might need it someday. One or two, possibly. But hundreds?

When I started clearing out the clutter, I took a huge gulp and eliminated all but a dozen used manilas. I've trained myself, with some effort, so that I put them in the recycling bin instead of bringing them into my office. Whenever the mail carrier delivers another one, I repeat to myself, slowly and with great feeling, *don't even think about saving this envelope.*

I've been able to let go of most of the inessentials. By using this mantra I now have merely a dozen used manila envelopes I'll never use, rather than hundreds of them. Well, nobody's perfect.

You might find it helpful to come up with a similar mantra for the times you're tempted to squirrel away any of the items you tend to stockpile. Things like used plastic wrap, newspaper clippings you'll never look at again, magazines with an article you'd like to read if you could only remember what relevance it had to your life, extensions of pipe that won't work for any plumbing repair job you'll ever attempt in this lifetime, milk cartons you'll never use to make candles, bits of fabric you'll never turn into quilts, twisties past their prime, the small pad of address labels sent by a worthy charity printed with your former address, the small boxes of business cards from a company you haven't worked for in five years, a 1992 telephone directory, ballpoint pens that no longer have ink, sprung paper clips, keys whose provenance is unknown, bald emery boards, broken sunglasses, ID tags for the previous dog, bus tokens for the Topeka Transit System when you live in Duluth and have no plans to return to Kansas, and the plastic doohickey that used to fit something though you haven't a clue what. You won't remember what it used to fit until you throw it out. If you ever could retrieve it, you'd find that it didn't fit what you thought it did anyway.

Next time you find yourself standing in front of the drawer into which you're planning to tuck away a bit of thrice-used foil too small to keep, let yourself go, and throw it out.

# 47. Use Your Public Library

I've used the library extensively for years, but it wasn't until I started getting letters from readers, especially from mothers with young children, that I began to recognize the extent to which it could minimize the clutter.

Public libraries are for most people an easy and readily available solution for cutting back on the amount of stuff that comes into our homes, not only in terms of the books we read, but also in terms of magazines, newspapers, newsletters, audiotapes, videotapes, CDs, reference sources, and information services of almost limitless variety.

In addition to providing an ever-ready source of the latest books and reading material at minimal or no cost, public libraries also, through the ever-impending due date, supply the impetus to read these materials in a timely fashion. While we may not read every single book or magazine we bring home from the library, at least they won't be cluttering up our night-stands and bookshelves on a permanent basis; at some point we have to take them back to the library.

Libraries also supply a practical way to offload the stacks of your own books and audio- and videotapes that are cluttering up your environment. Not only will donating books to the library free up space in your home and office, but it provides such a simple and satisfying way to share your resources with others.

At the very least, when you donate books to the library—if your library keeps them—you always know where they are should you want to read them again. You can thereby have your books and not have them at the same time. It's hard to get simpler than that.

## 48. Get Some Help

I hear from people all the time who, once they saw how much it would simplify their lives to get rid of the clutter, jumped right in and started throwing stuff out. But many are not inclined to move so quickly and could use some hand-holding through this process. If you need some help, get it.

Ask a family member, one of your simplicity buddies, or a friend who knows you well to help you. You want someone who has the strength of character to overlook your whines and half-hearted entreaties when you want to hold on to thirty years of *National Geographic* magazines and throws them out anyway, but who has the heart to let you keep your high school yearbooks.

Pick your starting point—the attic, the closets, or wherever. If you really want to be brave, take a deep breath, and have them go through the attic *without* you: Let them make the decisions about what to get rid of. You don't have a clue what's in those boxes anyway. So how can you possibly miss them?

Or establish some parameters ahead of time. They can throw out anything that was made prior to 1990. They can get rid of any clothes, but they can't touch the books.

I did this with a friend who couldn't bear to get rid of a lot of the clothes in her closet, even though she knew there were many things she'd never wear again. I went through the closet with her standing by, but we decided that I would make the initial decision regarding what stayed and what went out. (It's so much easier to toss it on the out pile when it's not yours.) When we were finished, she could go back through the stack and retrieve three items.

Then we made arrangements for a local thrift store to haul the rest away quickly, before she could change her mind. It was such a relief for her not to have to make the decisions about what had to go.

Not only does this relieve you of the responsibility of deciding what to get rid of, but you can always blame them if you decide later that there was something you would have kept!

If you don't trust your friends or family in this sometimes delicate task, another alternative is to hire a personal organizer to help you. If you can't locate one in the yellow pages, contact the National Association of Professional Organizers (512) 206-0151 to see if they can refer you to a professional organizer in your area.

# SIX

# Changing Our Consumer Habits

# 49. The Thirty-Day List

Now that we've addressed ways to get rid of some of your stuff, let's talk about what you can do to keep the clutter from piling up again.

Have you ever found yourself wandering through a department store and coming across something you felt you just had to have? It's entirely possible that until you saw it on display, you didn't even know it existed. But now that you've seen it, you want it. And you want it now.

Often, whether you need it or not, whether you can afford it or not, whether you truly want it or not, you buy it, and bring it home. Maybe you use it once or twice, or even half a dozen times.

Eventually you come across this thing lying around the house somewhere and you wonder why on earth you ever bought it to begin with. Invariably, it ends up on that back shelf.

This scenario is played out over and over again in the lives of millions of people every day. Why? Because advertisers spend billions of dollars each year training us to react this way. It's a safe bet for their money—experience has shown we can be convinced to buy *anything*.

After Gibbs and I got rid of a lot of clutter and moved to our smaller place, we noticed, as I mentioned earlier, that we were going out and buying stuff to fill it up again. We realized we were going to have to change our buying patterns.

We decided to set up a thirty-day list. If we came across a significant item we thought we wanted, we'd put it on this list before we'd rush out to buy it. If at the end of thirty days we could remember what it was for, we might consider acquiring it. Or, we had the option at that point to extend the date for another thirty days. More often than not, at the end of the first thirty days, we couldn't remember why we wanted this thing in the first place.

You might consider using a similar system to keep youself and other family members from rushing to buy the next thing you see advertised that you think you want. It does require a

modicum of discipline, but not only will it save you a considerable bundle of money, it will greatly reduce the amount of stuff
which comes into your home that you then eventually have to
get rid of.

## 50. Watch for the Early Warning Signs

Another thing we found helpful in the process of changing our buying habits was to become aware of the early warning signs of a potential buying transaction. There were at least two major signals we could learn to recognize and do something about.

First there are the physiological signs. You may find yourself innocently browsing when you quite unexpectedly come across something you think you'd like to buy. You'll begin to feel a slight palpitation of the heart. Soon your pulse starts to quicken. You feel a rush of adrenaline. Part of you wants to hold back. Another part of you is reaching for your credit card. You may experience shortness of breath. You might even salivate. In extreme cases you start to drool, though not so much that anyone would notice.

Then come the psychological rationalizations. You hear yourself listing all the reasons you should have this thing. You need it.

It'll make your life better. You deserve it. You've earned it, for godsake. It's on sale! It's been ages since you splurged a little. We only live once. It's only a hundred bucks. Your whole psyche is itching for this thing.

The itch is a critical juncture. Once you start to scratch it, it's all over.

This is where you train yourself to pull out your thirty-day list—the list on which you write down every significant item you feel you have to have but that you refuse to buy immediately. Keep it wrapped around your credit card, or in your check register.

When you reach for your thirty-day list, you can trick your mind into thinking you're reaching for your money, which gives you a slight relief from the itch and reduces the urge.

In that brief moment, the part of your brain that the advertiser has a hold of relaxes a little, and you come back to reality for a moment. The reality is that you don't really want this thing, you have no conceivable use for it, but an extremely clever advertising and marketing campaign has gotten you to think you do.

Immediately write down on your thirty-day list the date and the name of the item. Put the list back in your pocket. Turn around and leave the premises posthaste.

You'll be amazed at how just being aware of the warning signs will simplify your life.

## 51. Come Up with a Creative Solution Rather than a Buying Solution

One of the first pieces of gear we unloaded was our exercycle.

We had purchased it a number of years before, secondhand though barely used: a big, beautiful, shiny, monolithic testament to consumer gullibility. I rode it perhaps half a dozen times; then it sat in the corner of our bedroom collecting dust, making me feel guilty every time I walked by it.

We've congratulated ourselves many times over these past few years for having had the good sense to get rid of it when we were clearing out the clutter.

Recently, after five exercise-equipment-free years of walking along the beach every morning, we started thinking that we might be able to meet our exercise needs more effectively with a different shiny, monolithic testament to consumer gullibility: a treadmill.

Our puppies provided our excuse. Over the past year our walks had gradually regressed into doggie strolls with frequent pauses while the dogs do what dogs really prefer to do on walks: sniff. Gradually, we lost the aerobic and calorie-burning benefits of our daily walks.

We still enjoyed these strolls with the dogs and the opportunity they gave us to be outdoors together, watching sunrises or sunsets and delighting in the beauty of nature.

But they weren't exercise.

So we started thinking about an alternative approach. We came across a series of ads for a treadmill that seemed to address our very problem. The seduction had begun. So, even though we should know better, we succumbed once again to the lure of the advertising dollar.

Well, we *almost* succumbed. Thanks to our thirty-day list and the fact that we'd become aware of the changes in our vital signs, we stopped ourselves in the nick of time. We'd come so close to spending money for a six-foot-long, three-foot-wide piece of plug-in equipment that provided absolutely no benefit that a slight change in our schedule wouldn't provide much more simply and at no expense.

Our solution, after resisting the urge to acquire the treadmill, was simple and obvious: We stroll once around the half-mile length of the park with the dogs for our warm-up and their sniffs, and then we take them back to the car. We increase our speed to a brisk pace and walk twice more around the park for our aerobic exercise. It's so simple.

But I'm embarrassed to confess how close we came to capitulating to a complicated and ultimately ineffective buying solution.

I mention it because I suspect there are many people, perhaps even you, who are sometimes as susceptible as we are to an effective ad campaign.

I want to point out that our solution might not necessarily be your solution. When I asked the clerk in the aerobic equipment store what the benefit of this machine was over simply getting out and walking faster, he replied: "It's the time and inclement weather displacement factor."

Meaning, if you have to spend half an hour driving to the park to walk, or if you live in Minneapolis and can't walk outdoors six months out of the year because of the weather, a treadmill might provide a simple way to get your exercise.

But since our park is only a few minutes away and we live in a climate where it rains roughly three days a year, these reasons are not relevant for us. And an expensive treadmill is not the answer for us.

Take the time to come up with other solutions to your next perceived buying need, or at the very least, wait for a few days to let the immediate gratification impulse lose its hold on you. It's so easy to end up, as many of us have, with an expensive piece of machinery that does nothing more than sit idly collecting dust, while cluttering up our lives.

## 52. Recognize the Point of Diminishing Returns

When we were deciding what to get rid of, our stereo and record collection were high on the list.

Even though at that point we had invested a fair amount of money in our stereo system, and even though we'd enjoyed having it, we realized that since we'd acquired our VCR we seldom listened to the stereo anymore. The reality is that we can't watch videos and listen to records or tapes at the same time. And we'd reached a point in our lives where, if we're not watching old movies, we prefer a quiet evening of reading.

Most households now have one or more television sets, one or more radios, half a dozen tape players, a video camera, a VCR, a stereo system, a CD player, several Walkmans, and a dozen computer games that fill up the space and the time that used to be taken up by a single household radio. Isn't it ironic that we're acquiring more and more goods, but have less and less time to spend with them?

But even if we had the leisure time that our parents or our grandparents had, there is a point of diminishing returns. You might want to keep this in mind the next time you're considering the acquisition of one more item that will take up time and space in your life. At the very least, consider passing on to someone else the items you'll no longer have time for.

## 53. When You Bring In Something New, Throw Out Something Old

I got this idea from readers. It's such a basic concept. It's so simple. And it works. You can teach it to your kids. You can easily put it into practice in your own life.

Well, it's not always so easy; but it'll definitely help you keep the clutter to manageable limits.

It applies to clothes, books, toys, shoes, tools, dishes, glassware, kitchen gadgets, computers and other electronic equipment, telephones, eyeglasses, linens, towels, pillows, umbrellas, and among other things, furniture.

Furniture? Yes. And this is the one area where most people already put this idea into practice. Given the limitations of the average home, if you purchase a new couch, more often than not you'll pass the old one on to someone else who might be able to use it. Otherwise, the living room would quickly be quite obviously overcrowded.

But in other areas of our homes, the overcrowding is not so immediately apparent. Most bookcases can hold another book. Most closets can hold another outfit. Most kitchen pantries can hold another toaster oven. Most toy boxes can hold another Barbie doll. And so forth. Up to a point.

When we go beyond that point, our stuff starts to get out of hand. If we'd started way-back-when throwing out the old when we brought in the new, we wouldn't have tool chests so jammed we can never find a screwdriver, or lingerie drawers so crammed we can never find a decent pair of knee socks, or linen closets so full of everything else that we can't open the door without having half the contents come tumbling down around our ankles.

Gibbs and I have learned to use this method to keep our books within bounds. Now, when we acquire a new book, we go through the shelves and pick an old book to pass on to someone else. We also use this system with our clothes.

It's often difficult to predict ahead of time the point at which there's too much stuff for any given space. But if you get in the habit of throwing out the old when you bring in the new, you won't have to predict. You can simply enjoy the freedom of uncluttered spaces.

# 54. The Simple Souvenir

As a travel writer, Gibbs spends a good deal of time visiting interesting places around the globe.

It started to become obvious that we'd soon overload our family and friends and run out of space in our home if we continued to bring back shrunken heads from every place we visited. Aside from the expense, there was always the hassle of fitting one more thing into the luggage, maneuvering through customs, and arriving back home with the item still intact.

Early on we began keeping souvenir matchbook covers from the restaurants we visited on our travels. We now have one huge bowl that sits on our kitchen countertop that holds hundreds of matchbooks. Hardly a week goes by that one of us doesn't reach in, pull out a matchbook, read the inscription, and pull up a wonderful memory from our travels.

The Plow and Angel, the San Ysidro Ranch where we fell in love. The Three Georges, Georgetown, where we spent our honeymoon. The Pacific International Hotel, Cairns, Australia. Jumby Bay, Antigua. The Wakaya Club, Fiji Islands. Johnny Sesaws, Peru, Vermont. The Atlantic Inn, Block Island.

The matchbooks are colorful. They're lightweight. They're nonbreakable. They require no special packaging and they fit easily into a jacket pocket for the trip home. They're available everywhere. They're low maintenance. They don't need to be insured. They're functional. They're free. Eighteen years of memories that fit into a decorative bowl. The ideal souvenir for the simple life.

Other simple souvenirs that won't run you out of house and home and pocketbook include airline luggage tags, postcards, small flag insignia, or postage stamps from foreign countries.

## 55. What to Tell the Grandkids

Recently a woman pulled me aside after one of my speaking engagements and told me all the steps she and her husband had taken to simplify their lives. This included accepting an early retirement package offered by her husband's employer, selling their house, paring down their possessions to what would fit into their motor home, and setting out for two to three years to travel around the country to see the sights and to visit their four children and nine grandchildren who were scattered around the country.

Her problem was, what to tell the grandchildren when they asked what she and Grandpa wanted for Christmas, or birthdays, or as going away mementos.

Being supportive grandparents, they didn't want to discourage their grandchildren's creative endeavors. But they were so delighted to have reached a point where they were free of time- and energy-consuming possessions. They had exactly what they wanted, and they didn't have room in their scaled-back lifestyle to accommodate a lot of *chotchkes*, no matter how imaginative the object or well intentioned the thought behind it.

The answer seemed obvious to me: Ask for a box of home-made fudge, or a basket of Christmas cookies, or any other *consumable* items within the range of the kids' talents and their parents' patience.

A gift of this type encourages thoughtful and resource-conscious gift giving on the part of the children, while providing the grandparents with a sweet reminder of the gift bearer.

The gift would be short lived—only as long as it takes to consume a box of brownies—but the memory of it could last forever. ("Remember how delicious Sara's gingerbread men tasted that evening as we watched the sun set over the Grand Canyon?")

It wouldn't put a strain on their space limitations, nor would it ultimately be one more thing to discard into our overloaded ecosystem.

Also, it would be an excellent opportunity to propose to their children and grandchildren that the time has come in all our lives to think about scaling back on our purchasing and consuming habits.

Gift giving doesn't have to mean going to a store to purchase some item that the other person may or may not want, and may or may not have space for. A lovingly crafted card or the joy of quiet time spent together can add far more meaning to our lives than a bagatelle plucked off the consumer merry-go-round. What better way to teach succeeding generations how little we need to be happy.

And what better legacy to leave our kids than a new consumer ethic.

## 56. Put a Moratorium on Shopping

In Chapter Two, I mention that one way to save time is to limit your purchases over the next thirty days to groceries and basic essentials.

This practice has several obvious benefits. Not only will it save you time and money and minimize the clutter, but it will go a long way toward changing your consuming habits.

When Gibbs and I looked at the process we'd gone through to eliminate the stuff we no longer wanted in our lives, we saw that we'd made some fairly wise choices. We had minimized our stuff, and there wasn't much more we needed or wanted to acquire.

Even so, we found ourselves falling into some of our old buying patterns. Since we'd had such great success with our thirty-day list (#49), we decided to take that idea a step further. As an experiment, we put a moratorium on shopping. We decided we wouldn't purchase anything except groceries and personal necessities for three months.

If we began to feel there was something we might want to acquire, we'd either put it on a list for later or we'd come up with a creative solution rather than a buying solution (#51).

Going for three months without shopping for anything but our food and personal items turned out to be so liberating we extended the moratorium for another three months.

This was not about living in austerity or depriving ourselves of the things we need. We approached it as a challenge and an opportunity to break the buying habits that had been a force in our lives. Not only did we save time and money and reduce the clutter that comes into our home, but we drastically changed our consumer mentality. We simply don't acquire stuff like we used to.

When you look at the buying habits that have taken hold in our culture over the past thirty years or so, you can see that we made the decision somewhere along the line to work longer hours so we could acquire more things. We've exchanged our leisure time for stuff.

A lot of us are starting to question that exchange. It hasn't been a good trade-off. Not for us, not for our children, not for the environment.

I urge you to try this moratorium. Even if you do it for only thirty days it'll be an eye-opener. You'll see how little we really need, and how easy it is to get along without most of the things we feel we have to have.

Learning to step off the consumer treadmill has been one of the major benefits Gibbs and I have gotten from simplifying our lives.

# SEVEN

# Learning to
# Say No

# 57. The Truly Free Person

The playwright Jules Renard once said the truly free person is one who can turn down an invitation to dinner without giving an excuse.

It's difficult to imagine anyone actually doing that, and it's impossible for most of us to imagine doing it ourselves. In our culture it's more socially acceptable to be nice than it is to be honest or direct.

The social pressure to automatically say yes to invitations is a challenging one to overcome. There are so many considerations, and they're all mixed in together. At one level we're afraid the other person will feel rejected. At another level we're afraid that if we start saying no, people will reject us. And even though we may not want to go, there's frequently a part of us that wants to be included.

More often than not, our true desire to not accept an invitation has less to do with the invitation we'd like to decline, and more to do with our need or desire to do something else—such as spend time with our kids or a quiet evening with our partner.

But for many, it seems easier to spend an evening having dinner with people we'd rather not have dinner with than it is to put up with the guilt or the discomfort we'd feel if we turned down the invitation in the first place.

Then there are all the shoulds. It's obvious there are some things we feel we should do—like taking care of an ailing parent or helping a friend in need, among others—that we really should do. But there are often many things we feel we should do that, in fact, we don't really have to do. Getting to the point where we can tell the difference is a major milestone in the simplification process.

For some fortunate people this is not a problem. But for many the inability to graciously decline an invitation, or to stop doing all the things they feel they should do, is a major complication. It robs us of many hours we could spend doing something we'd rather do.

As you begin to simplify your life, you're going to be making a lot of changes in the way you spend your time. If saying no is a problem for you, go back to your short list (#21) and keep it firmly in mind. Your objective will be to get to the point where you see that by turning down an invitation you're not saying no to someone else; rather you're saying yes! to what you really want to do.

## 58. One Way to Deal with the Guilt of Saying No

One woman who attended a talk I gave suggested the following solution to the problem of social invitations and the guilt that often accompanies our desire to say no.

She'd been in the travel business for many years and had finally reached a point where she was fed up with constantly being on the go and feeling she had to say yes to every invitation that came across her desk.

When she first started out, she loved the social whirl. It gave her a chance to meet new people and to expand not only her social base but her client base as well. Over the years, both hosting and attending dinner meetings and cocktail parties became an integral part of her life.

But in recent years it had gotten to be too much. She realized she no longer knew where her business life ended and her personal life began.

She decided she needed a breather. So she stopped issuing and accepting social invitations entirely for six months. She said that what made it so easy—and eliminated the guilt—was that she said no to everyone, no exceptions.

Obviously, this freed up a lot of her time, which she used to evaluate where she was in her life. By stopping everything she had a chance to see that she was ready to make some changes in her career. She'd been moving so fast, she was unaware that she was close to burnout.

At the end of six months, she sold her business and moved across the country to start working for a small travel magazine where she could use and develop her writing talents.

Your desire to reduce the number of social activities in your life may have nothing to do with a career move, but you can still use her tactic. Simply decline any and all invitations for a month or two or more. The time you free up could provide a lot of clarity and direction for your life.

If you keep this plan in place long enough, the invitations may stop coming in altogether. This will give you a chance to clean the slate, and perhaps to start all over again. You might choose to do it differently next time.

# 59. Move Beyond the Guilt

Like many people, I used to have a problem with the guilt of saying no. And sometimes I still do.

But my friend, Sue, is much more realistic about dealing with invitations. Her philosophy has helped me eliminate a lot of the guilt that comes from saying no.

She points out that the one who's doing the asking might like you to join them, but if you don't accept the invitation, it won't be the end of the world for them. Someone else will accept, or they'll make other plans, so it's no big deal.

Now, they may *say* it's a big deal. After all, that's the socially acceptable thing to do—what else can one who's extending an invitation do if someone declines, say they're *glad* you're not coming? It's just not done.

So they make regretful noises ("So sorry you can't join us...maybe next time...we'll miss you" and the like). And usually they're sincere, but they're probably not devastated. Those kinds of comments were designed to get everyone off the hook gracefully, not to induce guilt in the one who is declining.

And so the one who gets declined moves on, and they don't think a whole lot about it. In truth, they're too busy getting on with their life or tracking down the next person on their list to hold your no against you. But certainly any momentary flash of regret a host might feel because someone declines is seldom worth the paroxysms of guilt felt by the one who's declining.

After all, when someone turns *you* down, you don't rush to the nearest cliff to leap off. No. You move on. Though you probably say things like you're so sorry they can't join you, you'll miss them, maybe next time, and you usually mean it. But you probably don't think enough about it to justify the guilt they might feel by saying no to you.

Also, keep in mind that you're not doing anyone a favor by showing up for a dinner party or any other type of gathering when your heart isn't in it. You'd be doing the host and everyone else a much greater service by staying home and freeing up the space for someone who'd love to be there.

# 60. Afraid You'll Miss Something?

I was talking to my cousin, Joanie, a while back about the issue of saying no. She and her husband, Joe, had just gone through a brief soul-searching exercise because they'd recently decided they'd been going out too much, and yet they kept finding themselves saying yes to invitations that they really didn't want to accept. When they thought more about it, they realized they were saying yes because they were afraid if they didn't go, they'd miss something.

So they'd go, and invariably they'd find that what they missed out on was a quiet, restful evening at home.

I knew exactly what she meant, because I've often felt that way, too. She said she'd always thought it was a family thing—because everyone in our family feels this way.

But I know from the letters I get and the people I talk to around the country, there are many others who have this problem, too. It's a cultural thing. There are so many opportunities out there, and we don't want to miss any of them. So we frequently find ourselves in the classic dilemma of wanting to go and not wanting to go at the same time.

I've finally reached a point where I know I have to be ready to miss some new things, if only so that I'll then have time to enjoy the old things.

## 61. The Reality of the Urgent Request

Gibbs, who has been an active volunteer for numerous organizations over the years, recently received a card from a group he used to do volunteer work for. On it was a very gracious handwritten note from the director of the group, telling him how much they had missed him and asking him to come back to join them as soon as he could.

Since he's actively involved with a different volunteer organization right now, he knew he couldn't commit to another assignment, but the friendly note gave him a moment's pause, and just a twang of guilt. Maybe he *should* go back and help.

But after he'd thought about it for a bit, he realized the card asking him to come back was merely a routine. His name just happened to come to the top of the list. This doesn't mean they wouldn't love to have him come back, but this was a call to reactivate volunteers, not a device to make anyone feel guilty if they couldn't participate.

The need to fill a spot also applies to many social and work-related requests as well. Keep this in mind the next time someone says you simply must join them (for something you're not interested in), that it just won't be the same without you. It won't, but they'll survive. And so will you.

Another area that is frequently a problem for people are the social functions, or any kind of an event, that people feel they should attend because someone has gone to so much trouble to put them on.

My feeling is that if someone has gone to a lot of trouble to put them on, they presumably did it because they enjoy doing that type of thing. There'll be enough people who show up because they want to be there, so you don't need to feel you have to.

Of course, if no one shows up at all, perhaps it's an indication that the gathering wasn't necessary in the first place.

# 62. How to Say No

$U$nless you're Jules Renard, how you respond to requests for your time depends to some extent on your relationship with the person who's asking.

With friends, just be honest. "Look, I'm simplifying my life right now, and I need to slow down. I'm not going to be going out as much as I have been. It's nothing personal, but I need some time to recharge my batteries."

When a new personal or business acquaintance suggests, "Hey! Let's do lunch sometime!" nip it in the bud. You can casually say you're not doing lunch these days and leave it at that. You don't need to get into a major discussion about it.

To the crazy-makers—the mother-in-law, the next-door neighbor, the hangers-on who are always creating havoc in your life and eating up the time you'd like to spend doing other things—you may simply have to get tough. Put your foot down. And keep putting it down until they get the picture. "Blanche, I'm starting a new project next week and won't be able to do coffee with you for a while. I'll give you a call when my schedule frees up."

When Blanche shows up anyway, be firm and persistent. "Blanche, maybe I didn't make myself clear the other day, but remember I'm starting my new schedule today. I don't have time to visit now. I'll call you later."

If it's someone you feel you should see, then set some parameters. "I'm available on Friday afternoon between one and two to see you," for example. But don't let them take over your life. To do this you may have to let go of your desire to be "nice." You can please some of the people some of the time, but you can't please them all, all of the time.

To requests for volunteer efforts you're not ready for yet, again, a simple explanation with a minimum of details is best. "Sorry. I don't have the time now. I'll call you when my schedule clears up."

For any other situations where you know you need to say no, be inventive. This is your life you're making time for.

# 63. Saying No in the Workplace

You may not have a problem saying no in social situations, but you might be a pushover at work. In *The Overworked American*, Harvard sociologist Juliet Schor reports that many fast trackers have continued to work longer and longer hours without a corresponding increase in pay because they don't know how to say no.

Somehow, in the workplace, corporate management has gotten us to believe that saying no to more work and longer hours is tantamount to being un-American. And there's always the fear that if we don't say yes to whatever time-demanding project is passed our way, someone else will, and we'll be without a job or won't get that next promotion.

Saying no to the boss. Ah, that's a tough one. There's so much at stake—namely our livelihood. If you're simplifying your life, there are other areas where you can free up time and energy which may help you put up with, for the time being, a demanding job that requires, or that you feel requires, long hours.

But this is simply another area where you may have to learn to say no. According to Professor Schor, a number of recent studies have shown that workers *are* starting to say no to longer hours. Many people are moving away from the frenzied work ethic of the 1980s to more traditional values.

Professor Schor points out, however, that shorter work schedules won't be handed over to us by management. Rather, we'll have to claim them for ourselves.

If you're tired of working ten- and twelve-hour days, reduce your workday by half an hour or more over the next couple of months. No one's going to miss you for that half hour. Besides, you may be amazed to find, as I did, that you're more productive when you're working less. You'll therefore be making more of a contribution. You can then cut back even more.

Your next challenge might be deciding how to spend your extra time. After you recuperate—with rest, quiet time, long walks, time in nature, time with your family, time at the movies, —check out your creative urges. You will be pleasantly surprised at what's been cooking away inside all this time.

## 64. So Why Haven't You Written Your Book?

Or painted your Mona Lisa? Or sculpted your David? Or written your play, or started any of the other creative pursuits you have in the back of your mind that you'd like to do?

We all have creative ideas we want to develop. We may have been too busy to explore them, or we may have believed they were impossible for us to do. But it's our heart's desire that we should be doing.

Ask anyone who's following their muse. That's when they're truly happy, that's when they're in love, that's when they have passion in their life. They do it because they heard the call. And they heard the call because they took the time to listen.

Georgia O'Keeffe once said that it takes time to see a flower. It also takes time to write a poem. It takes time to open up to our creativity. And that time has to be free of many of the distractions we so often allow to take over our lives, often because we haven't learned to say no.

In my experience the creative process works like a locomotive. It takes a tremendous amount of inner resources and energy to start the wheels moving, and they move very slowly at first. If something on the track stops the train, it takes a tremendous amount of energy to get it going again. But once it's going full bore, it takes a lot to stop it.

When I started writing, for example, I found that I couldn't write and do lunch at the same time. By the time I get up and running, if I stop for lunch, the writing is all over for the day. After years in the real estate business, where doing lunch was de rigueur, I had to change my practices and start saying no to luncheons and many other invitations. I simplified my work life so I could expand into my creativity.

If you've got a creative project that you'd like to begin, I urge you to learn to say no to as many of the social and cultural and consumer distractions as you possibly can, so you can begin to build up the steam you need to move forward with it.

# EIGHT

# Some Inner Stuff

# 65. One Reason We're Craving Simpler Lives

Dear Ms. St. James;

I am 14 years old, and this school year I will be in ninth grade. About two years ago, I started feeling like my life was missing something. At first I thought I was lonely. I would get sick and lie in bed and cry. Loneliness didn't really make sense though. My parents love me. I have a brother I get along with. I have a dog, and I have friends I can talk to and trust. Then, about a year ago, my parents sent me to a psychiatrist. I only went four or five times, and I didn't feel helped. But a few months ago I decided that I didn't have to feel so depressed all the time. I pulled myself out of my pit of despair. I am still pulling. I give myself pep talks when I need them. When I am angry, I climb a large tree in my backyard. I feel that I am making progress.

I finished your book *Inner Simplicity* about ten minutes ago. I now realize that I am lonely, but not for company. I am lonely for myself. All my life so far I have concentrated on school, and being good, and being other people's idea of perfect. But now I know that I need to not worry so much about what others think but to do things I like to do. I need to look inside myself for strength. I need to get in touch with my inner self. I want to thank you for helping me realize that. I plan to try everything in your book, and to read the books you recommended.

Very sincerely,
Erin Webreck
Somerset, PA

"I am lonely for myself."

Erin speaks eloquently for many of us. We've been so busy being the good wife, the good husband, the good mother, the good father, the good son, the good daughter, the outstanding employee, the successful entrepreneur, and everyone else's idea of what perfect is that we've lost touch with who we really are.

As you begin living a simpler life, you'll have the time to spend in solitude, to write in your journal, to get some counseling if you feel the need, to work on eliminating any addictions that may be getting in your way, to learn to forgive, to develop gratitude, to figure out your big issue, and to learn how to move through your life at a pace that allows you to enjoy each day to the fullest.

Go back to Chapter Two and take another look at some things you might do to free up some time to think about simplifying your life (#13, #14, #15, and #16).

Another benefit of having this newfound time will be the opportunity to begin to get reacquainted with yourself.

## 66. Why We Keep Our Lives So Hectic

One thing I've learned about maintaining a complicated life is that it's one of the best ways we have to avoid looking at some of the larger questions. It may not apply to everyone, but I believe it explains a lot about why we've been moving so fast. The prospect of getting reacquainted with ourselves can be daunting.

As long as we convince ourselves that we're so busy and our work is so vital and we can't afford to slow down, then we don't have to look at our own lives and the personal issues that are so difficult to address: a marriage that isn't working, a career that isn't satisfying, children we're out of touch with, friendships we've outgrown, associations we need to move on from, the creativity we've been afraid to explore, our deepest fears or childhood traumas that have been holding us back from leading truly fulfilled lives.

As you start to slow down, to cut back your work hours, and

to free yourself from some of your commitments, you're going to have some time on your hands.

To begin with you may feel the need to start nourishing your body by catching up on your sleep, cleaning up your eating patterns, restoring your energy, reestablishing an exercise regimen, spending some time in nature, learning how to laugh and how to have fun.

And then gradually, you may reach a point where there's nothing left to do but start to deal with some of those inner issues. With a blanket of time around you, you'll find they're not as monumental as they may once have seemed. Creating the inner strength to move through them will lighten you up.

An amazing thing happens when we slow down. We start to get flashes of inspiration. We reach a new level of understanding and even wisdom. In a quiet moment we can get an intuitive insight that can change our entire life and the lives of the people around us in incredibly positive ways. And those changes can last a lifetime.

Living more simply will make it possible to create those quiet moments. Out of those quiet moments miracles happen. Be open to them.

## 67. Find Your Life's Work

One of the greatest benefits I've derived from simplifying my life has been finding a new and satisfying career. I wish I could say it was easy. It wasn't. It was one of the biggest challenges I've ever had to meet. But as anyone knows who is doing something they truly love to do, there is nothing like it, and few things they would exchange for it.

I spent most of my life not knowing what I wanted to do when I grew up. I've taken a lot of the tests, I've read many of the books, I've talked to numerous career counselors. But the only career guidance that worked for me was the advice to take some time off and do nothing until I figured out what my next career move should be.

Perhaps the hardest part was coming to the decision that I could take the time off. As we know, when we're in the middle of a hectic life, we think we can't stop. But slowing down makes it possible to see many options that simply aren't apparent when we're moving at warp speed.

The next hardest part was figuring out how to arrange it financially. I've already mentioned *Your Money or Your Life* by Joe Dominguez and Vicki Robin. Their approach to achieving financial independence gave me an entirely new way of thinking about the time and effort it takes to earn the money we spend. And of course, if you're living more simply you'll be spending significantly less money in the process.

If you're considering taking steps to find your life's work, and finances are one of your considerations, I urge you to study some or all of the money books described on the Reading List. You'll find an almost unlimited number of ways to reduce your expenses or to rearrange your finances so you can explore new career options.

Once you put your mind to it, you'll begin to see that saying you can't afford to find a more satisfying career is only an excuse. It's the most deceptive excuse there is. The truth is, in terms of the quality of your life, you can't afford *not* to.

Once I moved beyond the excuses, I made the commitment

to myself that I wouldn't start anything new until I came up with something I wanted to do. Out of that commitment I started writing, just for the fun of it and because I loved doing it. It opened up new career possibilities for me that I never would have thought of if I hadn't made that promise and stuck to it.

Though Gibbs and I did a lot of rearranging so I could take some time off, you may not have to do that. I'm a slow learner. I had to completely change my pace before I could begin to ask the right questions. Then I had to listen for the answers.

Don't fall into the trap of thinking that if you're not now doing what you love to do, it's too late to figure it out. One thing I've realized is that everything I did previously prepared me for what I'm doing now. And what I'm doing now is no doubt preparing me for whatever I may do differently in the future.

With the rapid changes that are happening in the market-place, with the downshifting that's happening in the work-place with the increasing advances in all phases of technology, there perhaps has never been a better time to figure out what your best work is, if only as preparation for the next stage of your life.

If you're not doing work you love, the greatest contribution you can make to the world and to your own growth is to *take whatever time you need to figure out what you want to do.* Then start doing it.

## 68. Giving Back

Across the country, volunteer organizations have reported a significant decline over the past decade in the numbers of people who are willing to devote time to charitable or other worthy causes. Our ten- and twelve-hour workdays have not left much time for volunteer endeavors.

But as simplifying and downshifting take hold in this culture, the numbers of people who are ready to give back will start to rise again. I hear from many readers that one of the major benefits of simplifying their lives is that now they have time to devote to others through volunteering.

One reader said, "My own view is that getting out of the rat race through simplifying solves only half of the problem of lack of fulfilment that so many people experience. The other half is found in considering the needs of others as much as our own."

Volunteering may not be high on your short list as you begin to simplify your life. If you're feeling exhausted and depleted from the frenetic pace of your life in recent years, perhaps it shouldn't be. Charity begins at home. It's possible that one of the greatest services you can perform is to get your own house in shape and to spend time with your kids and your spouse and your extended family before you rush out to save the world.

But the time may soon come when you're ready to give back. Doing something for others can be a very powerful step toward getting to know yourself and for adding joy and value and a sense of accomplishment to your life. The distinguished historian Arnold Toynbee said that the future of mankind depends on every person withdrawing into himself and finding his own depths, then coming forth to serve his fellow men.

And remember, your greatest service and where you can make the greatest contribution is when you're doing what you love to do (#67).

# NINE

# Personal and Household Routines

# 69. Another Approach to Household Chores

Several readers of *Simplify Your Life* wrote to say they had learned to spread out the weekly routines into more easily manageable portions that take less time.

Margo Bogart of Dearborn, Michigan, put it this way:

"I have streamlined my household chores by having a major focus for each day of the week. This may sound trite, but it actually saves me the trouble of trying to remember how long it has been since I last did each major task. Each person can vary the concept to suit his or her needs and flex the schedule when circumstances require switching days for certain tasks. Here's my basic plan:

Monday: empty wastebaskets and put out trash for city garbage pickup. Do laundry.

Tuesday: Work on computer. Clean second floor and basement.

Wednesday: Volunteer. Shop on the way home.

Thursday: Clean bathrooms.

Friday: Vacuum carpets and mop floors. Plan activities to do together for the weekend.

Saturday: Spend as much time together as possible. If my husband brings work home from the office, I pay bills, write letters, clip coupons, dust, iron, mend, water plants, etc., until we can spend more time together.

Sunday: Work in the yard and garden together or do repairs together. Phone relatives together. Relax and read together.

"This system works for me. It's true that I don't have the best kept house in Dearborn, but I think I have one of the happiest marriages! The beauty of having a preestablished focus for each day of the week is that I never waste time trying to figure out what I should be accomplishing next.

"Also, this schedule helps me pace myself and not feel like I'm falling behind when responsibilities threaten to pile up. Once I have done the designated chores for the day, I feel more comfortable about allocating time for other tasks (or invitations to do fun things!) that come up unexpectedly. I feel more in control of my week and less stressed by the endless 'to-do' list."

As Margo says, such a plan can be adapted to your own circumstances.

Another reader said she completed one household task before she headed for the office each morning. This way, she didn't have to think about doing it at the end of her workday when she was tired and would thus be more inclined to skip it. She also pointed out that it meant she didn't have to lose a major part of her weekend to the drudgery of chores, and instead she looked forward all week to being able to spend her Saturday doing whatever she wanted to do.

# 70. A Simple Weekly Menu Plan

Though Gibbs and I both love to eat, neither one of us wants to spend a lot of time in the kitchen. So years ago we came up with a solution to the perennial question, "What are we having for dinner tonight?"

We didn't recognize how much it simplified our lives until I started hearing it as a tip from readers who do it, too. I know this won't work for everyone, and it's a flagrant violation of the get off automatic pilot suggestion (#30), but we got into the habit of eating pretty much the same thing each night of the week.

For example, on Mondays we have grilled chicken breasts with steamed veggies.

On Tuesdays we usually eat at one of our favorite local restaurants.

On Wednesdays we have either a large Greek salad or a salade Niçoise with one of Gibbs's muffins.

On Thursdays we have fresh crab or tuna gazpacho with a muffin in summer—or a hot veggie soup in winter. Or sometimes we really break loose and have grilled chicken with veggies again.

On Fridays we have Gibbs's scrambled eggs with whole wheat toast, turkey sausage, and fresh squeezed orange juice.

We like to keep it light on the weekends, so on Saturdays (our favorite) we have blue corn tortilla chips with fresh guacamole.

On Sundays we have popcorn and apples with cheese. This leaves room for our weekend dessert treat, maybe a fresh fruit cobbler or berries and cream.

We'll stick with this menu until we get tired of it; then we'll come up with another menu plan. As one reader pointed out, this simplifies not only the meal planning, but also the grocery list, the shopping, the provisioning, the cooking, and the cleanup. It's one less thing to have to occupy your mind with each day.

Another reader told me about a variation on this theme, which Ethel Kennedy has reportedly used for years: a menu plan based on simple roasts and broiled meats, omelets, and salads that rotates every two weeks instead of each week.

I know that for many people this approach would be boring beyond belief. Obviously, if you love to cook, you can do other things to simplify your life so you have the time to spend preparing your favorite meals.

But Gibbs and I enjoy knowing each morning what we're going to have for dinner that night. We eat only foods we're really fond of, so we tend to look forward all day to our predictable dinners.

## 71. Some Other Possibilities for Simple Meals

This idea, which I heard from many readers, is one I did for years: Cook up a week's supply of spaghetti sauce or lasagne or one of your favorite soups or casseroles, freeze it in meal-sized portions so it doesn't spoil, and have it every night for a week, perhaps with a different salad or a variety of rolls or fresh bread.

I recently came across another book that you might explore if the idea of cooking ahead and freezing appeals to you: *Once a Month Cooking* by Mimi Wilson and Mary Beth Lagerboard. It's a step-by-step guide for preparing a month's worth of dinner entrees in advance and freezing them.

Depending on the size of your family, the program might require the addition of some larger cooking pots, extra freezer space, and a lot of organization. And it definitely requires a complete day of your time each month to do the menu plan, the provisioning, and the cooking. If you're willing to put in that whole day, it would definitely save you money and simplify your life.

Another simple option for frozen meals might be Healthy Choice or Lean Cuisine or any of the other well-balanced, dietetically proportioned frozen dinners that are now available. These are not the standard TV dinners. A friend recommended these to us a while back and we found, to our surprise, that they are quite delicious. If you select carefully, you can find a variety that are well balanced in terms of protein, carbohydrates, and fat and the appropriate micronutrients.

Gibbs and I keep some of these on hand for evenings when we don't want to go out to eat and want the simplest meal possible. Yes, they are more expensive than using Mimi and Mary Beth's system of cooking from scratch and then freezing, but as a stopgap measure—and with the addition of a fresh salad—they're another simple solution.

And given that the major cause of overweight in this country is overeating, an added benefit we've found from having this type of frozen dinner from time to time is that it's a very simple way to limit our food intake. The preset portions serve as an excellent reminder of how little we need to eat to stay fit and healthy.

## 72. A Simple Way to Maintain Your Weight

I don't believe everyone needs to be pencil thin. But I have found that life is simpler if I can keep my weight to what for me is an acceptable level. When I do, I feel better, I look better, and I don't have to keep a thin wardrobe and a heavy wardrobe in my closet.

Gibbs and I have struggled for years with the problem of maintaining our ideal weight. A couple of years ago we discovered what has become for us a surefire way to keep our weight in check: We use a chart to track our weight each day.

We use plain graph paper taped to the wall above the bathroom scales, and we keep a red pen nearby.

It's amazing how easy it is to nip in the bud a small weight gain from a dinner out, or some indiscriminate snacking from the day before, when we're keeping track on a daily basis. If we're up a pound in the morning, we know we have to make some adjustment in our intake for the rest of the day in order to bring it back down by the next morning, or possibly the next.

Modifying our food intake based on the movement of that red line up the graph becomes an automatic, unconscious, and almost painless way to maintain the weight we want.

Time and again, if we slack off on using the chart—either we've been too lazy to make up a new one for the month or we've misplaced the pen—we can gain five pounds without batting an eye. It's so easy to convince ourselves that the piece of double chocolate mousse cake was only a small piece, or that the extra handful of M&Ms we pilfered at last night's meeting didn't count because we ate them standing up. But the chart isn't so easily convinced.

We've found it's not sufficient simply to weigh in every morning and not mark the weight on the graph. If we do that, we somehow conveniently forget what we weighed the day before and the day before that. But it's impossible to lose track when the weight is recorded in bright red ink on the bathroom wall, and difficult to ignore when it's moving inexorably up the graph.

Now we photocopy enough weight graphs to last the entire year, and we keep the red pen in a nearby drawer so it doesn't get misplaced. Maintain your ideal weight with a red pen. It's so simple.

# 73. Dealing with Unwanted Callers

$M$argo Bogart also had some good ideas for dealing with incoming phone calls and uninvited solicitors at the front door.

She says, "Our first line of defense against unwanted phone interruptions at home is an unlisted number. The reduction in dinner-time interruptions has been well worth the onetime $40 cost of switching from a listed to an unlisted number. Now all the people we want to hear from have our number, and most of those who would solicit us for purchases or contributions don't.

"Also, to keep your number out of the computer files of businesses with Caller ID, we begin by pressing *67 before we press the phone number. This defeats the Caller ID system, but only for that call, so we must remember to press *67 whenever we call an organization we don't necessarily want to hear from later. I've put a sticker on my telephone receiver to remind us to use this blocking code more often. (The blocking code number varies from region to region, depending on your phone service provider.)

"For those telephone solicitors who make it through our first line of defense, I have a foolproof response that brings their calls to a speedy conclusion. Years ago my husband and I made a pact to simplify our lives: We will not buy from any salesperson or contribute to any cause that approaches us by phone (or at our front door). This pact leaves no room for the salesperson to attempt to change our minds, so it really is foolproof. I simply say, 'Sorry, we don't accept any telephone offers,' or 'We don't contribute to any organizations through telephone solicitations.' My husband's response is even simpler: 'NO, thank you.' (Click.)

"Regarding your suggestion about not answering the doorbell, either, we have saved ourselves untold visits from the area Fuller Brush man, religious proselytizers, and kids selling candy and magazine subscriptions by posting a hand-lettered sign in plain sight near our front doorbell. It reads: 'No Soliciting. We don't do business at our front door.' As persistent as these callers are trained to be, they generally remove themselves from our front porch without even ringing or knocking when they see our sign."

A big part of learning to say no (#62) is learning to avoid the kinds of situations that put you in the position of refusing a request. If this is a problem in your neighborhood or in your life, preparing for them in advance will help. In life as in football the best defense is often a good offense.

## 74. The Simple Answering Machine

W̧e all know about using the answering machine to screen phone calls and about turning the phone off altogether if we need some uninterrupted time to work or spend time with our kids.

But I've found another effective way to utilize this true time-saving device. An associate and I keep in touch via our answering machines.

Monica and I know that if we get on the phone together, we can talk for ages. That's fine when we both have the time, but our lives are such now that one or the other of us is always on a deadline. So we agreed some years back that when one of us has some information to pass on to the other, we'll just leave a message on the machine.

Even if the other person is there and listening to the message as it's coming in, neither one of us has to feel compelled to pick up the phone. In fact, often we prefer that the other not pick up.

And so the one calling will say, "If you're there, don't pick up, but I just wanted you to know such and such."

If the other party has a need to respond to the message, she can then call back and leave any pertinent information on the other's machine.

I have since established similar answering machine relationships with people I have no need to talk to in person, but whom I have a need to keep in touch with. Think of it as audio E-mail.

Obviously, this arrangement wouldn't work for all your relationships, but learning to use the telephone effectively can free up an extrordinary amount of time that you might not even be aware you're losing.

Another way to keep incoming phone calls under control is simply to let people know when it's convenient to call you. If you want to avoid phone interruptions during your mealtime, have all the family members let their friends and associates know that they can reach you before 6 p.m. or after 7 p.m. or whenever your dinner slot is, and that any calls during that time will not be picked up.

Another option is to set up a phone date. Arrange, even through answering machine messages if necessary, to get together by phone at a prespecified time.

But perhaps one of the greatest advantages to having an answering machine pick up your calls is that telemarketers will hang up when a machine answers.

## 75. The Simple Fireplace

If you're a purist when it comes to wood-burning fires, please don't read this.

But if you are tired of the hassle of wood-burning fires and have access to natural gas, consider installing a gas-burning log in your existing hearth.

Gibbs and I love sitting quietly in front of a fire on a cold evening. But, except for special occasions, we went for years without enjoying our fireplace because of the inconvenience involved.

To begin with, unless you have your own source of wood, there's the expense and the bother of having the wood delivered to the house and stacked in a suitable place, away from the house to avoid termites, but not so far away that it's a bother to retrieve the logs when you need them.

Then you have to haul the wood—free of spiders and other

insects—into the house and build the fire, cleaning up the bits of bark and chipped wood as you go. Then you've got to get the fire lit and keep it burning without smoking out the living room in the process. You've got to make certain the fire screen is in place so that flying sparks don't burn holes in the carpet after you've gone to bed.

At some point you've got to clean out all the ash from the burned wood, and depending on how much wood you use through the season, you should have the chimney cleaned at least once a year.

Unless you particularly enjoy chopping wood, having a gas log means you can eliminate that chore from your list or cancel your standing order for wood for the winter.

Admittedly, Gibbs and I live in a mild climate, and though we wouldn't be able to do this if we lived in Wisconsin, we use our gas log through most of the heating season as our only source of heat for our home. The recent technological advances in ceramic logs have not only made gas-burning logs much more realistic looking and attractive, they're much more efficient as well. We light the fire early in the evening, let it burn for an hour or so, and then turn it off. Because of the heat-storing capability of the logs, it will continue to put out heat for at least another hour or more. Of course, we also keep sweaters and extra blankets nearby during the colder months.

Burning a gas log is considerably cheaper than burning wood, running roughly a quarter to a third the expense, depending on where you live. Best of all, gas burns much cleaner and is more environmentally friendly than burning wood.

Though a gas fire doesn't have that wonderful snap and crackle that a wood fire has, and you don't get the wood-burning aroma, we've found a gas fire is just as warm and just as romantic as a wood fire, much easier, and you never have to interrupt a cozy snuggle to stoke the logs.

## 76. The Simple Bed

Gibbs is a churner. He falls asleep easily and sleeps soundly, but tosses from one side to the other all night long, taking the covers with him at every turn.

It takes me a few minutes to get the covers and the pillow adjusted comfortably, but then I fall asleep and remain in exactly the same position until morning.

Gibbs is a heat machine and needs only a light cover. I'm usually cold at night and like a heavy quilt.

The standard bed with sheets and blankets tucked in at the bottom doesn't work for our different sleeping habits. After years of struggling, Gibbs and I have finally devised a much simpler way for each of us to get a good night's sleep.

Though it might not work for every couple with radically different sleeping habits, our solution to this common problem works well for us, and several readers wrote to describe variations on our approach to the simple bed.

We have a king-sized bed with a fitted sheet over the mattress. We each have a queen-sized comforter. Mine is heavyweight; Gibbs's is lightweight.

We fold each comforter in half—the lightweight one goes on his side of the bed and the heavyweight one goes on my side—and we use them as sleeping bags. The folded edge of each comforter runs down the center of the bed; the open edges run down the outside edge of the bed so they're easy to get into and out of.

Because the comforters are queen size, there's plenty of room for each of us to spread out within our own quilted envelope, and it holds the heat better than a blanket spread over the whole bed.

Making the bed up in the morning is a snap. You can either leave the top half of the "bag" in casual disarray, or with one flip of the top layer, each half of the bed is neatly made (well, sort of neatly made). Several couples I heard from who use this method fold up the comforters and place them on the foot of the bed each morning.

sleeping Bag style Bed

Also, by flipping the whole arrangement head to foot or inside out, the options for irregular laundering are greatly expanded. Let your conscience be your guide. Each comforter makes a full load for the standard-sized washer and dryer.

This system makes snuggling together more of a challenge, but it keeps the game interesting.

## 77. Simple Laundering Ideas

It was a relief to learn that Gibbs and I were not the only ones for whom socks have been a daily and weekly complication.

Not only are they a pain in the neck to find in a freshly laundered load of clothes (mine invariably find their way down a long dark sleeve or pant leg, or into the deepest recess of a pillowcase), but then you've got to find the mate and somehow tie them together so that when you want to wear them they'll both be in roughly the same vicinity in your chest of drawers.

Finally, in self-defense, I came up with a solution that works for us. Many people have written to me with variations on this approach, so this system can be adapted to suit your own circumstances.

I bought seven identical pairs of dark socks for each of us, one pair for each day of the week.

I also bought two zippered mesh bags for each of us. The bags are available at most hardware or variety stores.

No sock mating or Lose!

Arrange the bags side by side in your closet on a hanger or on a hook, or designate a sock drawer that will hold both bags. Fill one bag with clean socks. Since the socks are identical, you don't have to mate them. When you need a clean pair, take them from the clean bag. When you remove your socks at the end of the day, put them in the other bag. At the end of the week, toss the dirty sock bag into the laundry.

When it comes out of the dryer, it now becomes the clean bag, and the process starts all over again. You'll never have to match socks or hunt for the mate to your favorite pair again.

In terms of the rest of the laundry, several people wrote to say they never buy any launderable item in red because it *always* runs, even after many washings. I stopped buying red many years ago for this very reason.

And many people shared this idea about cutting drying time in half, which I'd never heard of before, but I now do regularly: Run your clothes through the dryer only long enough to get out the wrinkles (ten to twenty minutes, depending on the items and the dryer and the setting). Then hang them on hangers in your closet to dry completely.

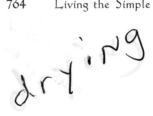

This won't work for every climate, but if you can do it, not only will it save you time and reduce either the gas or electricity used by your dryer, it also eliminates wrinkles, which eliminates ironing. It also reduces the damage and wear and tear to your clothes that are caused by extended exposure to high temperatures.

Then you can get rid of your iron.

Another great laundering tip I got from readers is to use laundry disks (available from Real Goods Trading Corporation, 555 Leslie Street, Ukiah, CA 95482 (800) 762-7325).

These are 2 1/2-inch-diameter disks filled with ionizing ceramic beads. You just toss them into the washer with a load of clothes and they eliminate the need for harsh detergents—in your clothes and down the drain. They also eliminate the rapid fading of dark colors that comes from using detergents with whiteners. They are recommended for everyday washing, but do require warm water. I've used them for over a year now and find them very effective for cleaning, though I do use a teaspoon or so of detergent when I launder our dusty trail-hiking clothes.

They come in a set of three disks for $49 and last for between 500 to 700 laundry loads (roughly two years for most people).

No detergent
washing

# TEN

# Lifestyle Issues

## 78. The Simple Computer

Frequently, people ask me, "Did you get rid of your computer when you simplified your life?"

I always explain that using a computer saves me untold hours and is a tremendous simplifier for me as a writer. I can't imagine being without one.

I began to realize that people who ask this question are of the "simplifying means getting rid of everything and moving to the cabin in the woods" mind-set.

But it's a fair question. Given the rapid pace of the technological advances that are taking place every day, we're all going to have to address the issue of whether or not the computer—and the Internet, E-mail, virtual reality, software for every conceivable application, and computer developments we haven't even thought of yet—will actually simplify our lives.

You can ask a dozen people whether or not any of these advances will make things simpler, and you'll get thirteen different answers. It's not an easy question, and I believe we each will have to answer it for ourselves. Some of us won't be able to move forward in our careers unless we're computer literate. Others will find limited computer applications for their lives. And still others will be dragged kicking and screaming into the computer age.

I recently conducted my own random and admittedly limited survey of a couple dozen acquaintances from around the country who are computer literate and who are active on the Internet. Even though they all agree that at the present moment the Internet has some sorting out to do before it actually becomes a useful tool for the average person, the consensus among all the people I spoke to was basically that, like it or not, the computer and Internet are here to stay, so we might as well get used to it.

Yes, perhaps. But the telephone is here to stay, too. And so is the television. That doesn't mean we have to allow them to take over our lives. For me, right now, a computer with a simple word processing program, a laser printer, and a fax are extremely helpful for my work as a writer. And I have no doubt that the Internet will someday soon prove to be a valuable reference tool.

But, knowing myself as I do, I will have to exercise a fair amount of discipline in my use of it, just as I do with television. I've already met a number of technocrats on the Internet who may never return to the real world.

Obviously that's their choice. (Or possibly not—there are addictive aspects to being on-line, similar to the addictive habits of sitting in front of a television screen, that we won't understand the effects of perhaps for some years to come).

But now that I've created a wonderfully simple life, I plan not to lose it to the Internet. We can keep abreast of the technology that is appropriate for our lives without losing our souls to it. All it takes is a clear vision of how we want our lives to be, and the discipline not to let them be overrun by so-called progress.

## 79. E-Mail

E-mail simplifies the mail and information handling for many of us.

But it can also complicate the process. I have a friend who uses E-mail exclusively now to keep in touch with her friends and business associates. It's so easy, she tells me. She can type a message, press a button, and send it to two hundred people in just a couple of minutes. And she does this now on a regular basis.

Yes, but she now spends several hours a day reading the return responses and then, in some cases, sending out another message. This is simple?

If you use E-mail a lot, you might take a quick moment to analyze how much more time you spend now dealing with the daily mail and various communications than you did before you incorporated E-mail into your life.

As one reader, Amy Newman, pointed out, "E-mail and voice mail were supposedly developed to make our lives simpler. This can be accomplished by responding immediately to 90 percent of all messages. E-mail should be responded to on-line, if possible, and should never be printed, responded to by hand, then retyped by yourself or an assistant—it amazes me how many people still do this. It takes practice to be confident enough to respond immediately, but it will save lots of time if you handle it on the spot."

E-mail is another convenience—just like the automatic washer and dryer—that is easy to overdo. It can complicate our lives precisely because it's so easy.

## 80. Automatic Payments

Gibbs and I reduced the complexity of our financial chores in a number of different ways, including closing out all but one bank account, eliminating all but a couple of credit cards, avoiding consumer debt, and consolidating our investment portfolio within just a couple of families of funds. And of course, our shopping moratorium (#56) has not only drastically decreased our spending but has also reduced the expenses we have to track.

After hearing from many readers that automatic payroll deposits and automatic payment withdrawals had greatly simplified their lives, I decided to explore those options.

It took a single phone call to set up the automatic payroll deposits. It took an hour or so to contact the companies I receive bills from each month—the mortgage, insurance, utilities, and so on. Each vendor mailed or faxed their own form requesting bank account information and our signatures so they could access our bank account for bill-paying purposes. It took a month or two to process this paperwork.

Now, payments for all but a few of the monthly bills are automatically deducted from our checking account. There are a couple of local utilities that are not, at this time, set up for automatic payments. Those I pay six months to a year in advance, so I only have to handle those bills once or twice a year.

The only check I write monthly is for the credit card bill, since at the present time the bank that services the card is not set up to utilize automatic payments.

The process of keeping track of the monthly charges is quite simple: I receive a statement each month from the utility companies, for example. Using the method of handling-it-only-once (#44), when the statement arrives in the mail I enter the amount that has been deducted from my checking account into my check register, which I keep at hand. At the end of the month I use the bank statement, which lists each automatic payment transaction, to reconcile the payments the bank made against the entries in the check register.

That's it. No check writing, no envelope addressing, no return addressing, no stamp licking, no having to get it into the mailbox on time. I've literally gone from spending a day or more each month on the bill-paying and record-keeping process to now spending little more than an hour each month.

One reason I hadn't pursued this avenue earlier was because I feared that by using automatic payments and deposits I'd lose control of the process. I imagined that deposits would get credited to someone else's account and that payments wouldn't get made by the bank, and then I'd have to spend hours straightening it all out. I clung too long to the belief that I could maintain better control if I was taking care of the payments myself each month. But I've been taking advantage of automatic payments and deposits for over a year now without a single glitch.

If there's any simpler way than this to pay bills, I'd love to hear about it.

# 81. Use a Monthly Spending Plan

O ne of the easiest ways I know to simplify your finances is to keep track of your monthly income and expenses so you can establish a workable spending plan to live within.

Numerous books are available today that will show you how to set up and maintain a budget. I describe several on the Reading List.

Or you can simply sit down and draw up your own system. I started years ago using a National Brand 14-column, double-page 11 x 8 1/2-inch analysis pad—available at any office supply store—to keep track of income and expenses.

It's quite simple. The various expense categories—mortgage, taxes, insurance, food, utilities, and so on, are set up vertically in the left-hand column; the months run across the top of the double-page spread.

At the end of the month I transfer the entries from our check register to the appropriate column in the budget book, total them, and deduct them from the monthly income.

At the end of the year, I total each expense for the year and divide by twelve to get the monthly average for each category. That number, adjusted up or down as needed, then becomes the budget figure for the coming year.

I keep this process very simple. This is not double-entry bookkeeping. It doesn't have to balance to the penny. In fact, to make it easier, I round up the numbers and never use the decimal point. It takes only a few minutes each month to total the columns and to keep up with the figures.

Tracking income and expenses makes it possible to increase your savings and control your spending, and it provides valuable information at the end of the year that can be used for the coming year's budgeting. It also greatly simplifies your tax records and reduces the time you have to spend gathering information for filing your tax return.

But probably the greatest advantage a spending plan offers is that it puts you in control of your money. Having that control will simplify your life.

## 82. The Simple Credit Card

When Gibbs and I were looking at ways to simplify our finances, we got rid of all but one or two of our credit cards. Not only did this drastically cut back on the hassle of keeping track of, rotating, and making payments on several different cards each month, but it cut back on the amount of junk mail we get each day.

Now that most grocery and department stores and even the U.S. Post Office accept credit cards, we use one card for all our routine monthly expenses such as groceries, gasoline, and any miscellaneous expenditures such as haircuts, personal items, office supplies, and so on. We keep a second card as a backup for traveling, since many hotels and car rental companies can tie up your available credit until your charges are finalized.

Since we know from our budget figures how much we spend in each category each month, it's easy to stay within our self-imposed limits. This way we don't have to carry excess cash around, which is more difficult to keep track of (and easier to slip through our fingers); and we don't have to carry a checkbook—though we do keep a couple of checks on hand for the rare vendor that doesn't accept credit cards.

It's a simple matter to use the monthly credit card statement to record the entries into our budget ledger (#81), and every expenditure we can put on a credit card means one less check we have to reconcile with the monthly bank statement.

We found that it does take some discipline not to get carried away with credit card expenditures, and it's vital that you know the parameters of your budget so you don't go over your monthly limits. We make certain to pay the amount in full each month so there are no interest charges.

Using our credit card this way has greatly simplified the monthly record keeping. Now, all of our regular monthly bills are deducted from our checking account through automatic payments(#80), and most of the remaining expenditures are paid for by one check to the credit card company.

A debit card, available from your bank, is another simple way to take care of miscellaneous purchases and eliminates the need to carry extra cash. It works like a credit card, except the charge is deducted directly from your checking account. The charges are shown on your bank statement each month, and so can be reconciled and entered into your spending record as expenses.

A debit card eliminates the monthly check to the credit card company and of course there's never any possibility of interest charges for unpaid balances or late payments. Most banks don't charge for this service. If you use a debit card, be sure to enter each transaction in a check register just as though you were writing a check, and deduct it from your running balance. This makes it possible to keep track of expenditures as you go through the month.

# 83. Is Quicken Quicker?

$A$ couple of years ago my accountant suggested that I could greatly simplify my annual tax preparation chore, as well as my monthly bill-paying process, by getting one of the mass-marketed computer bookkeeping programs that would automate these routines for me.

I consider myself to be moderately computer literate in terms of word processing systems, having used a variety of programs on various computers in the writing of my books.

But I hadn't gotten involved in computer bookkeeping systems because, even with my past involvement in real estate investing, most of the software available in those days seemed to be excessive for my needs. The fairly efficient bill-paying, budgeting, and end-of-year statements I did by hand were relatively easy and served my purpose well enough at that time.

But now that I'm simplifying, I'm always looking for easier approaches to time-consuming routines, so I decided to explore how the computer could simplify my life in this regard.

I spent roughly a hundred dollars on the software, checks, and envelopes, and a couple of hundred dollars on the consultant I hired to help me learn the program and to totally revamp my bill-paying methods.

After using the new system for roughly six months, I came to the conclusion that, for me, this is not simple. Since I don't keep the computer or the printer running when I'm not using them, it became far more trouble than it was worth to boot them up, replace the paper in the printer tray with computer checks, input the payment information into the program, print the check, pull out the computer envelopes, tear off the perforated checks, insert then into the envelopes, put a stamp on them, and drop them in the mail.

Now that all my monthly bills are handled by automatic payment through my bank, and I write only a couple of checks each month, using a computer program is overkill. Unless you're paying and tracking a significant volume of checks each month, now and even into the forseeable future, automatic payments are a much easier and less expensive way for the average household to simplify the bill-paying process.

Using a computer program for bill payments does, of course, eliminate the end-of-the-month number crunching, since the numbers are totaled instantaneously. And a computer program makes it possible to quickly analyze your income and expenses from many different angles.

If you've got a small in-home business and a significant number of bills to pay throughout the month, or if you have a complex tax picture, handling it all by computer would no doubt be simpler. But I accessed the system only once a month, so one consideration for me was the learning curve required to stay on top of it. In effect, I had to start all over again each month to get up to snuff with the program.

I also believe that, with the exception of monthly income and expense records, the charts, graphs, and reports that the software promoters tout as adding clarity to our financial picture are unnecessary for most of us. If you *want* those reports, or *enjoy* spending your time generating that type of data, that's one thing. But for those of us for whom that information is irrelevant, much of the advertising hoopla about the convenience of computer bookkeeping is overstated, at best. At worst, these programs can be far more complex than they appear.

No one can deny the incredible benefits computers offer us. And it seems possible that automated everything is just around the corner. But often, even with computers, we still need to evaluate objectively whether a particular application, or the way in which we utilize it, can really simplify or at least add something to our lives.

## 84. The Simple Time Management System

My system for time management parallels my system for keeping stuff organized. If we reduce the amount of stuff we allow to accumulate in our lives, we won't have to organize it. If we cut back on the number of things we have to do each day, we don't need a large double-page spread on which to track them.

If you take a close look at your system, you'll see that the things which are the most important aren't scheduled in there anyway. How many of us ever write in "Spend time with my kids today." Or "Take time for my soul this afternoon." Or "Have sex tonight."

Many people are finding a smaller date book is much more compatible with the simple life. As reader Melissa Keane wrote, "I moved out of my Filofax calendar with a full page per day because it led me to believe I could really *do* all that in one day. I'm a writer-historian-researcher, so most of my days can be filled with a one- to two-word notation: 'library,' 'archives,' or 'write.' I don't need hour-by-hour appointments noted."

The hectic lives we've created have become an acceptable and, in many circles, a respectable way to fill up complex and expensive time management systems. Have you ever added up how much time you spend keeping one of those systems up to date? Most of the time is spent *rewriting* on tomorrow's schedule the things you didn't get done today.

Getting to the point where we don't have dozens of things to do each day is a big part of what simplifying is all about. If you're thinking of going to a simpler system, it may take you several successively smaller sizes to get to simple. And obviously it will mean taking steps to cut back on the number of things you feel you have to do each day.

A hectic schedule is a lifestyle choice. We don't *have* to be chained to a huge time management system. As one proponent of the simple life, an executive from New York wrote, "I know I'm in trouble if I've got so many things to do that I have to make a list."

# ELEVEN

# Simple Parenting

## 85. Keep *Your* Life Simple

Simple parenting is an oxymoron, of course, since there are no simple kids. But our lives with our kids can be made simpler than they now are.

Simplifying with kids requires exactly the same things that simplifying without kids requires: time, energy, awareness of the problems, an understanding of the relevant issues, self-discipline, the ability to set boundaries (for both ourselves and our children), the strength of character to say no and stick to it, and the willingness to do whatever it takes to make the adjustments and rearrangements in our lives so we can bring about the desired changes.

The only difference is that simplifying with kids requires *more* of all this. Much more.

I want to point out that I don't have children of my own, though I do give myself some credit for marrying a man who has two terrific kids. Looking back, I see that simplified my life a good deal. They were 9 and 14 when I came on the scene, so I've never experienced the joy of changing a baby's diaper or the bliss of waking up for a 2 a.m. feeding (though I did share in a couple of sleepless nights with Gibbs when, at 2 a.m., it was clear our 16-year-old was not going to be home at midnight as we'd all agreed!).

Since the boys were with us only on the weekends and for vacations, I've never had to deal firsthand with the full-time, ongoing issues of laundry, chores, television watching, car pooling, day care, homework, drugs, teen sex, pregnancy, and the myriad other issues that full-time parents with kids face today.

But I've been surrounded my entire adult life with friends who have kids, so over the years I've observed some things that work and some things that don't work, and I have a couple of admittedly quite biased opinions of my own to share as well.

The best advice I, as a nonparent, can give to someone with children is this: Simplify your own life. In the process, the complications of having children will become more manageable.

If you could free up ten or twenty hours a week to spend with your kids or to eliminate or reduce some of the pressures you face—which simpifying will enable you to do— at the very least you can clear away enough of the day-to-day concerns so the dilemmas you have to deal with as a parent can be put in their proper perspective: Your kids are the most important issue of your life right now.

Continue to ask the question, "What do I need to do to simplify my life?" (#18). Just asking that question and taking the time to listen for the answer will provide you with the right solutions for your particular circumstances.

The suggestions that follow in this chapter are obviously not the only things parents can do to simplify their lives with kids. But, in terms of simplicity, they are, in my opinion, some of the most important ones to get started on.

## 86. Involve Your Kids in the Household Chores

**M**any parents wrote to say they had simplified their lives by requiring their children to help with routine household duties.

One mother, Jennifer Sellers, a secondary school teacher who has taken a sabbatical to be with her children, put it beautifully.

"This may seem like a no-brainer to anyone without children, but it is *rare* to find children who help with household chores today.

"I was at a talk given by John Rosemond, who writes about parenthood, and he asked the audience, 'How many of you have children over five who have regularly assigned chores that must be done to certain standards—and they don't get paid to do them?'

"In a full auditorium only half a dozen hands went up.

"He then asked how many of those present had chores when they were kids. Every hand went up. 'That's one generation, folks,' he responded.

"My children do a lot willingly and for no monetary pay. We achieve this by:

1. Letting them 'help' when they were little. It would actually take me twice as long to accomplish the task with this 'help,' but it gave me time to talk with my children, and the task eventually did get accomplished. The payoff is that now I have excellently trained assistants who truly do help today.

2. Use working together as an opportunity to be together. When you've finished playing Candyland, your work still waits. When you've made soup together, you've gotten dinner accomplished, trained a future cook, visited together, and your child will blossom from the pride of making dinner.

3. Being profuse with thanks and gratitude and compliments and comments.

4. I've found it's better to give young children several short chores rather than one long task. My youngest wipes off the cat's mat and the trash can lid, takes out the recycling and compost,

washes the compost bucket, wipes off the counter where the recycling piles up, and changes the kitchen linens daily.

All of these are things I used to do and don't do now. None in themselves are time consuming, but collectively they save me time and energy and don't overwhelm my 7-year-old. He dries dishes every third night (three children), but I don't ask him to wash the evening dishes. I feel it would be too much for him and stifle his desire to help.

My teenagers do longer tasks. Sometimes I pay them to help, but only for a special usually strenuous task, never for a regular chore.

5. I stress how lucky they are to be learning how to do things and how to work. They'll be the ones getting the jobs in the future.

"I always try to remember that a child's self-esteem is not built by silly stickers that say, 'You are special!' but rather by having achieved a genuine sense of accomplishment and a sense of being a contributing and valuable member of the community (family)."

A friend of mine who has three children simplifies the household chores by posting a chart of duties on the fridge door each month. If there's any question about whose turn it is to do the dishes, for example, she can point to the chart as the authority. This eliminates any discussion. (She does end up with a fair amount of graffiti on the chart, however.).

## 87. Curtail Their Extracurricular Activities

I hear from both parents and kids on this one. And it's heartening to learn that people are starting to figure out that even though *everything* is available to kids today, kids don't have to *do* everything.

One mother of two teenage children wrote to say they had finally sat down together as a family and made a group decision: only one or two extracurricular activities per season per kid.

Both parents were surprised at first at how readily the kids agreed to this seeming restriction. But as time went on, they found that not only were the kids amenable to the idea of fewer after-school activities, they were actually relieved at the prospect of not having to compete and/or perform in so many different areas: dance, golf, gymnastics, hockey, and voice lessons for her; football, hockey, track, and chess for him.

Over the course of the two years since they began this cutback, they've all become aware of the following benefits.

The kids are no longer exhausted from being constantly on the go. Their mother is relieved of the responsibility of being on call as the family chauffeur. Both kids' academic performance has improved dramatically and so has their performance in their chosen activity.

They get along better with each other and with their two younger siblings. The mother's private explanation for this is that they all now have more of her time, so their innate need to compete for her attention has diminished.

The family as a whole is happier because they're less stressed out and each has more quiet time on their own.

We've been so imbued in recent years with the belief that we have to take advantage of all the opportunities out there. The urge to *do everything* complicates our lives. We've lost the ability to distinguish between the things we'd like to do and the things we feel we should be doing.

We've passed this complication on to our kids. Often we allow peer pressure—our peers and our children's peers—to in-

fluence our decisions. We want our kids to have the same opportunities that all the other kids have, or opportunities we didn't
have. But it's so easy to get carried away. We don't have to do it
all. Our kids don't either.

You could start by cutting back on even one or two after-school
activities to see if it doesn't greatly simplify your lives.

## 88. Monitor Your Children's Television Viewing

In psychologist John Rosemond's excellent book, *Six-Point Plan for Raising Happy, Healthy Children*, he makes a strong case for heavily monitoring what our children are watching on television.

The fact that much of the television programming for kids—not to mention for adults—is of questionable value is not at issue here; though the quality of the material available should be sufficient reason for any caring parent to curtail television usage.

According to Dr. Rosemond, even programs like *Sesame Street* and other socially acceptable educational kids' shows foster passive learning traits that are detrimental to a child's future learning abilities.

But there are other issues here that are not often addressed. We think allowing a child to sit in front of the television screen simplifies our lives because it gives us a break. But according to

Dr. Rosemond, not only does regular television viewing stifle initiative and creativity, but it develops addictive patterns and children who depend on you, rather than on themselves, for their entertainment. Children who grow up not knowing how to create their own happiness and sense of well-being are going to be entering the real world with a major handicap.

And any child who has developed the ability to think and do for himself or herself is going to have a decided advantage over all those developmentally impaired kids who spent an average of seven hours a day in front of the tube.

Because of the harmful effects of television on a child's ability to learn, Dr. Rosemond believes no child should be allowed to watch television until they've learned to read well. Then, if permitted at all, television should be closely monitored and greatly curtailed.

Set parameters. They can watch an hour a day of a program you approve of. And perhaps another hour of a quality educational program. Then the set gets turned off. My friend Vera bought a television with a hidden control switch, so the set can't be turned on in her absence.

Pick up a copy of Steven and Ruth Bennet's *365 TV-Free Activities You Can Do with Your Child*. If you need some outside support in eliminating television, contact TV-Free America, 1322 18th Street NW, Suite #300, Washington, DC 20036 (202) 887-0436 for a free booklet that will show you how to organize and participate in a TV-free week in your community.

## 89. Teach Your Kids How to Handle Money at an Early Age

When I was 8 years old, my dad started giving me an allowance of fifty cents a week. The only advice he gave me at the time was to save half of it. I could do whatever I wanted with the other half, but it was to take care of any extras I might want. If I spent it all in one place, which I did for the first couple of weeks (all twenty-five cents of it), I couldn't go running back to Dad for more. I had to wait until the next weekly infusion of cash. I learned pretty quickly how to set aside money for unexpected contingencies—the double feature and popcorn on Saturday mornings—and how to budget my income.

This allowance was not connected to any household chores I was required to participate in. I had long been expected to do basic tasks like making my bed, helping set the table for dinner, and hanging up my clothes after school.

My involvement in chores increased as I got older; they were what I was expected to contribute as a member of the household. My allowance was my parents' way of getting me accustomed to handling money wisely. They provided all of my basic needs, but expected me to budget for and pay for any extras I might want.

By the time I entered high school I had my own checking account and a savings account and knew how to reconcile them both. Thanks to Dad's guidance, and his willingness to let me fall on my face a couple of times, I grew up confident about my ability to handle money so I could always take care of my basic needs and have money left over. The habit of saving part of my income has stayed with me through all my working years.

Mary Hunt, in her book *The Cheapskate Monthly*, outlines a similar program she and her husband used to get themselves out of debt and to set up their two boys with a program for handling their own expenses at an early age.

There are a couple basic differences in her program and my dad's. The first is that each child was required to save 10 percent and also to give away 10 percent of their income to a cause of their choice. It could be to a needy friend, to the local library fund, or to a charity.

Secondly, they gave the boys a larger amount of money, which was to cover *everything* above the basic room and board provided by the parents. And they gave them a raise at the beginning of each school year that was appropriate to the expenses each child would be encountering. So the boys had to learn to budget for *all* their expenses, including clothes, school books, entertainment, school trips, bus money, birthday gifts for friends, family presents, and everything else.

The parents agreed not to interfere with how the kids spent their money. But they made it clear that the boys couldn't come to them for more money if they spent it all early in the month and needed more to get them through. If they ran out before the next "payday," that was tough; they'd just have to wait.

While Mary admits it was hard to refuse her kids the extra money they thought they needed when they spent it all on the first day, they stood by their rule.

As a result, both boys quickly learned how to handle money

at an early age. By the time the boys were old enough to drive, they each paid for their own cars—and the gas and insurance needed to run them—and also had money set aside for continuing their education.

Mary's book lists some guidelines in terms of the amount of money that would be appropriate for various age groups. Any of her principles could be adapted to your children and your own circumstances.

For example, not every child is mature enough to be trusted with a month's allowance. If you have a child who would spend it all on candy (or beer, or drugs), you'd need to dole the money out more carefully and perhaps require a strict and detailed accounting of how the money is spent.

Teaching your kids how to handle money wisely will not only simplify your life, it could be one of the most powerful gifts you give them.

## 90. Set Buying Limits for Toys and Candy and Stick to Them

One of the more publicly visible complications that parents have with children is played out in supermarket checkout lines across the country week after week. It's the chilling scream of the distraught child whose mother has not yet agreed to allow him to purchase both the gummi bears and the space cadet suckers.

One solution is to leave the kids at home when you go shopping. Obviously, there are times when it's not possible to do this. And besides, kids need to be taught how to behave in public. So in one sense, grocery shopping is a good training ground.

I've discussed this with dozens of parents, and they all agree the answer seems so simple: Just say no. But the trick is to say no or let your kids know what you will allow them to buy, if anything, *before* you go into the store, and then stick to that decision.

Describe ahead of time what the consequences will be if they cry or throw a tantrum, and stick to that, too.

Another approach is to start as early as possible to use an appropriate variation of Mary Hunt's allowance system (#89), and, within reason, let each child learn to make his or her own decisions about how to spend the money they have available.

## 91. Set Limits for Your Parents and Other Well-Intentioned Relatives, Too

It's one thing to set parameters for items you buy for your kids or what you allow them to purchase, but it's just as important to set the parameters for what your parents and grandparents can buy for your kids.

For years, my friend Liz has purchased extravagant Christmas gifts for her niece and nephew who live several thousand miles away from her. Several years ago she had an unavoidable business trip that took her out of the country for most of December. Since she was going to be away over the holidays, she made her gift selections early and sent them off to her sister at the end of November.

She called several days later, just before she was to leave the country, to wish them all Merry Christmas and was shocked to find out that the kids had already opened her presents.

"But why didn't you wait until Christmas?" she wailed to her sister.

"Liz, they get so many presents from the grandparents and the stepgrandparents and the aunts and uncles and other assorted family members that if they don't open a package or two each night, starting several weeks before Christmas, they'd still be opening presents halfway through January."

This sounds like a situation that's gotten out of control. But it's not all that unusual. Not only does this excess of gift giving complicate the parents' lives because of all the toys, games, and other paraphernalia that are taking up space in their home, but it complicates the children's lives as well. It becomes overwhelming. They don't know what to play with first. It numbs their sensitivity and their creativity.

If you're watching, you'll see that invariably they pick one or two toys that become their favorites, and the rest sit idly, taking up room and cluttering up their space.

It also sets up unrealistic expectations that can never be fulfilled in the real world. And it certainly gives them a negative message in terms of consumerism and the habits of responding to television advertising (100 percent of the ten best-selling toys are tied to television shows).

You might want to start setting some parameters for your parents—the kids' grandparents—as well as aunts and uncles and friends and relatives. "Look, Mom, we appreciate all the things you do for the boys, but we feel we need to set some limits on the number of toys that come into the house and complicate our lives. We'd like to limit the number of presents to one or two, and any other money you want to spend will go into a college fund."

It's that simple.

## 92. Cultivate Simple Values

Relaxing on some of the household chores; reducing your social commitments; cutting back to eight-hour workdays if you are employed outside the home; reducing your commute time; spending less time shopping and consuming; changing your expectations about the size of your house, the green of your lawn, and the whiteness of your laundry will make it possible for you to create the time to teach your kids simple, mind-expanding, soul-filling activities.

In addition to teaching them to cook and sew and do their own laundry as Jennifer Sellers has done (#86), try taking them on nature walks and bike rides, and teaching them to use the public library and spend quiet time there. Plant a garden, build castles in the sand or castles in the air, watch sunsets and sunrises. Teach them to seek out quiet time each day and to enjoy developing their own inner resources as appropriate to their age, through reading, writing, journal writing, and their own creativity through music, drawing, painting, and any other artistic leanings they might have.

As reader Ann Hopson wrote, "As the parent of two young children, I feel lucky to have found this avenue to explore. My girls, 5 and 7, love nature, new experiences, and freedom, so your suggestions are a happy alternative to Chuck E Cheese, amusement parks, and costly mall shopping. We love visiting free places like botanical gardens, local historical sites and museums, and even doing genealogical studies in libraries, which have become our family's favorite resource. Luckily, my girls are happily entertained at home with our own simplistic activities."

Yes, these activities will take more of your time, certainly in the beginning, than sitting them in front of the television. But in the long run, having happy children who love simple pleasures and who can be their own source for entertainment will make life simpler for you and for them.

# TWELVE

## Simple Wardrobe
## Ideas for Women

# 93. Make Your Own Rules

I gave a talk on simplifying recently and when it came to the subject of simple clothing, the women in the group were commiserating on how difficult it is to deal with the vagaries of women's fashion. Many of us are fed up with the herculean task of putting together a suitable look that is functional and versatile and doesn't cost an arm and a leg.

One of the men in the audience announced that he was an investment banker who puts together venture capital for the fashion industry. He said the women's clothing designers and manufacturers were going through some very tough times and a lot of restructuring because sales have been down considerably in recent years, far more than the overall downturn in the economy would explain.

He was hearing over and over again that women were tired of struggling with the frustration of trying to find clothes that worked for them. He said the feeling in many parts of the industry was that women had simply stopped buying clothes the way they used to. As he saw it, the entire fashion industry was going to have to make some drastic changes in the way they designed and produced clothes for our rapidly changing lifestyles.

I hope he's right. But it would be surprising to see any monumental changes in the promulgation of fashion trends in our lifetime. Clothing designers and manufacturers have spent too many billions of dollars creating the epidemic feelings of discontent in American women. It would be a major turnaround for them to suddenly start producing clothing that actually works for the majority of women.

If you've reached a point in your pursuit of the simple life where you can move to that cabin in the woods or in some other way arrange your life so you can ignore even the minimum decrees of the fashion industry, you can probably limit yourself to a couple of sets of jeans and a pair of boots—which is my ultimate ideal—and get away with it.

But those of us who plan to remain in the swing of commerce—either by choice or by circumstance—will probably continue to play the fashion game to one degree or another. The objective, as far as I'm concerned, is to set as many of my own rules as I can, and to play the rest of them as simply as possible.

There are many women out there who feel as I do about this issue. We're not interested in being fashion plates, but we want or need to look presentable, and we'd like to do so with the least amount of fuss, bother, and expense.

Needless to say, it'd be a lot easier if we could just say to hell with Madison Avenue and ignore the incredibly powerful dictates of the fashion industry. If you've been able to do that, congratulations. You're ahead of the game.

I haven't yet reached the point where I can disregard all those edicts, but, with some effort, I have gotten to a point where I can turn my back on a lot of them.

After some months of pondering this issue I finally put together a simple look that works for me. And I learned a few things in the process.

I discovered that when it comes to clothes—as with many other things—less is definitely more. It's so much simpler to work with a few classic pieces that are always in style and work with each other than to have a closet jammed with the latest fashions that, if they ever look good, don't look good for long and seldom work together.

I figured out that I don't need a multitude of colors in my closet. I've greatly reduced the complexity of putting together a suitable look by limiting my palette to two or three basic colors that are always in style.

I see no reason to have more than a few pairs of shoes in my closet at any one time. And they all have the same heel height.

I've eliminated the accessories that have cluttered up my drawers for years, most of them seldom used.

I've found the simplicity of a couple of pairs of earrings liberating beyond belief.

I've learned to make certain that every piece of clothing I buy has pockets so I don't have to carry a purse.

I built a simple wardrobe around a couple of outfits that I already had in my closet and I liked. I wanted one basic look that I could use as a uniform, which I could layer to take me through the seasons.

One of my challenges was to find out why these particular outfits worked for me, so I could easily add to them through the years as one piece wore out, and so I could repeat the process when I needed to (which I hope won't have to be any time soon).

I know many women would not be happy with the limited range of colors and styles this approach embraces. But if you're looking to create your own simple look, I hope there will be some principles here that you can adapt to your own set of rules, based on your own needs and circumstances, rather than on the whims of fashion.

# 94. Start with What You Already Have

**O**ne of the rules we used to get rid of the clutter in our home was "If you haven't used it in a year, throw it out." The first place we started with was our closets.

I was strongly tempted, when I looked into my closet and saw all the things I hadn't worn in over a year—some for many years—to throw out everything but the clothes on my back and start over from scratch.

Though I got rid of a lot of stuff on that first attempt, I didn't quite have the nerve to get rid of everything. Later, I was awfully glad I hadn't.

It turned out that, mixed in with all the clothes I hadn't worn recently—and with a lot of things I had worn but wasn't crazy about—there were several treasures. These were outfits—a couple of jackets, a long skirt, a pair of slacks, some simple tops—that I'd had for a number of years that I quite liked and I had continued to wear over and over again. I wore them so much because I always felt good in them. They were comfortable. The colors, the style, the fabric, and the look all suited me. So I kept them and got rid of most, though at this point, not all, of the other clothes—the sweaters, suits, blouses, shirts, jackets, shoes, boots, and several drawers of accessories that I knew I'd never wear again.

Those few pieces I liked became the starting point for my new simplified wardrobe and stayed in the front part of my closet. There were other items that I wasn't sure about, which I hung in the back of the closet as a safety net, just in case my ideas for my simple look didn't pan out. Eventually, as my new wardrobe took shape, I felt more comfortable about letting go of the fall-back pieces altogether.

If it feels as though your closet is out of control and you've been thinking you'd like to take some steps to simplify it, start slowly, and don't jettison *everything* just yet. The chances are good that you, too, have some old favorites that you wear over and over again. If so, keep them.

If you know why you like them and why they work for you,

the job of building from them (or replacing them with similiar pieces if need be) will be much easier. But if, as I didn't, you don't have a clue why they work, don't worry about that part just yet. There is help available. But you might find it useful to sort through a couple of other questions first.

## 95. Limit Your Color Scheme

A few years back I had my colors done by one of the color consultants that were in vogue at the time. I came away from that session with a two-foot-square display board that I could hang in my closet, to which was attached at least four dozen color swatches, representing all the different shades of colors that would be suitable for my skin tones.

I was also given a credit card–size, accordian-type, color-swatch holder containing these same colors, which I could conveniently keep in my purse so I could stay within my range of colors when I went clothes shopping. You probably know the type of color charts I mean.

When I started weeding clothes out of my closet in my first attempt to simplify my wardrobe, it dawned on me that just because this consultant said I *could* wear all these different colors, it didn't mean I *had* to. I didn't have all those colors in my closet of course, but it felt like I did.

In theory, each color in one's palette could be worn with every other color in one's palette. But in my experience, it never quite worked out that way. I've always suspected that all the clothing manufacturers got together and conspired to make sure that none of their colors worked with the palettes the color consultants were working with.

But if they don't do that, there's no doubt that many of them go to great lengths to figure out how to formulate this year's "in" colors so that, not only do they not work with last year's "in" colors, but they don't work with any previous year's "in" colors either. Though those color palettes are now somewhat passé, many women still buy clothes with their color charts in mind.

The result is that millions of us have ended up season after season with numerous outfits in our closets, no one piece of which ever blends with any other piece. It's just one of the many ways clothing manufacturers lure us into starting all over again each year in our seldom attainable attempt to create an acceptable fashion statement.

I began to see that having such a wide range of colors was a major complication for my wardrobe. So I narrowed my palette down to three colors.

The colors I chose, black, white, and shades of gray—with complements of taupe—would not be everyone's choices and, in fact, I'm not certain they're my first choices. I decided on these colors because my favorite outfits—the ones I wore over and over again, and that I always felt good in, and were therefore the ones I wanted to build my simple wardrobe from—were in these colors.

Also, I stayed with these mostly darker colors because, as several readers with the same idea pointed out, darker colors are easier to work with from season to season and lend an aura of quality and professionalism to your total look.

(Since my simple puppies are black and white and gray, I figured I could simplify the dog hair issue at the same time: The black hairs would end up on the black clothes, the white hairs would end up on the white clothes, the gray hairs would end up on the gray clothes, and, as we all know, taupe goes with everything. It doesn't quite work out that way, but if I alter my expectations slightly, I can overlook the dog hair.)

I don't feel I have to stick with these colors for the rest of my life, but they work for me now and into the forseeable future. And with basic colors like these, I can always add a splash of color in a vest or a top to put a bit of zip into my palette from one year to the next should I feel so inclined.

Limiting your palette also simplifies your accessories—your jewelry, scarves, belts, purses, and shoes.

Take a moment right now to imagine how much simpler shopping for clothes would be if you limited yourself to three or four of the colors that look best on you. Just think of the tremendous number of clothes you could pass right by because they don't fit into your color scheme.

## 96. Figure Out Your Clothing Needs

For years I had hoped to find one classic all-purpose outfit that would be suitable for my work life, my social life, my exercise regimen, and every other possible event.

I would then acquire seven copies of that magic outfit—one for each day of the week as Einstein reportedly did—and that would be it. I'd never again, well, almost never again, have to bother with the task of building a suitable wardrobe or with spending time each day figuring out what to wear.

It's possible my life will one day be so simple that one outfit will work for everything I do. But I've finally figured out that for now I need clothes for at least three separate circumstances: casual clothes for my morning walks and for my day-to-day work at the computer in my home office; business attire; and something in between—not dressy but not sweats—for wearing into town for a luncheon meeting or for a casual dinner out.

Since we simplified our lives, formal attire has become a non-issue. On the rare occasion I attend a formal gathering, one of my business suits has to do. Otherwise, as Thoreau did, I tend to avoid events that require fancy garb.

If you don't already know what they are, it might be helpful to take some time to figure out the kinds of clothes you actually need for the types of activities you engage in.

This seems so obvious, but I see this mismatching of form to function over and over again. I know many women, for example, who love business suits and who therefore have a closet full of them, but whose work life actually calls for more casual attire. They have a closet full of clothes and nothing to wear.

## 97. Find Your Best Silhouette

The factor that moves the subject of fashion up a couple of notches on the complexity scale is the tremendous variety of styles that are available for women. Men's fashion options are fairly limited and predictable. But the possibilities for women know no bounds. Consequently, it's a tremendous challenge for most of us to find an acceptable style, or silhouette, that works for our particular body type.

Pulling together a suitable silhouette seems like it should be easy. But how many times have you gone clothes shopping and fallen in love with an outfit because it looked terrific on a mannequin, or even on the hanger, only to get home and find it doesn't look all that great on you.

You love the fabric, you love the color, you love the idea of it, it's exactly the type of thing you think you need. But even though you tried it on in the dressing room, the fact is it simply doesn't work.

More likely than not you keep it because it's just too much trouble to take it back and start all over again. Then it's guaranteed to be one of those outfits that ends up in the back of your closet that you never wear or is not comfortable when you do wear it.

Often the reason it doesn't work is that, even though it may fit size-wise, it doesn't fit silhouette-wise. It's either too long in the waist, or too short in the length, or too narrow in the shoulders, or too broad in the hips, or too frilly, or too severe, or *something* else is wrong with it.

Whether you're short or tall, large or small, young or old, broad or narrow, there is at least one silhouette that can make you look and feel like a million bucks. Finding it may not be simple—though it can be done—but *having* it will be.

Zeroing in on one or two silhouettes that work for you will simplify your present and future wardrobe immeasurably. Once you find a look you're comfortable with, you can build on it forever. You can add a piece one year and drop a piece the next year, or fill in pieces as you need them. You can dress it up or down. Using layers, you can take it from season to season.

Finding one of your ideal silhouettes will eliminate the continual frustration of never being satisfied with how you look. It will make it possible for you to get up in the morning, get dressed, and not have to think about clothes for the rest of the day. It'll save you time. It'll save you money. It'll be one less thing to complicate your life.

You may already know what silhouettes suit you best. But if the prospect of figuring it out has always been one of life's great mysteries, you can simplify the process by getting some help.

## 98. If You Need Help, Get It

After struggling with the problem of trying to figure out what clothes work for me and why, I finally decided to bite the bullet and get some help.

My plan was to find a salesperson in one of our local stores who had put together a good look for herself and who would be able to help me do the same.

Over a couple of weeks, I spoke with three or four different women in various clothing departments, outlining what I was looking for. The first two made some halfhearted attempts to help, but were obviously not all that interested.

The third young woman was enthusiastic but, after I saw what she had pulled together from the racks, it was clear that she didn't have a clue what she was doing for me, even though she had quite a good look for herself.

On the fourth try in as many weeks I hit the jackpot. I found a woman who was enthusiastic and knowledgeable, and clearly understood what I was trying to do in creating a simple look. Very briefly I outlined what I was looking for in terms of my various clothing needs and the colors I wanted to work with.

We set up an appointment for later in the week—to give her some time to pull some possibilities together—and she asked me to bring in the outfits that I liked from my own wardrobe so we could build from them.

Maryke spent several hours with me over the next couple of weeks. She showed me what worked from my closet and from the clothing she had selected from the racks and what didn't and why—either a jacket was too short, or a skirt too long, or the cut wasn't right for my shape, for example.

With her help I was able to zero in on the best silhouette for my body type. She helped me add a couple of pieces to my existing business outfits and to find a comfortable, washable, work-at-home look that, with some easy layering, I can use year round. And we added a couple of other pieces that dress down the business look or dress up the casual look so I can greatly expand the serviceability of each piece in my closet.

Building a simple wardrobe with the help of a personal shopper has made it possible for me to reduce my clothes shopping excursions to once a year, or less. It's been over a year and a half, and the only new items I've acquired are some T-shirts to take me through the summer.

Now that I understand my silhouette and know what pieces I need to make it work for me, I can avoid the impulse shopping which contributes to corporate profits but seldom does anything positive for my wardrobe.

Getting some professional advice saved me an incredible amount of time, energy, and money, and it has immeasurably simplified my life.

If you can't find a knowledgeable salesperson to help you, perhaps you have a friend who has an innate sense of style who can steer you in the right direction. Or you may be able to find a personal shopper listed in the yellow pages. Or simply ask around for the name of someone who can guide you once you carefully explain your parameters. Just remember to keep in touch with your own intuition through the process.

And don't overlook consignment shops as an excellent source of quality clothing for your simple wardrobe.

## 99. The Simple Purse

Ohe day several years ago I pulled into the parking lot of my neighborhood grocery store. As I was getting out of the car to go in to do my shopping, I happened to look over at the car that had pulled in beside me.

I watched a woman get out of the car, sling her duffle bag–sized purse over her shoulder, and walk across the lot into the store.

I knew for a fact that she was going to spend the next twenty minutes or so walking around the store with that bag over her shoulder. She'd come to the checkout counter, pay for her groceries, bring everything out to the car, climb in, and drive off.

She would have spent all that time carrying that huge bag around with her, and the only thing she would use from it would be a check or a two-inch by three-inch plastic credit card that weighs a fraction of an ounce.

I knew this because it was exactly the same thing I was going to do, and exactly what I had been doing for years.

I went home that night and emptied the contents of my bag onto the dining table. I sorted through every item and pulled out only the things I had actually used during the past week: my wallet, a pen, my lipstick, and a huge ring of keys. I put everything else back in the big bag, and found a smaller bag to hold the items I had actually used.

I put the large bag in the trunk of my car, in case I might actually need a pair of packaged rain slippers, a serrated knife, a small bottle of hand cream, a slightly shredded package of tissues, an empty perfume atomizer, a large hairbrush, a slightly mangled miniature tube of toothpaste, a small flashlight, a handheld calculator, or any of the other vital accoutrements we tuck away in those gargantuan totes.

Six months went by. The emergency supplies in the trunk of the car went untouched. The strap-shaped crease in my right shoulder gradually faded. It occurred to me that I could possibly pare down some more.

I went through the same exercise with the smaller bag. What

had I used from that bag recently? Four plastic credit card–sized cards: my driver's license, my library card, one credit card, and a triple A card—which I hadn't actually used, but you never know.

I pulled the money out of my wallet and set aside the wallet, with all its miscellaneous photos, old receipts, mangled business cards, and tattered pieces of paper with cryptic notes. I folded the green money, along with a couple of checks, and put these with the plastic cards. I ringed them all with a wide rubber band on which, just for the heck of it, I wrote "Gucci" in black ink.

I got rid of all the keys except a single car key, for which I don't need a ring. (I use a garage door opener to get into my house.) Since I seldom write checks anymore (#80), I don't require a pen—though there's always one attached to a counter with a plastic cord should the need arise.

I had already stopped wearing sunglasses because it had become such a hassle to change them back and forth and to find them in the bottom of my bag.

I keep any spare change I might pick up from a folded money transaction in the car's ashtray.

I keep a small emergency supply of tissues in the glove compartment.

Eventually, I got rid of the emergency bag from the trunk of the car.

I will say that even though I was delighted to be free of having to carry a heavy bag around all the time, I did go through some withdrawal pangs. Not only had I been in the habit of having a purse with me for many years—so for a brief time I felt almost undressed without it; but it had also become my security blanket. There lingered the small nagging concern that I might need one of those mostly useless items I had always carried with me. But, having seen all those items strewn over the dining table, I knew that I hadn't actually used any of that stuff for a very long time, in some cases, ever.

It didn't take long to get comfortable without a purse. Once I began to experience the freedom of not having to deal with that huge bag of stuff, there was no going back to carrying a handbag.

So now, in the pocket of whatever I happen to be wearing, I keep my "Gucci" rubber-banded cards/check/folded green stuff, my car key, and the one thing I would need above all else should I ever be stranded on a deserted island, my lipstick.

That's it. It's so simple. It's so liberating.

# THIRTEEN

# Simple Wardrobe
# Ideas for Men

# 100. Gibbs's Ideas for Simple Clothes for Men

Gibbs has volunteered to share his own thoughts about simple clothes for men. Here they are:

"When it comes to business clothing, men have it a lot easier than women. Unless they're actors, they need only look neat, clean, and like everyone else they work with. The simple fact men's clothing manufacturers would like you to forget is this: Nobody notices what a man is wearing unless it's weird.

"Years ago, a friend of mine simplified his business wardrobe by restricting it to one gray suit with two pairs of pants, three blue shirts, one tie, one pair of shoes, and several identical pairs of socks. Nobody noticed.

"I asked him if there was anything he'd do differently. He said next time he'd get a suit with three pairs of pants, because pants wear out much faster than jackets.

"Clothing that isn't for work can be chosen mostly for its function—fishing, woodchopping, ballroom dancing, for example. Pick it primarily for how well it does the job.

"As far as appearance is concerned, just don't buy anything that glitters."

There's probably not a whole lot more that needs to be said about simple clothes for men. That in itself says a lot.

# A FINAL THOUGHT

It's been more than five years since Gibbs and I first made the decision to begin living simpler lives. Looking back, we see it as one of the better decisions we've made. Not only has it been a fun and challenging adventure, but it's given us the incredible opportunity to step back and take life a little less seriously. We've come to see that even though we'll never get to do it all, we can still be happy and fulfilled. In truth, it's more often than not the quiet, simple moments that bring depth and meaning to our lives.

At its most basic level, the process of simplifying allows us to cut back on the incredible number of time- and energy-consuming options that confront us every day.

It was only a few years ago that when you wanted an ice cream cone, you could choose vanilla, chocolate, or strawberry. Now there are dozens of flavors to choose from. It was only a few years ago that when you wanted a new car, there were only a couple of dozen models to choose from. Now there are hundreds of models to choose from. You can apply this same expansion of options to nearly every area of our lives: the food we eat, the clothes we wear, the television programs we watch, the music we listen to, the sports we participate in, the web sites we frequent, and so on.

It's gotten to the point for many of us that taking the time to consider all the flavors takes away a good portion of the time we have to enjoy the ice cream. As reader Kathy Louv said, "I'm learning to take the Baskin-Robbins out of my life."

How do we do that? We start by becoming aware that the problem exists. Then we train ourselves to minimize the number of options we get exposed to through the clutter we accumulate, the activities we participate in, the expectations we try to meet, and our excursions through the mall.

But of course, having no options can complicate our lives, too. One of the greatest challenges we all face is to find a happy balance between the opportunities that are available to us, the media-implanted urge to have them all, and our own desire to keep focused on the things that really matter.

# READING LIST

## Household/Family

Campbell, Jeff. *Clutter Control: Putting Your Home on a Diet.* New York: Dell Trade Paperback, 1992. Dozens of books on the market tell you how to get organized. In my opinion this is one of the best. It's a basic, no-nonsense approach. It's also a great companion book to *Speed Cleaning,* listed next. But remember, the best way to control clutter is to get rid of it, and keep rid of it. That's one of the basic tenets of the simple life.

Campbell, Jeff, and the Clean Team. *Speed Cleaning.* New York: Dell Trade Paperback, 1987. A delightfully easy system for simplifying household cleaning chores.

Rosemond, John. *Six-Point Plan for Raising Happy, Healthy Children.* Kansas City: Andrews and McMeel, 1989. Paperback. Outlines a simple, basic approach to raising children who are responsible and depend on themselves for their entertainment and, ultimately, their happiness. Also spells out Rosemond's guidelines for family television use.

Wilson, Mimi, and Mary Beth Lagerborg. *Once-a-Month Cooking.* New York: St. Martin's Press, 1986. Paperback. Describes a step-by-step plan for preparing two weeks or a whole month of main-meal dishes at a time.

## Work/Creativity

Boldt, Laurence G. *How to Find the Work You Love.* New York: Penguin, 1996. This book won't give you the answers but it will guide you to the right questions. It explains beautifully why, for your own growth and peace of mind, you have the duty and responsibility to find your life's work.

Cameron, Julia. *The Artist's Way: A Spiritual Path to Higher Creativity.* Los Angeles: Jeremy P. Tarcher, 1992. Paperback. Following the steps outlined in this book may help you find the work you love.

Orsborn, Carol. *Enough Is Enough: Exploding the Myth of Having It All.* New York: Putnam, 1986. A delightfully readable story of one superwoman's decision to start living with a saner scale of expectations.

Saltzman, Amy. *Downshifting: Reinventing Success on a Slower Track.* New York: HarperCollins, 1991. A business journalist's look at how our attitudes toward work and leisure are changing for the better. Outlines five strategies for downshifting. Includes interviews with people who've made the decision to lead more balanced lives and tells how they did it.

Schor, Juliet B. *The Overworked American: The Unexpected Decline of Leisure.* New York: Basic Books, 1991. A scholarly documentation showing how the demands of employers and the addictive nature of consumption tie us to longer work schedules and reduced leisure time. A real eye-opener regarding our present-day work habits.

## Money

Dacyczyn, Amy. *Tightwad Gazette II.* New York: Villard Books, 1995. Paperback. This book, along with Dacyczyn's first book, *Tightwad Gazette*, lists hundreds of ways to spend less money. These books embrace and celebrate frugality, and offer many practical, thought-provoking, upbeat, and amusing discussions on saving money that everyone can use.

Dominguez, Joe, and Vicki Robin. *Your Money or Your Life: Transforming Your Relationship with Money and Achieving Financial Independence.* New York: Viking, 1993. Paperback. This book will change the way you think about money and offers a practical plan for simplifying both your financial life and your work life. Shows how to set up a monthly budget and how to use a graph for keeping track of income and expenses.

The Green Group. *101 Ways to Save Money and Save our Planet*. New Orleans: Paper Chase Press, 1992. Paperback. The emphasis in this little book is on saving money through sensible practices that are good for the planet.

Hunt, Mary. *The Cheapskate Monthly Money Makeover*. New York: St. Martin's Press, 1995. Offers a palatable approach for reorganizing your financial life and for developing a healthy attitude about money. Also outlines a workable system for establishing a monthly spending plan.

Long, Charles. *How to Survive Without a Salary*. Toronto: Warwick Publishing Group, 1991. Paperback. Some interesting ideas on how to get along with less and make do with what you have. Not a lifestyle that will necessarily work for everyone, but it shows what's possible.

Terhorst, Paul. *Cashing in on the American Dream: How to Retire at 35*. New York: Bantam, 1990. Written by a CPA and a former partner at Peat Marwick Mitchell & Co. who cashed in and retired at 35. Assumes you have equity either in your home or stocks that you can put to work for supporting an early retirement. The numbers and rates of return he cites aren't realistic in today's financial climate, but if you have the equity available, his plan can be adapted to other circumstances.

## Lifestyle

Bennet, Steven, and Ruth Bennet. *365 TV-Free Activities You Can Do with Your Child*. Holbrook, MA: Bob Adams Publishing, 1991. Paperback. Includes both indoor and outdoor activities that require little or no preparation and that will provide hours of entertainment which otherwise might be spent in front of the television.

Eisenson, Marc, Nancy Castleman, and March Ross. *Stop Junk Mail Forever*. 1994. Available from Good Advice Press, Box 78, Elizaville, NY 12523 (914) 758-1400. $3. The best program I've come across for eliminating junk mail.

Kelly, Jack and Marcia. *Sanctuaries*. Bell Tower, 1994. A guide to monasteries and retreat houses. Published in both an East Coast and a West Coast edition.

Lindbergh, Anne Morrow. *Gift from the Sea*. New York: Vintage Books, 1978. Another perspective on simple living and what complicates our lives.

*Peace Pilgram: Her Life and Work in Her Own Words*. Available from Ocean Tree Books, Post Office Box 1295, Santa Fe, New Mexico 87504. Paperback, 1992. This is the incredible story of a woman who simplified her life down to a comb and a nail file, and then carried a message of love and peace around the country. Anyone who longs for a truly simple life will love this book.

*Simple Living Journal.* Available from Publisher Janet Luhrs, 2319 North 45th Street, Box 149, Seattle, WA 98103 (206) 464-4800. $14 per year (U. S.). This is a quarterly newsletter that shares ideas about simplifying and tells personal stories of people from around the country who are doing it.

Stoll, Clifford. *Silicon Snake Oil: Second Thoughts on the Information Highway.* New York: Doubleday, 1995. A fascinating look at computers and the hype surrounding the Internet, written by a computer expert. A witty and perceptive explanation about how and why computers can both simplify and complicate our lives.

# REFERENCES

Mail Preference Service, P. O. Box 9008, Farmingdale, NY 22735-9008. Write and request that your name and any variation of your name not be sold to mailing list companies. This is a first step in the process of reducing the amount of junk mail you receive. Many other effective steps you can take are outlined in *Stop Junk Mail Forever*, listed above.

National Association of Professional Organizers, 1033 La Posada Drive, Austin, TX 78752 (512) 206-0151. With over 700 members around the country, this association may be able to help you locate a professional organizer in your area to help you get rid of the clutter in your life.

Real Goods Trading Corporation, 555 Leslie Street, Ukiah, CA 95482 (800) 762-7325. Source for laundry disks and other environmentally friendly household products.

TV-Free America, 1322 18th Street, NW #300, Washington, DC 20036 (202) 887-0436. This national nonprofit organization was founded to raise awareness about the harmful effects of excessive television watching. They will send you a free booklet that will help you organize a TV-free week in your community.

UNPLUG, 360 Grand Avenue, #385, Oakland, CA 94610 (510) 268-1100. If Channel One with its heavy commercial loading is in the schools in your area, contact UNPLUG for information about what you can do to keep your schools commercial free and to limit your child's media-induced wants.